CONSTITUT.

Most Muslim-majority countries have legal s͟   ͟ ͟ ͟ͅ that enshrine both Islam and liberal rights. While not necessarily at odds, these dual commitments nonetheless provide legal and symbolic resources for activists to advance contending visions for their states and societies. Using the case study of Malaysia, *Constituting Religion* examines how these legal arrangements enable litigation and feed the construction of a "rights-versus-rites binary" in law, politics, and the popular imagination. By drawing on extensive primary source material and tracing controversial cases from the court of law to the court of public opinion, this study theorizes the "judicialization of religion" and examines the radiating effects of courts on popular legal and religious consciousness. The book documents how legal institutions catalyze ideological struggles that stand to redefine the nation and its politics. Probing the links between legal pluralism, social movements, secularism, and political Islamism, *Constituting Religion* sheds new light on the confluence of law, religion, politics, and society.

This title is also available as Open Access on Cambridge Core at https://doi.org/10.1017/9781108539296.

Tamir Moustafa is Professor of International Studies and Stephen Jarislowsky Chair at Simon Fraser University in Vancouver, Canada. His research stands at the intersection of law, religion, and politics. Among other works, he is the author of *The Struggle for Constitutional Power: Law, Politics, and Economic Development in Egypt* (Cambridge University Press, 2007) and the co-editor of *Rule by Law: The Politics of Law and Courts in Authoritarian Regimes*, with Tom Ginsburg (Cambridge University Press, 2008).

CAMBRIDGE STUDIES IN LAW AND SOCIETY

Founded in 1997, Cambridge Studies in Law and Society is a hub for leading scholarship in socio-legal studies. Located at the intersection of law, the humanities, and the social sciences, it publishes empirically innovative and theoretically sophisticated work on law's manifestations in everyday life: from discourses to practices, and from institutions to cultures. The series editors have longstanding expertise in the interdisciplinary study of law, and welcome contributions that place legal phenomena in national, comparative, or international perspective. Series authors come from a range of disciplines, including anthropology, history, law, literature, political science, and sociology.

Series Editors
Mark Fathi Massoud, *University of California, Santa Cruz*
Jens Meierhenrich, *London School of Economics and Political Science*
Rachel E. Stern, *University of California, Berkeley*

A list of books in the series can be found at the back of this book.

Constituting Religion

ISLAM, LIBERAL RIGHTS, AND THE MALAYSIAN STATE

TAMIR MOUSTAFA

Simon Fraser University

CAMBRIDGE
UNIVERSITY PRESS

University Printing House, Cambridge CB2 8BS, United Kingdom

One Liberty Plaza, 20th Floor, New York, NY 10006, USA

477 Williamstown Road, Port Melbourne, VIC 3207, Australia

314–321, 3rd Floor, Plot 3, Splendor Forum, Jasola District Centre,
New Delhi – 110025, India

79 Anson Road, #06–04/06, Singapore 079906

Cambridge University Press is part of the University of Cambridge.

It furthers the University's mission by disseminating knowledge in the pursuit of
education, learning, and research at the highest international levels of excellence.

www.cambridge.org
Information on this title: www.cambridge.org/9781108423946
DOI: 10.1017/9781108539296

First published 2018

A catalogue record for this publication is available from the British Library.

Library of Congress Cataloging-in-Publication Data
NAMES: Moustafa, Tamir, author.
TITLE: Constituting religion : Islam, liberal rights, and the Malaysian state /
Tamir Moustafa.
DESCRIPTION: New York : Cambridge University Press, 2018. | Series:
Cambridge studies in law and society
IDENTIFIERS: LCCN 2018010094 | ISBN 9781108423946 (hardback)
SUBJECTS: LCSH: Muslims – Legal status, laws, etc. – Malaysia. | Civil rights – Malaysia. | Constitutional
law – Malaysia | BISAC: LAW / General.
CLASSIFICATION: LCC KPG511.3 .M68 2018 | DDC 342.59508/5297–dc23
LC record available at https://lccn.loc.gov/2018010094

ISBN 978-1-108-42394-6 Hardback
ISBN 978-1-108-43917-6 Paperback

Contents

Figures

Tables

Acknowledgments

This book has been a long time coming. *Constituting Religion* was initially conceived as a comparative study of Islamist litigation in Egypt, Malaysia, and Pakistan. However, I quickly realized that a significant treatment of the nexus of law, religion, politics, and society in any one of these three countries would require an enormous investment of time and energy. Having already been captivated by initial fieldwork in Malaysia, I chose to shift my full attention to understanding the Malaysian experience as best I could. It is a decision that I have not regretted for a minute.

Nearly a decade later, I am indebted to dozens of Malaysian activists, academics, lawyers, journalists, and others, many of whom invested considerable time and energy helping me with this project. I am especially indebted to Shanmuga Kanesalingam, Ahmed Farouk Musa, Jacqueline Surin, Shanon Shah, Norani Othman, Zainah Anwar, Masjaliza Hamza, Ibrahim Suffian, Azmil Tayeb, Clive Kessler, and Sharaad Kuttan for their patience with my endless questions, and their warm companionship during my time in Malaysia. I am also grateful to Damina Khaira, Aston Paiva, Seh Lih Long, Ravi Nekoo, Zaid Kamaruddin, Philip Koh Tong Ngee, Tan Beng Hui, Malik Imtiaz Sarwar, Patricia Martinez, Yusri Mohamad, Abdul Rahim Sinwan, Tun Hamid Abdul Mohamad, Edmund Bon Tai Soon, Fadiah Nadwa Fikri, Haji Mahamad Naser Bin Disa, Haji Mohamed Haniff Khatri Abdulla, Nandita Solomon, Dato Cyrus V. Das, Nizam Bashir bin Abdul Kariem Bashir, Chin Oy Sim, Suriani Kempe, Chandra Muzaffar, Andrew Khoo, Noraida Endut, Latheefa Koya, Azmi Sharom, Reverend Sivin Kit, Uthayakumar Ponnusamy, Mazeni Alwi, Reverend Thomas Philips, Prematilaka Serisena, Goh Keat-Peng, Norhayati Kaprawi, Al Mustaqeem Mahmod Radhi, Mohamad Hashim Kamali, Benjamin Dawson, KJ John, Zaid Ibrahim, Rozana Isa, Ratna Osman, Marina Mahathir, Ivy Josiah, and Tan Kong Beng. Finally, parts of this study could not have been completed without superb research assistance in Malaysia from Azmil Tayeb, Chang Chee Er, and Dinash Kathirkama, and in Vancouver from Tracy Lim Sim Yee and Erin Morissette.

Financial support for this project came from the Carnegie Corporation of New York, through the Carnegie Scholars Program on Islam and Muslim Societies; the Social Sciences and Humanities Research Council of Canada (SSHRC), through an Insight Grant; and the Stephen Jarislowsky Chair in Religion and Cultural Change at Simon Fraser University.

The Islamic Legal Studies Program at Harvard Law School provided an ideal environment to organize my thoughts and to write. I am also grateful for having had the opportunity to present draft chapters at the Law and Public Affairs Program (LAPA) at Princeton; the Islamic Law and Society Workshop organized by the Department of Middle East and Islamic Studies at New York University; the Islamic Legal Studies Program (ILSP) at Harvard Law School; the Comparative Law and Society Studies (CLASS) Center at the University of Washington; and through invited lectures at the University of British Columbia, McGill University, and Concordia University. I was especially honored by the opportunity to share research findings with the Malaysian advocacy group, Sisters in Islam, and with the Malaysian Bar Council through their National Strategic Litigation Consultation on Freedom of Religion.

This book was also enriched by my participation in two extraordinary research groups. The first group, convened by Mirjam Künkler, Hanna Lerner, and Shylashri Shankar at the Center for Interdisciplinary Research (ZiF), Bielefeld University, focused on the theme of "Balancing Religious Accommodation and Human Rights in Constitutional Frameworks." The second research group, convened by Saba Mahmood, Elizabeth Shakman Hurd, Winnifred Sullivan, and Peter Danchin and funded by the Henry R. Luce Initiative on Religion and International Affairs, focused on the "Politics of Religious Freedom."

I am also grateful to many friends and colleagues who stimulated my thinking along the way. I would like to thank Hussein Agrama, Rumee Ahmed, Onur Bakiner, Asli Bâli, Azza Bassarudin, Felicitas Becker, John Bowen, Nathan Brown, Ayesha Chaudhry, Jeffrey Dudas, Zachary Elkins, Mohammad Fadl, Kambiz GhaneaBassiri, Ellis Goldberg, Andrew Harding, Laura Hatcher, Iza Hussin, Ahmed Fekry Ibrahim, David Leheny, Hanna Lerner, Saba Mahmood, Mark Massoud, David Mednicoff, Sally Engle Merry, Michael McCann, Jamie Meyerfeld, Joel Migdal, Matthew Nelson, Jaclyn L. Neo, Mona Oraby, Arzoo Osanloo, Michael Peletz, Asifa Quraishi-Landes, Intisar Rabb, Jeffrey Sachs, Kim Scheppele, Benjamin Schonthal, Yuksel Sezgin, Elizabeth Shakman Hurd, Rachel Stern, Kristen Stilt, Frank Vogel, Amanda Whiting, Malika Zeghal, and my colleagues at Simon Fraser University, particularly Elizabeth Cooper, John Harriss, Michael Hathaway, and Geoff Mann. I am especially indebted to those friends and colleagues who provided extensive feedback on draft chapters: Onur Bakiner, Ceren Belge, Shanmuga Kanesalingam, Mirjam Künkler, Jeremy Menchik, Matthew Nelson, Jeffrey Sachs, Benjamin Schonthal, Elizabeth Shakman Hurd, and Winnifred Sullivan. John Berger at Cambridge University

Press served, once again, as a wonderful editor. Emma Collison, also at Cambridge University Press, was a terrific help during the production process. I hope I have not left anyone out, but fear that it is all too easy given the number of people who assisted me and pushed my thinking along the way.

Finally, I want to thank my wife, Nina Lobo, for the love and support that helped me to see this project through to completion. This book is dedicated to her, to our daughter, Salma, and in loving memory of my father, Mohamed Eid Moustafa.

Introduction

Constituting Religion

Over half of all Muslim-majority countries have constitutions that proclaim Islam the religion of state. Many also require that state law adhere to Islamic law.[1] For instance, the Malaysian Constitution declares that "Islam is the religion of the Federation. ... "[2] The Constitution of Pakistan goes further by requiring that state law conform to "the injunctions of Islam as laid down in the Holy Quran .... "[3] And the Egyptian Constitution affirms that "Islam is the religion of the state ... and the principles of Islamic jurisprudence are the chief source of legislation."[4] These sorts of provisions are not likely to change anytime soon. In fact, all the constitutions written in Muslim-majority countries since the turn of the millennium – including those of Afghanistan (2004), Iraq (2005), Somalia (2012), Egypt (2012, 2014), Libya (2013), and Tunisia (2014) – declare Islam the religion of the state. Most of these countries also have substantive laws and regulations that claim fidelity to Islam (Otto 2010). This is most common in Muslim family law (An-Na'im 2002), but state claims to Islam sometimes extend to other areas, such as criminal law (Peters 2005). Whether by way of constitutional proclamations or substantive laws, Muslim-majority states have endeavored to "constitute" Islam.

At the same time, most of these legal systems contain provisions that one expects to find in a liberal legal order, including constitutional guarantees for civil liberties, religious freedom, and equal rights before the law. These dual commitments to Islam and liberal rights are not necessarily at odds. With multiple schools of Islamic thought and jurisprudence, and an ever-expanding corpus of substantive legal opinions, the Islamic legal tradition is diverse, open-ended, and is by no means locked in an inevitable tug-of-war with liberal rights. Moreover, the Islamic legal tradition is only one facet of a complex and multi-layered religious tradition.

---

[1] An inventory of such provisions for all Muslim-majority countries is provided in Appendix A. See Stahnke and Blitt (2005) for an earlier iteration of this exercise.

[2] The full clause reads, "Islam is the religion of the Federation; but other religions may be practised in peace and harmony in any part of the Federation." Many regard Article 3 as symbolic, but Schedule 9 of the Malaysian Constitution also details specific areas of law that fall under the purview of state-level religious councils and shariah courts.

[3] Article 227. Article 2 also provides that "Islam shall be the state religion of Pakistan."   [4] Article 2.

1

Nevertheless, dual commitments to Islam and liberal rights provide vital resources – both legal and symbolic – for those who wish to advance contending visions for their states and societies. In diverse contexts, from Egypt to Malaysia to Pakistan, activists have seized upon state religion clauses to push for a more expansive role for Islam in the political order, even while other activists challenge the laws that are legislated in the name of Islam. The result is a "judicialization of religion," which I define as a circumstance wherein courts increasingly adjudicate questions and controversies over religion.[5]

Academic and popular accounts tend to frame these struggles as the product of a collision between ascendant religious movements and liberal legal orders. In other words, conflict is understood as originating from *outside* the legal system. This conception of the problem (religion) and what is at stake (liberty) comes easily because it aligns with the prevailing notion that courts serve as defenders of fundamental liberties and strongholds of secularism.[6] This common assumption is made explicit in one of the most ambitious book-length studies on the topic, Ran Hirschl's *Constitutional Theocracy*. Hirschl contends that constitutional review provides an important bulwark against a worldwide trend towards religiosity. He explains that "constitutional law and courts ... have become bastions of relative secularism, pragmatism, and moderation, thereby emerging as effective shields against the spread of religiosity and increased popular support for principles of theocratic governance" (2011:13). Hirschl's thesis reflects a conventional wisdom that courts safeguard secularism, resolve conflict, and protect fundamental rights.

In contrast with this expectation, a central argument of this book is that legal institutions play important roles in *constituting* struggle over religion. As suggested in the opening paragraph of this book, the leaders of most Muslim-majority states have sought to constitute Islam by way of state law to harness the legitimating power of Islamic symbolism. But rather than unequivocally shoring up state legitimacy, these provisions frequently open new avenues of contestation.

Building on recent work from socio-legal studies, religious studies, and comparative judicial politics, *Constituting Religion* examines the judicialization of religion and, crucially, the radiating effects of judicialization on political life. *Constituting*

---

[5] This term has been used in a few prior studies, including Sezgin and Künkler (2014) and Fokas (2015). In this study, a judicialization of religion is not derivative of a more general "judicialization of politics," which is defined by Tate (1995: 28) as "the process by which courts and judges come to make or increasingly to dominate the making of public policies that had previously been made ... by other governmental agencies, especially legislatures and executives." Instead, judicialization of religion, by contrast, is used in this study to describe a circumstance wherein courts assume the functions of religious authorities, thereby authorizing an "official" religion, and/or rendering judgment on the appropriate place for religion in the legal and political order. Activist litigation is one of several mechanisms that can produce a judicialization of religion. I examine others in the following chapters.

[6] This framing finds particular resonance in regard to Islam, specifically, due to the considerable baggage with which it is frequently associated these days.

Religion shows that, far from consistently resolving disputes and defending liberties, legal institutions can intensify controversy and augment ideological polarization. Explanations that start and end with the "problem" of religion, without examining the intervening work of law and courts, will fail to appreciate these conflict-generative functions. Simplified explanations that lay blame on a reified "religion" will fail to grasp the myriad ways that the state is itself implicated in the politics of religion and in modern constructions of religion more generally. Law and courts do not simply stand above religion and politics. Instead, they enable and catalyze ideological conflict. An important objective of this book is to make visible the role of courts in constituting the very ideological conflicts that they are charged with resolving. This objective encourages reflection on deeply held assumptions about religion as a perennial troublemaker, and deeply rooted expectations about the role of law vis-à-vis religion.[7] This focus on legal institutions is not meant to minimize the ideological cleavages that have gripped many Muslim-majority countries over the place of religion in the legal and political order. Rather, it is to better understand the role of modern law in catalyzing and fueling those struggles.

Constituting Religion departs from conventional accounts of the law-religion-politics nexus by theorizing the interface between courts and the broader social and political domains in which they operate. This focus on the "radiating effects" of courts (Galanter 1983) contributes to a number of research agendas at the intersection of law, religion, and politics.[8] Here I wish to highlight two bodies of work in particular: studies of Islamist mobilization and legal studies at the intersection of law and religion. Regarding studies of Islamist mobilization, the lion's share of scholarly attention is focused on the electoral arena.[9] This attention to electoral politics may spring from a scholarly interest in the way that political participation shapes the trajectory of Islamist parties. And it likely reflects scholarly interest in challenging the "one-man, one-vote, one-time dilemma" that casts a shadow over policy discussions. The relative neglect of law may also stem from an assumption that courts serve as little more than window dressing in Muslim-majority contexts.[10] Whatever the reason, research

---

[7] Schonthal (2016) identifies striking parallels in the Sri Lankan context. These parallels immediately suggest that a reductive focus on an essentialized Islam as a perennial source of trouble is ill-conceived.

[8] Marc Galanter coined this term in his critique of doctrine-centric legal scholarship and judicial impact studies, which, he argues, assume that "the authoritative pronouncements of the highest courts penetrate automatically – swiftly, costlessly, without distortion – to all corners of the legal world." Galanter explains that "such influence cannot be ascertained by attending only to the messages propounded by the courts. It depends on the resources and capacities of their various audiences and on the normative orderings indigenous to the various social locations where messages from the courts impinge" (1983: 118).

[9] This body of research is too large to cite in its entirety. Representative studies include Schwedler (2006), Brown (2012), Masoud (2014), Nasr (2005), Mecham and Hwang (2014), and Rosefsky Wickham (2004).

[10] Even considering that there is a relative democracy deficit in Muslim-majority counties, recent work suggests that courts nonetheless serve as important sites of political contestation in many authoritarian or hybrid polities. For a theoretical framework and empirical treatment focused on the Egyptian case, see Moustafa (2007). For a series of comparative case studies that engage this framework, see Ginsburg

on Islamist mobilization has paid insufficient attention to courts as a political forum. Among the studies of Islamist litigation that do exist, ideological formation is typically assumed to occur prior to (and exogenous from) engagement with legal institutions.

There is a different lacuna in legal scholarship on the subject. Here, research examines the proliferation of "religion of the state" clauses, or the various ways that courts work to negotiate and reconcile constitutional commitments to both Islam and liberal rights.[11] These doctrine-centric and court-centric approaches are valuable. However, they leave the radiating effects of law almost entirely unexplored. In contrast, this book considers the ways that courts serve as important sites of ideological formation. Beyond the direct legal impact of judicial decisions, *Constituting Religion* examines the ways that courts provide a platform from which activists can challenge the status quo, attract public attention, and assert broad claims about Islam, liberal rights, and the role of the state.

The arguments developed here are relevant to the experience of many countries, but I ground a more general theory of the judicialization of religion through a detailed examination of the Malaysian case. Why? Because Malaysia has one of the most tightly regulated religious spheres in the world. The country offers a clear example of the way that leaders of many Muslim-majority states have sought to define and regulate religion through law, and it provides a cautionary tale of the unintended consequences of those efforts. Malaysia provides a striking example of how judicialization can construct religion and liberal rights as binary opposites.

CONSTITUTING RELIGION IN MALAYSIA: THE CONSTRUCTION OF A "RIGHTS-VERSUS-RITES BINARY"

Long defined by its ethnic cleavages, Malaysian politics is increasingly divided by questions and controversies over religion. Tensions have simmered for decades, but a series of high-profile court cases, beginning in 2004, pit the jurisdiction of state-level shariah courts against the federal civil courts. Each of these court cases – dealing with issues of religious conversion, divorce, and child custody – was significant in a legal sense, but their collective impact was felt most strongly outside the courts. The cases generated a flood of media coverage, and they became important focal points in a fierce national debate. Competing groups of lawyers, judges, politicians, media outlets, and civil society groups channeled public discourse into two competing frames. Liberals presented the cases as grave challenges to the authority and position of the civil courts, which they cast as the last bastion for the protection of liberal rights vis-à-vis the *dakwah*

and Moustafa (2008). For a more recent review of the literature on law and courts in authoritarian regimes, see Moustafa (2014b).

[11] Arjomand (2007); Stahnke and Blitt (2005); Stilt (2004, 2015); Rabb (2008); Redding (2003), Lombardi (2006), Lombardi and Brown (2005); Hirschl (2011).

(religious revival) movement. [12] Conservatives, on the other hand, framed the cases as grave threats to the authority and position of the shariah courts, which they cast as the last bastion of religious law vis-à-vis the secular state. Each claim was a mirror image of the other. These "injustice frames" (Gamson 1992) resonated with different constituencies and exacerbated longstanding grievances, even as they shifted political identities and loyalties in new directions.

Academic treatments of these developments (e.g., Liow 2009; Hirschl 2011) nearly always assume a liberal/secularist frame. That is, controversy is attributed to the *dakwah* movement, the most dynamic social and political trend in Malaysia since the 1970s. While the *dakwah* movement is certainly an important part of the story, this book suggests a different point of origin: the formulation of "Anglo-Muslim" law in British Malaya (Horowitz 1994; Hussin 2016). [13] A direct legacy of this legal regime is that state-level shariah courts administer Anglo-Muslim law for Muslims on select matters such as family law, whereas the federal civil courts administer the common law. [14] This bifurcated legal order is premised on a clear division of jurisdiction between federal civil courts and state-level shariah courts. But given the complex social realities of a multiethnic and multi-religious society, this legal framework began to produce vexing conundrums.

Shamala v. Jeyaganesh provides a striking example of these difficulties. [15] This case, litigated between 2003 and 2010, concerned a Hindu couple who had been married under the Marriage and Divorce Act, the statute that regulates non-Muslim marriages in Malaysia. Shamala and Jeyaganesh had two children together, but a few years into the marriage Jeyaganesh left Shamala and converted to Islam. As a Muslim, Jeyaganesh was now subject to the jurisdiction of the shariah courts. As a non-Muslim, Shamala remained subject to the jurisdiction of the civil courts. Each managed to secure interim custody orders from these alternate jurisdictions, but the court orders came to opposite conclusions: the shariah court awarded custody of the children to Jeyaganesh, while the civil court awarded custody of the children to Shamala. To make matters worse, because official religious status determines which court one can use, neither parent could directly contest the competing court order. This absurd situation was the beginning of an epic legal battle that remained in the courts – and in the press – for years. The case turned on

[12] The term *dakwah* comes from the Arabic *"da'wah,"* which carries the literal meaning of "making an invitation." In Islamic theology, *da'wah* is the practice of inviting people to dedicate themselves to a deeper level of piety. In contemporary Malaysian politics, the term stands in for the various manifestations, both social and political, of the piety movement.

[13] The term Anglo-Muslim law has fallen out of use in preference for the term Islamic law. I mostly use the term Anglo-Muslim law throughout this book because I believe it signals an important distinction between the diverse body of Islamic jurisprudence (*fiqh*) and efforts to codify and operationalize select fragments of *fiqh* through a common law or civil law framework. The term "Islamic law" tends to conflate the two.

[14] Malaysia is part of the common law tradition, but the federal courts are commonly referred to as the "civil courts" when contrasted with the shariah court administration.

[15] *Shamala Sathiyaseelan v. Jeyaganesh Mogarajah & Anor* [2004] 2 MLJ 648; [2011] 2 MLJ 281.

technical issues of court jurisdiction, rules of standing, and other features of Malaysian judicial process. When discussed by activists and politicians, however, the cases were presented as a zero-sum conflict between religious law and secular law.

As a direct result of *Shamala v. Jeyaganesh*, liberal rights groups formed a coalition to rally against the erosion of civil court jurisdiction and to "ensure that Malaysia does not become a theocratic state."[16] Not long after, a broad array of over fifty conservative NGOs united in a countervailing coalition calling itself Muslim Organizations for the Defense of Islam (*Pertubuhan-Pertubuhan Pembela Islam*) or Defender (*Pembela*) for short. In its founding statement, Pembela announced that it was mobilizing to defend "the position of Islam in the Constitution and the legal system of this country."[17] Both coalitions worked tirelessly to lobby the government and to shape public understanding of what was at stake in *Shamala v. Jeyaganesh* and in dozens of other cases. The two sides found agreement only in the proposition that Malaysia faced a stark choice between secularism and Islam, between rights and rites.

Each side derived legitimacy, purpose, and power from an oppositional stance vis-à-vis the other. Liberal rights activists rallied supporters by sounding the alarm that secularism was under siege and that Malaysia was on the way to becoming an Islamic state. On the other side, conservative organizations rallied support by contending that liberal rights groups wished to undermine the autonomy of the shariah courts and that they worked in cooperation with foreign interests that were intent on weakening Islam. Both groups told the public that Islam and liberal rights were incompatible, and that Malaysians must stand for one or the other. These efforts worked to *(re)constitute* popular understandings of Islam, liberal rights, and their imagined relationship to one another – this time in starkly adversarial terms.

Constituting Religion drills deep into the Malaysian experience to trace *when*, *why*, and *how* a sharp rights-versus-religion binary emerged, first within the legal system, and subsequently radiating outwards through political discourse and popular legal consciousness. By tracing the development of this spectacle, the book shows that the dichotomies of liberal rights versus Islamic law, individual rights versus collective rights, and secularism versus religion are contingent on institutional design and political agency. Malaysian law and legal institutions produced vexing legal questions, which competing groups of activists transformed into compelling narratives of injustice. Examining the legal, political, and social construction of these binaries is not to minimize their significance. On the contrary, this book aims to show how these constructions facilitate the political agenda of some actors while they disempower others, shaping the terms of debate around a host of important substantive issues.

---

[16] Founding statement of the Article 11 Coalition. http://www.article11.org/ (last accessed March 2, 2010). The website has since closed.

[17] Pembela (2006a).

WHY MALAYSIA?

There are good reasons why Malaysia is the primary focus of this book. As suggested above, Malaysia provides a striking example of the judicialization of religion and the emergence of what I call a "rights-versus-rites binary."[18] More broadly, the Malaysian case also sheds light on diverse contexts beyond Malaysia. Before specifying the more detailed causal argument in Chapter 1, let us briefly consider the most salient features of the Malaysian legal order and situate those features within a broader comparative context.

First, Malaysia regulates religion far more than the global average. The Pew Government Restrictions on Religion Index places Malaysia at number five among 198 countries (Pew Research Center 2017). In the more detailed Government Involvement in Religion Index, which examines 175 countries world-wide, there are only ten countries with a higher ranking than Malaysia.[19] Malaysia is also something of an archetype among Muslim-majority countries, which, as a group, regulate religion more than the global average. Consider, for example, that among the twenty-three countries in the "very high" category of the Pew Government Restrictions on Religion Index, eighteen (78 percent) are Muslim-majority countries. Likewise, a full 66 percent of countries in the "very high" and "high" categories are Muslim-majority countries, whereas Muslim-majority countries comprise only 12 percent of those in the "moderate" and "low" categories. The Malaysian experience is therefore particularly relevant to this subset of countries.

A second and related feature of the Malaysian legal system is that religious difference is regulated by way of state law. Distinct personal status laws for different religious communities govern a range of life events from the cradle to the grave, including whom one can marry, how one can worship, and how one must bury the dead. Malays, who constitute just over half of the country's population of 31 million, are defined as Muslim by way of the Federal Constitution. This official religious designation imposes distinct legal rights and duties. The second-largest ethnic group is Chinese, which stands at approximately 25 percent of the total population. Most ethnic Chinese are Buddhist (76 percent), with substantial numbers identifying as Taoist (11 percent) and Christian (10 percent), while less than 1 percent are Muslim. The third-largest ethnic group is Indian, which stands at approximately 8 percent of the total population.[20] This community is also diverse in regard to religion, with most ethnic Indian Malaysians identifying as Hindu (85 percent) and smaller numbers identifying as Christian (7.7 percent) and Muslim (3.8 percent). The overall breakdown of the population by religion is approximately 60 percent

---

[18] This term was inspired, in part, by John Comaroff's (2009) reflections on the rise of "theo-legality."

[19] See Fox (2008) and http://www.religionandstate.org

[20] There is considerable ethnic and linguistic diversity within each of these groupings. This is detailed with further precision and historical context in Chapter 3.

Muslim, 19 percent Buddhist, 9 percent Christian, 6 percent Hindu, and 5 percent of other faiths. In Malaysia's bifurcated legal order, the federal civil courts administer family and personal status law for non-Muslims, while state-level shariah courts manage a separate legal framework for Muslims.[21] While some of these institutional configurations are distinctive, segmented personal status laws are by no means unique to Malaysia. Roughly one-third of all countries have plural family law arrangements (Sezgin 2013: 3; Ahmed 2015). To the extent that segmented personal status laws fuel legal quandaries and political polarization, Malaysia offers valuable insights for the sorts of legal conundrums that emerge in many other countries.

Finally, as previously noted, the Malaysian Constitution contains provisions for both liberal rights and Islamic law. While this is also the case in most other Muslim-majority countries, what sets Malaysia apart from most of its peers is that the country also enjoys a relatively robust legal system, with broad public access to the courts. The relative strength of the legal system is suggested by Malaysia's rank at 39 of 102 countries in the 2015 Rule of Law Index of the World Justice Project.[22] To be sure, the Malaysian judiciary has its problems, but the legal profession and the courts are undeniably strong in comparison with other countries that tightly regulate religion. I shall argue that religion is easily judicialized in these circumstances. What is more, with its vocal NGOs and vibrant online media, Malaysia provides fertile soil for legal controversies to move swiftly from the court of law to the court of public opinion. Countries with similar legal and institutional features can expect a vigorous judicialization of religion and, with it, the politicization of religion via the radiating effects of courts. A careful study of the judicialization of religion in Malaysia offers valuable insights into how law and courts can catalyze the emergence of a rights-versus-rites binary.

DATA AND METHOD

Fieldwork for the project was conducted in the summer and fall of 2009, in the fall of 2010, and over several subsequent stretches between 2012 and 2015. A total of 170 semi-structured interviews were conducted, seventy with lawyers, judges, activists, politicians, and journalists, and an additional 100 with "everyday Malaysians." Findings also rest on an extensive textual analysis of court decisions and press coverage of prominent cases.[23] I examined the full universe of cases where there was a question of jurisdiction between the civil courts and the shariah courts.[24]

---

[21] Until the 1980s, Malaysia had five distinct laws governing marriage and divorce for different ethnic and religious communities. These were repealed and replaced with a new marriage and divorce law for non-Muslims, leaving Anglo-Muslim law as the only distinct personal status and family law system.

[22] For a contextual analysis of the Malaysian legal system, see Harding (2012) and Harding and Whiting (2011).

[23] To gain a more general sense of the daily operations of both the shariah and civil courts, I attended court hearings in Kuala Lumpur, Putrajaya, and Selangor.

[24] To be more precise, I examined the full universe of Article 121 (1A) cases reported in the *Current Law Journal* and the *Malayan Law Journal*, two of the major databases that report Malaysian court decisions.

A context-rich, process-tracing method (Bennett and Checkel 2014) was adopted to map the development of legal institutions over time, as well as the flow of individual cases through the courts. This two-level (institutional and case-specific) process-tracing approach facilitated careful consideration of the continuities and critical junctures where legal/institutional change produced new patterns of contention inside and outside the courts. I examined the full life cycle of each case, from its first appearance in court through to the public spectacle that emerged around certain of those cases. I considered the origin of each case and the legal logics invoked, as civil court judges navigated complex entanglements and contending claims concerning shariah court jurisdiction. Next, I noted whether cases became subjects of popular debate. For those cases that did gain political salience, I examined *how* they came into the public spotlight. I then studied the contending frames of understanding that were crafted for consumption in the court of public opinion. Here, I examined the public statements issued by non-governmental organizations, political parties, and various state officials (including the religious establishment) to understand the role of different actors in the construction of a rights-versus-rites binary. With the assistance of a research team, I also compared press coverage of select court cases across Malaysia's diverse media landscape, from the Malay-language newspapers *Utusan Malaysia, Berita Harian*, and *Harakah*, to the Tamil-language papers *Makkal Osai* and *Malaysia Nanban*, to the Chinese-language *Sin Chew*, and the English-language press. This comparison suggested the extent to which Malaysia's segmented ethnolinguistic media environment further refracts competing frames of understanding across variously situated communities. Finally, I circled back to examine the extent to which these frames differed from the logics that were at work in court. Studying the full life cycle of these disputes provided an empirically grounded examination of how the rights-versus-rites binary is continually inscribed in the Malaysian public imagination.

Elite-level interviews enabled a deeper understanding of the various positions and strategies of civil society organizations, which had mobilized around controversial cases, both inside and outside formal legal intuitions. I was mindful of the need to seek out views from across the political and ideological spectrum to consider the full range of thinking about the cases and the controversies they produced. I therefore interviewed lawyers litigating on opposite sides of the same cases, as well as activists from the most prominent liberal rights and conservative NGOs who had staked out opposite sides of public lobbying efforts. (The absence of a middle ground was striking, and it speaks to the ways that judicial institutions frame a binary logic that is hard to escape.) I found it relatively easy to empathize with the views and positions of liberal rights lawyers and activists, as their frames of understanding aligned closely with my own. Yet I was cognizant that a better understanding of the concerns, anxieties, and aims of conservative groups and their audiences is essential for a deeper appreciation of the legal entanglements and their polarizing effects on popular legal consciousness. Many of the lawyers, activists, and journalists whom

I interviewed became key sources of information. The lawyers among them provided access to case files and legal briefs. Repeated discussions with all key actors helped to round out my understanding of important cases and controversies beyond what was available through official court records and press archives.

To assess the radiating effect of courts on popular legal consciousness, I organized a multiethnic research team to conduct semi-structured interviews with "everyday Malaysians." The aim of these informal interviews was to study popular under-standings of court cases and legal controversies. I was interested in assessing whether popular understandings of prominent cases matched the legal logics that are deployed in court, or if they matched the frames that political activists constructed for media consumption. I supplemented these semi-structured interviews with several structured focus groups and a nationwide, stratified survey of popular under-standings of the Islamic legal tradition.[25]

Given that this is a single-country case study, with only brief reference to the experiences of other cases, this book serves primarily as an exercise in theory generation. I acknowledge the limitations of the study in terms of theory testing and establishing wider generalizability. Nonetheless, the diachronic, context-rich, process-tracing approach I embrace here generates important insights into the judicialization of religion and the construction of a rights-versus-rites binary that might otherwise go unanalyzed with a different research design.

OVERVIEW OF THE BOOK

Chapter 1, *The Constitutive Power of Law and Legal Institutions*, details the central theoretical claims and situates the comparative significance of the book. Building on recent work from the fields of socio-legal studies, religious studies, and comparative judicial politics, I challenge the conventional view that the judicialization of religion is the result of a straightforward collision between ascendant religious movements and liberal legal orders. Instead, I suggest that law and courts constitute these struggles in at least four important ways: by establishing categories of meaning (such as "secular" and "religious"), by shaping the identity of variously situated actors, by opening an institutional framework that enables and even encourages legal conflict, and by providing a focal point for political mobilization outside the courts. While contention over religion can be expected as a matter of course in any legal system, I argue that judicialization is exacerbated when religion is tightly regulated (particularly along religious lines, as it is in Malaysia) and when dual constitutional commitments are made to religion and liberal rights. Working induc-tively through comparative examples and deductively through the institutional logic of segmented legal regimes, I theorize the ways that legal institutions catalyze ideological contestation.

---

[25]   The research methods for this part of the study are detailed in Chapter 6.

Chapter 2, *The Secular Roots of Islamic Law in Malaysia*, moves to the empirical analysis, tracing the construction of religious authority by way of state law from the colonial era to the present. The chapter presents a brief primer on Islamic legal theory, focusing on core features of the Islamic legal tradition, including the place of human agency, mechanisms of evolution, and a pluralist orientation. Against this backdrop, I examine the way that religious authority is configured by way of state law in contemporary Malaysia. I argue that the state monopoly on religious authority should not be understood as the achievement of an "Islamic state" or the "implementation" of Islamic law. Instead, I examine significant tensions between the state monopoly on religious interpretation and core epistemological commitments in the Islamic legal tradition. I argue that we should not view the parallel shariah and civil court jurisdictions as "religious" versus "secular," but rather, as parallel formations of state law.

Chapter 3, *Islam and Liberal Rights in the Federal Constitution*, examines key provisions in the Malaysian Constitution. This constitutional ethnography (Scheppele 2004) provides essential historical background for understanding (a) the legal construction of race and religion in British Malaya, (b) the dual constitutional provisions for liberal rights and Anglo-Muslim law, and (c) the formation of separate jurisdictions for Muslims and non-Muslims in areas of personal status and family law. Each of these arrangements is the product of past political struggles, even as they continue to structure legal and political contention in the present. The chapter closes with an examination of an important constitutional amendment, Article 121 (1A). Introduced in 1988, the clause became a central flashpoint of contention around civil versus shariah court jurisdictions.

Chapter 4, *The Judicialization of Religion*, moves from the legal-institutional structure to a series of controversial cases that concerned the jurisdiction of the federal civil courts vis-à-vis the state-level shariah courts from the 1980s to the present. Tracing the cases from their inception, I examine how Malaysia's bifurcated legal system and tightly regulated religious sphere hardwired legal struggles. I show that the cases had little to do with religion (as a practice of faith) and everything to do with the regulation of religion (as a state project). I also examine how legal conundrums provided openings for a handful of legal activists to challenge the status quo and to advance new visions of religion and its role in the legal order.

Chapter 5, *Constructing the Political Spectacle*, moves from the court of law to the court of public opinion. Through extensive analysis of newspaper archives, press releases, and interviews with activists, I show that legal disputes concerning court jurisdiction were virtually unknown to the public until they were brought into the media spotlight, beginning in 2004. Political activists – liberals and conservatives alike – advanced competing frames of understanding for popular consumption. Taken from the court of law and deployed in the court of public opinion, the controversies assumed a different character altogether. I examine how the cases gave new energy to variously situated civil society groups, catalyzed the formation of entirely new NGOs, and provided a focal point for political mobiliza-tion outside the courts. I trace how self-positioned secularists and Islamists both derived power, legitimacy, and purpose from their oppositional stance vis-à-vis the other. Finally, I examine how these efforts constructed and affirmed a series of "rights-versus-rites" binaries, helping to shift the inflection of longstanding poli-tical cleavages from ethnicity (Malay, Chinese, Indian) to religion (Muslim, non-Muslim).

Chapter 6, *The Rights-versus-Rites Binary in Popular Legal Consciousness*, turns from the political spectacle to popular understanding of the cases. I draw upon open-ended interviews, focus group discussions, and original national survey data to explore the various ways that the cases were understood across religious and ethnic commu-nities. The data suggest that the political spectacle conditioned popular understand-ings of the cases. More consequentially, the sharp binary frames reinforced a popular understanding that Islam and liberal rights are in fundamental tension with one another. The second half of the chapter turns to the efforts of Sisters in Islam, a Malaysian NGO that works to deactivate these binaries and expand women's rights *from within* the framework of the Islamic legal tradition. I examine the challenges they face and the strategies they pursue to overcome the rights-versus-rites binary that is now deeply entrenched in the popular imagination.

Chapter 7 turns to recent litigation involving Article 3(1) of the Federal Constitution, which declares, in part, that "Islam is the religion of the Federation." The clause received little attention for decades. The federal judiciary had understood the clause to carry ceremonial and symbolic meaning only. However, recent years have seen increasing litigation around the meaning and intent of the clause. More significantly, recent Federal Court decisions introduce a far more robust meaning, one that practically elevates the role of Islamic law in the Malaysian legal system to a new *grundnorm*. Jurisprudence on the matter is still unfolding, but what is clear is the formation of two legal camps that hold radically divergent visions of the appropriate place for Islamic law and liberal rights in the legal and political order. I argue that the Article 121 (1A) cases provided a unique opportunity for a handful of Islamist lawyers to push for a sweeping new interpreta-tion of Article 3, one that has gained surprising traction in the civil courts.

1

The Constitutive Power of Law and Courts

Why do courts frequently stand at the center of heated debates involving religion? According to many accounts, legal struggles over religion are a product of religious challenges to secular legal orders. In the most alarmist narratives, courts are depicted as front-line defenders in a virtual clash of civilizations. Consider, for example, the view of jurist and academic, András Sajó. In a 2008 article, Sajó warns his readers that "constitutional arrangements are now facing new forms of religiousness ... that aspire to control or reclaim the public space" (2008: 605). What is required to meet this challenge, according to Sajó, is "a robust notion of secularism ... capable of patrolling the borders of the public square" (605). This understanding of the problem ("strong religion") and what is at stake (liberty) is compelling because it affirms a nearly hegemonic assumption that courts play important roles in resolving conflict, defending fundamental freedoms, and sustaining secularism.[1]

In this chapter, I wish to argue that this conventional view offers an incomplete understanding of legal conflict involving religion because it fails to consider the constitutive power of law and courts. Building on frameworks from religious studies, socio-legal studies, and comparative judicial politics, I maintain that law and courts do not simply stand above politics. Instead, they *constitute* political struggle over religion in at least four important ways: by delineating categories of meaning (such as "secular" and "religious"), by shaping the identity of variously situated actors, by providing an institutional framework that enables and even encourages legal disputes, and by providing a focal point for political mobilization. Long before claims

---

[1] Lempert (1978: 99–100) summarizes the various ways that courts are thought to settle conflict: "(1) courts define norms that influence or control the private settlement of disputes; (2) courts ratify private settlements, providing guarantees of compliance without which one or both parties might have been unwilling to reach a private settlement; (3) courts enable parties to legitimately escalate the costs of disputing, thereby increasing the likelihood of private dispute settlement; (4) courts provide devices that enable parties to learn more about each other's cases, thus increasing the likelihood of private dispute settlement by decreasing mutual uncertainty; (5) court personnel act as mediators to encourage the consensual settlement of disputes; (6) courts resolve certain issues in the case, leading the parties to agree on others, and (7) courts authoritatively resolve disputes where parties cannot agree on a settlement."

over religion emerge in the courtroom, law establishes the conditions that make legal contention possible. This is not immediately visible, it turns out, precisely because a secularist vision of law and courts is so hegemonic. Not only is religion cast as a perennial source of trouble, but other explanations for ideological polarization are obscured. A constitutive approach to law helps to uncover the various ways that law and courts catalyze ideological contestation.

THE SECULAR AND THE RELIGIOUS AS LEGAL CATEGORIES

An important step in appreciating the constitutive power of state law is to recognize the secular/religious binary as a construction. As Cady and Hurd (2010) note, a conventional view regards these categories as objective, neutral, ahistorical, and universal. Recent work questions these assumptions and shows that the secular and the religious are constructed categories that are historically specific and multivalent, with varied permutations across time and space (see, for instance, Agrama 2012; Cavanaugh 2009; Hurd 2008; Dressler and Mandair 2011; Mahmood 2016; Sullivan 2005). Talal Asad first problematized the twin categories by examining the historical context from which they first emerged in Western Europe.[2] He traces the development of a secular sensibility that generates identity *from what it is not* – the constructed category of religion.[3] For Asad and those who have followed his lead, the very idea that religion constitutes a distinct field of human activity is a notion that is socially and politically constructed. It is a conception that is unique to the contemporary world.[4]

To be sure, the twin categories of the secular and the religious are constructed both inside and outside state institutions, by state and non-state actors alike. However, modern law plays a particularly important role in delineating the secular/religious dichotomy in the machinery of the modern state. Demarcating categories is, after all, what law does best. But law does not merely discover preexisting boundaries between the secular and the religious. Rather, law is an instrument that constructs the twin categories in opposition to one another. As Hussein Agrama observes, the secular/religious binary is "an expression of the state's sovereign power" (2012: 26). As the administrative capacity of the state increases, so too does the centrality of the secular/religious binary to political life, and the role of state law

---

[2] Asad builds upon Wilfred Cantwell Smith's seminal book, *The Meaning and End of Religion* (1963), in which Smith argues that religion is a conceptually reified term that is estranged from personal faith. See Asad (2001) for his direct engagement with Smith.

[3] For more on religion as a constructed category, see Asad's *Genealogies of Religion* (2009), Harrison's *'Religion' and the Religions in the English Enlightenment* (1990), Masuzawa's *The Invention of World Religions* (2005), Cavanaugh's *The Myth of Religious Violence* (2009), and Nongbri's *Before Religion: A History of a Modern Concept* (2013).

[4] Recognizing that the secular and the religious are constructed categories does not require one to abandon a commitment to the secular (or to the religious for that matter). One should nonetheless be mindful that secularism is not a value-neutral space.

in delineating that binary. A central preoccupation of courts – whether in so-called secular states or self-proclaimed religious states – is to define the "religious" and, hence, to distinguish it from the "non-religious," if only to police those boundaries.[5] This is an undertaking without end, not only because competing claims are inevitable, but also because the "secular" and the "religious" are not stable and objective classifications that are waiting to be discovered.[6] Returning to Asad's central insight, these categories are constructed against one another, and they are in a constant state of flux.

These are important insights. However, the literature on the genealogies of secularism is often theorized at a high level of conceptual abstraction. Moreover, this literature is not as engaged as it should be with other bodies of relevant scholarship. This includes a growing body of research in comparative judicial politics, which offers valuable insights into how different judicial systems produce divergent legal and political outcomes. Similarly, a rich body of sociolegal scholarship has a good deal to say about legal consciousness – that is, how people come to understand concepts like secularism and religion in different legal and political contexts (e.g., Engel and Engel 2010). One of the hoped-for contributions of this book is to put these bodies of scholarship in conversation while taking the concerns and insights of each approach seriously.

Malaysia provides a concrete example of how courts shape the secular/religious dichotomy in law, politics, and popular legal consciousness. The Malaysian case also illustrates how this dichotomy obscures its own institutional origins. Most Malaysians – even those who regard themselves as staunch secularists – take it for granted that the shariah courts apply religious law, whereas the civil courts apply secular law. This dichotomy is misleading because it sidesteps the way that state law constructs religious authority in the first place. The shariah courts did not drop from the heavens. Rather, they are creatures of state law, and the codes they apply are what the state declares Islamic law to be.[7] First introduced in the colonial era and further institutionalized after independence, "Anglo-Muslim law" imposed a state monopoly on religious interpretation.[8]

These legal constructions are not unique to Malaysia. Nor are they exclusive to Muslim-majority countries, or even to state-religion configurations more generally. As Mahmood Mamdani (1996, 2012) explains, efforts to "define and rule" were

---

5   As Winnifred Sullivan insightfully notes, "modern law wants an essentialized religion" (2005: 155).
6   Zeghal (2013) observes that these binaries were briefly disrupted in the Tunisian Revolution, only to reemerge with a vengeance once the state's lawmaking functions were reengaged.
7   This is not to suggest that the state acts with a free hand, autonomous from social forces. This book embraces a "state-in-society" approach (Migdal 1998, 2001; Migdal et al. 1994). As the empirical chapters demonstrate, ongoing struggles continue to shape the content of family law codes. What I wish to highlight in this passage is not the autonomy of the state, but rather the fact that the codification of Muslim family law belies the deep pluralism and rich diversity of the Islamic legal tradition.
8   As examined in Chapter 2, this state monopoly is in tension with the pluralism of *fiqh* (Islamic jurisprudence) and *usul al-fiqh* (Islamic legal theory).

standard features of indirect rule in the late colonial era. Colonial authorities drew distinctions along what they considered "tribal" and "racial" lines in some contexts, just as they defined socio-political cleavages along religious lines in others.[9] In all cases, state law did not simply recognize preexisting realities of race, tribe, and religion. Rather, state law constituted those communities vis-à-vis one another by demarcating sharp boundaries that had been more porous, permeable, and ambiguous (if they existed at all) before state regulation. State law also defined and regulated norms and power relations *within* those respective communities, frequently authorizing and entrenching hierarchical, patriarchal, and authoritarian readings of culture.[10] In doing so, state law worked to replace the fluid, contradictory, and contentious impulses that are inherent in any cultural formation with the fixity and stability of codified law.[11]

There is now a considerable body of research on the formation of contemporary Muslim family law that affirms Mamdani's more general insights. In most Muslim-majority countries, the codification of laws governing marriage, divorce, and other aspects of Muslim family law provided women with fewer rights than men.[12] State law reflected the patriarchy built into Islamic jurisprudence (*fiqh*) as well as the patriarchal choices made in the codification process itself.[13] Far from uniformly advancing women's rights, codification more typically narrowed the range of rights that women could claim (at least in theory) in classical Islamic jurisprudence (Quraishi and Vogel 2008; Sonbol 2008). In place of the multiple positions that one might find in Islamic jurisprudence on any given matter, codification entrenched patriarchal understandings and elevated them above all other possibilities.

These legal constructions also situate the Islamic legal tradition above other normative practices that are equally integral to Islam. As Shahab Ahmed explains in his important book *What is Islam?* an excessive focus on the Islamic legal tradition "has the consequence of putting out of focus the central place of non-legal discourses in the historical constitution of normative Islam ... " (2016: 124). Ahmed cites theology, philosophy, ethics, the arts, poetics, Sufism, the sciences, and the diverse lived traditions of Muslim communities around the world as some of the constitutive elements of Islam. The Islamic legal tradition, responsive as it is (or can be) to diverse Muslim communities across time, is but one component of Islam

---

9   To be sure, many of the same trends were present outside of the colonial context, such as the efforts to streamline and codify Islamic law in the late Ottoman Empire.

10   As Dirks observes, "much of what has been taken to be timeless tradition is, in fact, the paradoxical effect of colonial rule, where culture was carefully depoliticized and reified ... " (Dirks 1992: 8; 2000).

11   See Merry (2006) for an insightful discussion of "culture as contentious."

12   This is not because Islam is inherently incompatible with women's rights or liberal rights more generally. See Wadud (1999); An-Na'im (2008); Souaiaia (2009). For more on state codification of Muslim family law, see Charrad (2001); Tucker (2008); An-Na'im (2002); Mir Hosseini (2000); Quraishi and Vogel (2008).

13   Of course, the same can be said about codification in European family law.

among many others. Elevating select fragments of *fiqh* through state codification contributes to a "legal-supremacist" conceptualization of "Islam as law" (116).

To be sure, different norms and practices will continue to percolate despite the best efforts of the state.[14] Nonetheless, state institutions demonstrated a growing capacity to define, authorize, and enforce Anglo-Muslim law over other possible formations of Islamic law and other understandings of Islam more generally. Put simply, Anglo-Muslim law advanced an authoritarian and illiberal reading of the Islamic legal tradition: authoritarian in the sense that it "usurps and subjugates the mechanisms of producing meaning [from the Islamic legal tradition] ... to a highly subjective and selective reading" (Abou El Fadl 2001: 5) and illiberal in the sense that it prescribes inequality and privileges collective duties over individual autonomy.

A further consequence of codification is that it invokes a sharp dichotomy. It presents law in a binary form: law is either Islamic, or it is not. As Ahmed explains, "How and when we use the word 'Islamic' is important because the act of naming is a *meaningful* act: the act of naming is an act of identification, designation, characterization, constitution, and valorization." Conversely, " ... by *not* labeling something 'Islamic' (or by the stronger act of labeling it un-Islamic) we are excluding that thing from being representative of the normative values of 'Islam'" (107, emphasis added).[15]

It bears repeating that although Anglo-Muslim law in Malaysia (and most everywhere else) is illiberal, there is no necessary or essential tension between Islam and liberal rights. To be clear, this is not to say that those who work within (or draw upon) the Islamic legal tradition cannot make, or do not make, illiberal claims. They can, and they do. It is simply to suggest that illiberal constructions of Islamic law are not the only or inevitable products of the Islamic legal tradition. Indeed, the oft-cited bedrock principles of equality and justice in Islam comport well with contemporary notions of liberal rights.[16] Like all religious traditions, the Islamic legal tradition is complex and multivocal.[17] And, as with religion more generally, the relationship between Islamic law and liberal rights is best understood as indeterminate and contested, but not fundamentally incompatible. It follows, then, that when state actors choose to codify an illiberal formula, it does not represent Islam or the Islamic legal tradition in all its diversity. It only gives binding force to one among many possibilities. It is therefore inaccurate to characterize the parallel shariah and civil

---

[14] Elizabeth Shakman Hurd's (2017) distinction between "lived religion" and "governed religion" is useful for capturing this difference.

[15] For others, including some strident secularists, the act of naming is also an act of identification. Rather than valorization, however, naming may function as an act of identification, designation, characterization, constitution, and *demonization*.

[16] For compelling arguments on the compatibility of liberal rights and the Islamic legal tradition, see Abou El Fadl (2004); Baderin (2003); Kamali (2008); Sachedina (2009); Ali (2000); March (2009).

[17] Stated differently to recognize the centrality of human agency, it is Muslim legal scholars and Muslim communities that are complex and multivocal.

court jurisdictions in Malaysia as "religious" versus "secular." Rather, they are simply *two formations of state law*.[18]

LEGAL PLURALISM AND ITS DISCONTENTS

The formation of Anglo-Muslim law as a distinct field of state law necessarily entails parallel provisions for non-Muslim communities.[19] Some celebrate family law pluralism as an opportunity for communities to realize concrete expressions of "multiple modernities" (Eisenstadt 2000) in place of a uniform, homogenizing legal code applied to all citizens. But these institutional configurations can produce significant legal dilemmas. This is not only because separate family law provisions can entrench illiberal norms that are in tension with state commitments to equal citizenship. Additionally, courts are put in a position where they must "see like a state" (Scott 1998) and categorize individuals in order to apply the appropriate personal status and family law regime.

For the vast bulk of the population, the application of legal regulation is a straightforward exercise, as one's official religious status is "inherited" at birth and is usually uncontested. If one leads a conventional life, these legal arrangements are stable and coherent. However, various scenarios can complicate matters. For instance, consider the situation in which a person wishes to change his or her official religious status. How might a court determine whether the motivation springs from sincerely held religious conviction or an attempt to maneuver from one family law regime to another for strategic advantage in divorce proceedings? Or, consider another issue: in many plural family law systems, there is no legal avenue to register a cross-communal marriage. How, then, do courts address a situation in which a person wishes to marry a partner of a different religious status, and who is, therefore, subject to a different legal regime? To complicate matters further, what happens if this mixed couple has a child out of wedlock? What is the official religious

---

[18] Some readers might insist that the shariah courts nonetheless apply a legal code that has a religious basis. My point here is not that the civil courts and the shariah courts apply codes derived from comparable legal traditions. Rather, my point is that any legal code with a religious basis is, by definition, one possible formulation among myriad (perhaps infinite) possible permutations. What distinguishes Anglo-Muslim law in Malaysia is not its religious content, but the fact that it is enabled by the coercive power of the state.

[19] Plural-legal systems apply different personal status and family law codes to different (legally constituted) communities. A variety of institutional arrangements is possible. In some countries, various family law provisions are applied to distinct religious communities, using the same court system (as in Egypt). In other countries, there may be a separate court administration (as in Malaysia). In still other countries, family law pluralism operates outside of formal state institutions, with varying degrees of state recognition and enforcement (Sezgin 2015). Plural personal status laws are not unique or exclusive to Muslim-majority countries, although they are more common in those settings. The preponderance of plural family law systems in Muslim-majority countries is in part a legacy of the Millet system in the Ottoman Empire (Barkey 2008). For countries like Malaysia, which had not been part of the Ottoman legal order, British colonial rule played a formative role in the institutionalization of pluri-legal arrangements (Chapters 2 and 3).

status of the child and what are the legal rights and duties of the biological parents? And what happens if the parents register this child under one faith (making the child subject to the personal status and family law provisions applied to that community), but raise the child in a different faith tradition? Now consider a third dilemma: how do courts handle a situation where a woman wishes to contest patriarchal family laws by way of constitutional provisions that guarantee equality of citizenship? In this circumstance, collective and individual rights provisions may come into conflict, especially when the constitution authorizes both collective and individual rights, and both have the vocal support of entrenched constituencies. These circumstances are not hypothetical. They are examples of the sorts of legal dilemmas that plural family law and personal status systems produce in many contemporary contexts today.[20] And, as we will see in the chapters to come, these legal conundrums regularly crop up in contemporary Malaysia.

Some legal systems may offer creative solutions that can accommodate the complex, lived realities of the societies they regulate.[21] However, these scenarios can just as easily generate legal difficulties that courts are ill-equipped to handle. When individuals do not conform to the neat categories of race and religion envisioned by the law, they may attempt to evade state regulation. Others may challenge the rigid logic of the legal regime directly. Because such quandaries are inherently tied to identity politics, they can spark intense controversies well outside of the courts.

For a concrete example of the difficulties that legal pluralist systems can produce, consider *Lina Joy v. Islamic Religious Council*, a case that continued in the Malaysian courts for nearly a decade and became a public spectacle at home and abroad. The case concerned a woman who had converted from Islam to Christianity and subsequently sought to change her official religious status so that she could marry a non-Muslim man. In litigating Joy's right to religious freedom, her attorney argued that the state failed to provide a viable avenue for official conversion out of Islam. Joy's legal team argued that this lacuna in the law restricted her right to religious freedom, a right enshrined in Article 11 of the Malaysian Constitution, which states (in part) that *"Every person* has the right to profess and practice his religion . . . ." [emphasis added]. However, Joy's opponents invoked another clause from the same article, which states, *"Every religious group* has the right . . . to manage its own religious affairs . . ." [emphasis added]. This second set of attorneys also claimed the right to religious freedom, but they argued that Article 11 safeguards the ability of *religious groups* to craft their own rules and regulations (including rules of

---

[20]   See Aks (2004), Maclean and Eekelaar (2013), Bottoni, et al. (2016), Ahmed (2015).

[21]   I recognize that some institutional arrangements might avoid the impasses examined in this book. For more on the potential tensions between multicultural accommodation and liberal rights, as well as possible institutional solutions, see Shachar (2001). For a sanguine account of the "shared adjudication model" in India, see Solanki (2011). In contrast, Sezgin and Künkler (2014) find that the judicialization of religion exacerbated identity politics and deepened ethno-religious schisms in India.

entry and exit) free from outside interference. Ironically, advocates on both sides of the controversy invoked "religious freedom." Both sides grounded their claims in constitutional texts, and both sides called upon the state to secure their contrasting visions for Malaysian state and society. *Lina Joy v. Religious Council* is a complicated case that receives comprehensive treatment in the chapters to come. The point here is simply to highlight the fact that these legal tensions originate from the way that the Malaysian state regulates religion as a category of law.

Religious minorities (Buddhist, Christian, Hindu, Sikh, Taoist, and heterodox Muslims) regularly field claims to religious freedom vis-à-vis the state. However, state-appointed (and self-appointed) spokespersons for the Muslim majority deploy "rights talk" (Glendon 1991) of their own. Moreover, claims to religious freedom are not only voiced across communal lines. They are also heard *within* religious communities, as individuals assert their right to religious liberty for their own persons, whereas spokespersons of religious communities invoke religious freedom in their claims to defend collective norms from state interference. The frequency of these cases and the repeated appeals for state action by a variety of actors working at cross-purposes suggests that these sorts of pitfalls are inherent in legal systems like that of Malaysia. Conundrums of this kind are virtually inevitable when legal systems are premised upon idealized categories of race and religion. They have difficulty anticipating and accommodating the complex realities of the diverse and dynamic societies that they govern.

COURTS AS CATALYSTS

When individuals encounter the sorts of legal predicaments described above, their formal avenue for recourse is, ironically, the same legal system that produced the dilemma in the first place. And when the wheels of justice start to turn, the state's legal machinery is likely to crush them once more. This is because litigation tends to activate and further entrench the same problematic categories, identities, and competing interests. Cases such as *Lina Joy v. Religious Council* are never about the fate of one person alone. Litigation challenges the status and entitlements of whole groups, as well as the entrenched positions of state-appointed gatekeepers of those legally-constituted communities. Whether intended or not, these cases challenge the logic of the legal order and bring its contradictions into high relief.

Once these sorts of cases go to court, the dispute is transformed further. To better understand the legal (as opposed to religious) catalyst of conflict, I adapt Richard Alba's (2005) distinction between blurred and bright boundaries. Alba suggests that we can think of the boundaries between religious or ethnic communities as being sustained in two different ways. In the first, "blurred" boundaries are constructed in a dense web of social relations. As a result, they are porous and ambiguous, leaving them amenable to negotiation, compromise, and incremental change over time. In contrast, state law defines, demarcates, and regulates "bright" boundaries. Here, sharp and institutionalized distinctions entrench religious or ethnic difference. Group membership takes on a dichotomous character: one is either a member of a religious group or not. Of course, social and legal constructions of community and difference are often linked. Here, I wish to draw attention to the way that legal institutions work to brighten social boundaries that would otherwise remain blurred, were they not regulated by way of state law.

A long-running tradition of law and society scholarship suggests that judicial process transforms the character of disputes in important ways. Mather and Yngvesson's (1980) model of the "narrowing" and "expansion" of grievances is particularly helpful.[22] Mather and Yngvesson observe that lawyers typically narrow the circumstances of their client's predicament in order to render claims justiciable by the courts. Legal claims assume specific forms, with specialized legal discourse. Mather and Yngvesson define narrowing as, " ... the process through which established categories for classifying events and relationships are imposed on an event or series of events [to make them] amenable to conventional management procedures" (783). In disputes involving religion, litigants typically invoke fundamental rights provisions. However, as this book demonstrates, advocates on both sides of freedom of religion cases can effectively ground their claims in constitutional texts. Even when judges strive to interpret constitutional texts in a harmonious manner, the law provides activists with a powerful vocabulary.[23] Law and legal institutions enable and even encourage the construction of rights claims in absolute terms, elevating and sharpening contention, rather than resolving the conflict. This is particularly true in contexts where institutions encourage formal legal contestation and litigant activism, the two components that define "adversarial legalism" (Kagan 2001: 9).

As Benjamin Schonthal explains, litigation also tends to preclude certain compromises that might otherwise take place outside of a legal context. In the case of Sri Lanka, he finds that " ... those who rely on the language of constitutional law tend to discard over time other idioms of difference (often with more flexible notions of religious identity) for a rigid grammar of discrete rights and fixed communities" (2016: 14). This privileging of singular and exclusive identities is generally associated with religious and ethnic conflict (Sen 2006; Chandra 2012). Indeed, when ethnic and religious communities are legally constituted, and conflict is adjudicated through courts, communal tensions are institutionally hardwired. Given the path dependence of judicial reasoning, courts are made to rehash the same antagonisms time and again, keeping controversy alive in the

---

[22] To be sure, Mather and Yngvesson built upon a good deal of law and society scholarship that had focused on dispute transformation.

[23] The promise and pathologies of "rights talk" were first observed in the American political context, but the shift towards rights consciousness is now seen as a global phenomenon. For early works focused on the dynamics of rights claims and rights consciousness in American politics, see Scheingold (1974) and McCann (1994). For an early work on the pathologies of rights talk, see Glendon (1991).

public imagination.[24] When communal boundaries are socially constructed and informally mediated, on the other hand, episodes of communal conflict may very well have shorter half-lives. The specifics of conflict fade with time.

Returning to Mather and Yngvesson's model of dispute transformation, courts can likewise fuel an "expansion" of audience. Mather and Yngvesson define expansion as the widening of issues that are associated with a dispute, along with a broadening of the audience. Expansion can come about as the result of concerted efforts of litigants and lawyers to draw public attention to the immediate case at hand. However, it is often third-party actors, such as advocacy groups, political parties, and the media, that expand the audience and the grievances that come to be associated with a case. These third-party actors need not have the same goals as the litigants. In fact, their objectives are frequently misaligned. For instance, media outlets are usually not concerned with the legal outcomes of cases so much as they are interested in finding compelling stories that will titillate their audiences. Advocacy groups and political parties also have strong incentives to raise the profile of cases that promise to advance the long-term objectives of their organizations. Even when a case is loosely related to an advocacy group's long-term goals, careful framing can induce resonance with a target audience. Unlike the narrowing of a dispute to a specialized legal form, which requires technical legal knowledge, the expansion of grievances to the political realm is driven by an entirely different skillset.

Activists and the media provide interpretive frames that link specific cases with broader constellations of grievances, controversies, and political positions.[25] In the most extreme form, cases serve as metonyms for the most pressing social and political issues of the day, including fundamental questions of state identity. In such a circumstance, the audience for a case can extend to the entire nation, with most everyone invested in the outcome. It is important to note that the broadening of grievances and the expansion of audience is not inevitable. Rather, cases will remain out of public view unless and until the media or activists bring them into the public spotlight. It is, therefore, incumbent on the researcher to explain *why* certain cases become linked to broader grievances and *how* they come to command an expanded audience, while others do not.

Disputes involving religion may be particularly prone to narrowing and expansion due to the inherent multivocality and indeterminacy of religious traditions themselves. Even seemingly straightforward claims to religious freedom are inextricably linked to questions about religion itself (what does a given religious tradition *really* prescribe?) and religious authority (whose version is *really* correct?). Here, Winnifred Sullivan's (2005) focus on indeterminacy is particularly illuminating.

[24] This may be especially true in common law systems where judges engage established case law.
[25] Gamson and Modigliani (1987: 143) define a frame as "a central organizing idea or story line that provides meaning to an unfolding strip of events ... The frame suggests what the controversy is about, the essence of the issue."

She shows that, even in so-called secular legal systems such as that of the United States, "the instability of religion as a category ... limits the capacity of law to enforce rights to religious freedom" (154–55). To be sure, the United States is not unique in this regard. Religious freedom carries multiple and contested meanings across a variety of legal systems (Sullivan et al. 2015). However, competing claims over religion gain traction in constitutional orders that entrench commitments to religion.

In these circumstances, competing claims about religion and religious liberty can quickly assume a binary form: Islam is pit against liberal rights; individual rights are pit against collective rights; religion against secularism, and so on. These binaries further elevate the "legal-supremacist" conceptualization of "Islam as law" (Ahmed 2016: 116), and they further position Anglo-Muslim law as the full and exclusive embodiment of the Islamic legal tradition. Likewise, these binaries elevate "secularism" and "liberalism" as monolithic ideological formations of their own, which appear as inherently inimical to religion. Given the ease with which state law constructs these binaries, it is crucial to remain mindful that they are, in fact, *constructions*. That is, they appear in this binary form as a function of the institutional environment through which they emerge.

For these reasons and more, we should not consider Islam and liberal rights as pure, coherent, and autonomous formations. People understand Islam and liberal rights in relation to one another *in specific political contexts*. Given that courts are key institutional sites where the proverbial rubber hits the road, they play an important constitutive role in this process. They help constitute the identities and interests of variously situated actors. And they facilitate ideological conflict, even as they paper over their critical role in "hardwiring" legal and political struggle. As will become clear in the chapters to come, these legal tensions become entirely predictable, because they originate from the same legal/institutional source.[26] All of this underlines the fact that legal institutions do not sit above the fray of religion and politics.[27] Rather, they constitute the fray from start to finish. The binary formations of Islam versus liberal rights, religion versus secularism, and collective versus individual rights encourage binary claims-making. Cases like *Lina Joy* and *Shamala* work to destabilize the fragile equilibrium,

[26]   This is perhaps especially the case in common law systems, where judges often follow established legal precedent.

[27]   Working in the North American context, Benjamin Berger (2015: 13) puts it well. He observes that "[t]he cultural pluralism imagined by legal multiculturalism never includes the constitutional rule of law itself; rather, law sits in a managerial role above the realm of culture ... This positioning ... is essential to prevailing public stories about the interaction of law and religion." An earlier analog of this argument is found in *The Mythology of Modern Law*, wherein Fitzpatrick (1992) argues that we should not take modern law to be a system that stands apart from, or above religion. Rather, Fitzpatrick strives to show that contemporary law and legal thought embody all the hallmark characteristics of religion itself. One among many is the myth that modern law occupies " ... a transcendent position where it has no specific connection with society but nonetheless exercises a general domination over it" (6).

and they provide openings for partisans to go for broke and to press for a new *Grundnorm*.[28]

COURTS AS AVENUES FOR IDEOLOGICAL MOBILIZATION

Given the volume of scholarship on Islamist mobilization, it is striking how few studies examine courts as sites of ideological mobilization. Most research on Islamist mobilization is focused on the electoral arena. This near-exclusive focus on the ballot box is surprising considering the stated goal of many activists is to transform the legal order. Litigation serves as a direct pathway to induce a change in the law. Moreover, Islamist activists are not the only actors who strategically engage the legal system. In Malaysia and elsewhere, self-styled liberals and secularists also mobilize through courts to advance their own visions for state and society.[29] Dual constitutional commitments to Islam and liberal rights facilitate these divergent claims.

There are a variety of pragmatic reasons why activists might choose litigation. Compared with electoral campaigns, litigation typically requires fewer fiscal and organizational resources. The work of one skilled lawyer paired with a like-minded judge can shift the law without having to overcome the collective action problems of broad-based social movements.[30] Perhaps more important, litigation can spur change in popular discourse. Although litigants may fight legal battles in the court of law, political activists know that they can win or lose ideological struggles in the court of public opinion. This calculation explains why litigation is initiated even when activists have every reason to expect that they will *lose* in court. The fact that extensive press campaigns frequently accompany litigation also suggests an extrajudicial strategy. Publicity generated by high-profile cases can be useful for a variety of purposes, from raising the salience of an issue, to publicly discrediting the government for not living up to its stated commitments. Litigation can also attract international media and bring external pressure to bear on government. Over and above the direct impact of court rulings, high-profile cases serve as important focal points that can provoke and exacerbate national debates.

The "radiating effects" of litigation can reach far beyond the courtroom. Here, I draw on Mark Galanter's seminal observation that the impact of litigation "cannot be ascertained by attending only to the messages propounded by the courts." Rather, Galanter suggests that the resonance of court decisions "depends on the resources and capacities of their various audiences and on the normative orderings indigenous to the various social locations where messages from the courts impinge" (1983: 118). From this, we can understand that the same court decision can be understood in

---

[28] *Grundnorm* (German: Basic norm) is a concept developed by the German legal scholar and jurist Hans Kelsen in his 1934 work "The Pure Theory of Law" (Kelsen 1967). The *Grundnorm* is the basic rule norm that serves as the bedrock and foundation of an entire legal order.

[29] To be sure, liberal and secular activism is no less "political."

[30] Tarrow (1998) provides a useful introduction to the fundamentals of social movement theory.

radically different ways. McCann (1994) develops the concept of radiating effects in his study of the pay equity movement in the United States. He shows that even when litigation failed to produce change in the law, it nonetheless raised legal consciousness of actors inside and outside the movement.

Similar radiating effects have been noted in litigation involving questions of religion. In Egypt, for example, Islamist lawyers set their sights on Article 2 of the Egyptian Constitution, which declares, " ... the principles of Islamic jurisprudence are the chief source of legislation."[31] President Anwar Sadat introduced Article 2 as a symbolic gesture to bolster the religious credentials of his government. However, activists called his bluff and engaged the courts as a new political forum to test those very credentials (Moustafa 2007, 2010). Islamist litigation yielded few legal victories, but the radiating effects were profound.

For a specific illustration of this dynamic, consider the controversy that arose from the infamous lawsuit against Nasr Hamid Abu Zayd, a Cairo University professor who was accused of apostasy. Islamist lawyers found allies in court who were willing to accept a *hisba* lawsuit, wherein the litigants had no direct interest in the case. The court pronounced Abu Zayd an apostate, precipitating his departure from the country after his appeals were exhausted. The public debate overshadowed the facts of the case and polemics raged in the press for years (Glicksberg 2003). The spectacle acted as a powerful catalyst for a discursive shift that was already underway in Egyptian society. Secularists did not lose many such cases, but they had lost their footing in a "war of position" (Gramsci 1971).[32] It was widely recognized that the Abu Zayd case had become a crucial focal point in Egypt's culture wars.[33] Less frequently noted, but just as significant is that the political spectacle elevated *particular voices* – the most strident Islamist and secularist voices – above all the others. Given this prominent public platform, which was otherwise inaccessible in Egypt's authoritarian political system (Moustafa 2007), it is not surprising that Islamist lawyers continued to launch *hisba* lawsuits by the hundreds, even when the cases held little promise of legal victory. Even when Islamist lawyers lost in court, they advanced their narrative in the court of public

---

[31] The original text of Article 2 of Egypt's 1971 Constitution declared that " ... the principles of Islamic jurisprudence are a chief source." But an amendment in 1980 changed the text to "*the*" chief source.

[32] It is important to note that dual constitutional commitments do not automatically result in legal tension. Islam and liberal rights are not inherently oppositional, and judges typically work to interpret constitutional provisions in a harmonious manner (Lombardi and Brown 2005). Moreover, legal claims invoking religion are not always illiberal claims. For example, litigants frequently invoked Article 2 in Egypt to challenge the constitutionality of illiberal laws, essentially invoking a liberal inflection of the Islamic legal tradition. Yet it is notable that these are *not* the cases that come to mind in discussions of Egypt's Article 2 jurisprudence. This is a telling indication that binary assertions of Islamic law versus liberal rights draw attention because of the spectacle that is often generated around them.

[33] For more on how the Abu Zayd case fits into a broader field of ideological contestation, see Mehrez (2008). For more on legal aspects of the case, see Agrama (2012: 42–68).

opinion. They claimed that their defeat in court was further confirmation that the government had failed to fulfill its stated commitment to Islam and Islamic law.

The Abu Zayd case illustrates the radiating effects of litigation and the powerful dynamic of discursive polarization. The likeness with the Malaysian case suggests that we need to pay attention to the indirect and radiating effects of the judicialization, and the strategic use of litigation to facilitate the claims that are made outside of courts.

MOBILIZING IN THE COURT OF PUBLIC OPINION

The radiating effects of courts are facilitated by the technical nature of law and legal institutions. The vast bulk of the population in every country does not have the legal training that is necessary to understand legal argumentation. The work of courts is, therefore, anything but self-evident to the lay public. In the more general typology provided by Charles Tilly, judicial decisions have the characteristics of "technical accounts" as opposed to "stories" (2006). According to Tilly, technical accounts are not accessible to lay audiences, by their very nature. This inaccessibility provides opportunities for political entrepreneurs to recast court decisions along stylized and emotive frames for public consumption. The technical aspects of legal process and legal decisions lend themselves to being transformed into compelling political narratives in the court of public opinion. Complexity not only makes competing narratives possible; it virtually guarantees that they will proliferate. As Merry (1990: 111) notes in her seminal study of legal consciousness, "the same event, person, action, and so forth can be named and interpreted in very different ways. The naming... is therefore an act of power. Each naming points to a solution." In translating technical accounts into stories, political entrepreneurs define the terms of debate. And in doing so, they make complicated issues legible for a general audience. Complexity gives political entrepreneurs the opportunity to frame legal problems in ways that advance their competing political agendas.[34]

The media is the primary avenue through which political actors work to broaden their audience. Efforts to draw the public's attention come in the form of "impromptu" statements on courthouse steps, press conferences at NGO headquarters, extended interviews with journalists, appearances on television and radio, open letters to the government that run in the newspapers, and more. Given the fact that a dispute typically involves multiple hearings and appeals, a single conflict has the potential to generate fresh press stories for upwards of a decade. For instance, a child custody/conversion dispute that first went to court when I began fieldwork for this project in 2009 is still working its way through the courts after the better part of a decade. *Indira Gandhi v. Muhammad Ridzuan Abdullah* has, by the time of writing, produced eighteen separate court decisions and thirty-five

---

[34]   See Benford and Snow (2010) for more on the importance of framing processes to social movements.

"newsworthy" court appearances. The dispute advanced through multiple hearings in the Shariah Court, the High Court, the Court of Appeal, and the Federal Court of Malaysia. Each hearing was covered as a distinct media event – the next installment in a politically charged and emotive drama. With each court decision, dozens of NGOs mobilized on opposite sides of a rights-versus-rites binary. Conservative Muslim organizations and liberal rights groups held watching briefs, submitted *amicus curia* briefs, and worked overtime outside the courts to frame the significance of the cases through public statements and media events.

The profound effect of the mass media on popular legal consciousness is underlined in Haltom and McCann's (2004) *Distorting the Law*. In their study of US tort litigation, they find that the American media played a central role in shaping popular (mis)conceptions of tort law, and attitudes towards the law more generally. Haltom and McCann help us make sense of the disconnect between popular legal consciousness and the actual work of courts. They also show us that skewed media representations tend to reflect and perpetuate existing power relations and ideological formations. Although Haltom and McCann examine popular legal knowledge rather than *competing* legal knowledges, they recognize that "a wide variety of legal knowledges and narratives circulates in modern society" and they suggest that even the same narrative can " … mean different things to different people in different situations" (12).

I embrace this nod to rival narratives and competing legal knowledges in this study. In that vein, I wish to draw the reader's attention to the ways that ethnolinguistic media segmentation amplifies distinct media narratives. In the flurry of coverage in Malaysia, media outlets frame court decisions differently in distinct ethnolinguistic markets, further refracting the radiating effects of judicialization across ethnolinguistic communities. Coverage of cases in the Malay-language newspapers *Utusan Malaysia*, *Berita Harian*, and *Harakah* is thus radically different from the Tamil-language newspapers *Makkal Osai* and *Malaysia Nanban*, which are different again from the Chinese *Sin Chew*, which in turn diverges from the English-language press. Over and above the ethnolinguistic diversity of the traditional media, social media platforms and a variety of other digital media tools increasingly empower advocacy groups by enabling them to operate outside the legal and fiscal constraints that saddle traditional media outlets. These digital platforms provide opportunities to engage the public directly and to build specific constituencies with targeted narratives of the law. Social media also provide spaces where everyday citizens actively participate in the production of divergent polemics and narratives of injustice.

(RE)CONSTITUTING RELIGION?

The opening pages of this book note that many Muslim-majority states have adopted constitutional provisions and substantive regulations in an effort to constitute Islam by way of state law. But rather than providing fixity to the amorphous category of religion, efforts to legislate Islam open new fields of contestation that draw new participants into the production of religious knowledge. If we accept the Asadian position that " ... religion is produced discursively rather than objectively found ... " (Dressler and Mandair 2011: 19) as many scholars have come to argue, then we should direct our attention to the specific institutional spaces where binary frames are produced, circulated, and sustained.[35] Courts are not the only settings where binary frames are constructed, but they are among the most important.[36]

What is remarkable about judicialization is that it draws in (and provides a platform for) a variety of actors who have little or no expertise in matters of religion. Claims and counter-claims are fielded by litigants, lawyers, judges, political activists, journalists, and government officials. Most of these actors have little (if any) specialized knowledge of Islamic law or the Islamic legal tradition. Yet their competing claims are nonetheless consequential. In fact, judicialization positions these actors as central agents in the production of new religious knowledge – often displacing, or at least competing alongside "traditional" religious authorities. What is so striking in the Malaysian case is that these actors increasingly define Islam *vis-à-vis* liberalism, or, more to the point, *against* liberalism.[37] As Murray Edelman (1988: 69) observes, "In polarizing public opinion, enemies paradoxically cooperate with each other, though the cooperation may be unintentional." The goals of self-positioned secularists and Islamists were enabled by the stance of the other. Each is an "enemy in the mirror" (Euben 1999).

We have already noted that claims in the court of law and in the court of public opinion construct Islam and liberalism as binary opposites. But do these elite-level claims shape popular religious knowledge and popular legal consciousness? This question receives extensive attention in the empirical chapters to come, but the answer may already be apparent. Increasingly in Malaysia, Islam is understood as being in fundamental tension with liberal rights. The binaries that are advanced by political activists and circulated in the media elevate the "legal-supremacist" conceptualization of "Islam as law" (Ahmed 2016: 116) and they position Anglo-Muslim law as the full and exclusive embodiment of the Islamic legal tradition. Likewise, these binaries elevate secularism and liberalism as monolithic ideological formations of their own and position them as inherently inimical to religion. As illustrated

---

[35] This approach answers Talal Asad's call for an "anthropology of Islam." In his seminal 1986 paper, Asad explains that "The variety of traditional Muslim practices in different times, places, and populations indicate the different Islamic reasonings that different social and historical conditions can or cannot sustain .... An anthropology of Islam will therefore seek to understand the historical conditions that enable the production and maintenance of specific discursive traditions or their transformation ... " (Asad 1986: 23).

[36] See Bayat (2007) for an empirically grounded example of how contestation shapes and reshapes religious knowledge outside the bounds of judicial institutions.

[37] This is the mirror image of Joseph Massad's (2015) *Islam in Liberalism*, wherein he works to show that liberalism is often defined against Islam.

throughout this book, self-positioned Islamists frequently claim that liberalism, secularism, and pluralism are inimical to Islam. Rather than challenge the basis of these claims, liberal rights activists more frequently reinforce and validate this Manichean worldview by emphasizing the incompatibility of Islamic law with liberal rights and secularism. This binary then underwrites the rationale of each side, and it consolidates the rhetorical position of individuals and groups who embrace the dichotomy. Given the ease with which these polarities emerge and the degree to which these binaries are normalized in popular legal consciousness, we must remain mindful that they are not inevitable. These binaries emerge as a function of the institutional environment through which Islam and liberal rights are enacted, and as a function of how they are situated vis-à-vis one another. Islam and liberal rights are not autonomous, pure, and coherent formations. What is more, in contexts like that of Malaysia, Islam and liberal rights are increasingly co-constitutive. Vernacular associations between Islam and liberalism are shaped by the political environment in which actors are situated.[38]

These binary constructions are not unique to Malaysia or Muslim-majority countries.[39] In the United States, conservative activists shifted away from promoting "traditional values" to a rights-oriented discourse (Dudas 2008). This move has long been evident in the adoption of a "right to life" frame among anti-abortion activists (Jelen 2005). More recently, there has been a shift towards a "religious liberty" frame (Jelen 2005; Djupe et al. 2014). The Religious Freedom Restoration Acts, which were proposed or signed into law in dozens of US states in 2015, illustrate this shift. The Acts reengineered the logic of federal legislation that Congress had intended as a shield for the *rites* of religious minorities into a *rights*-based rationale for denial of service to same-sex couples in the name of religious liberty. While criticism of religion-based exemptions turned around the implications for civil rights, these controversies also provided openings for conservatives to field assertions *about religion itself*. That is, the spectacle provides opportunities for groups and individuals to advance claims about the requirements of the faith. So, when a bakery-owner refuses to sell a wedding cake to a gay couple, there is more at stake than the legal question of religious liberty versus civil rights. The case also provides an occasion for social conservatives to amplify their position that homosexuality is inimical to Christianity. Similarly, when the United States Supreme Court adjudicated *Burwell v. Hobby Lobby Stores Inc.*, there was more at stake than the reproductive rights of employees versus the faith-based exemptions sought by their employers.[40]

---

[38] Menchik (2016: 8) puts it well when he explains that "actors' interests and beliefs are rooted in local history rather than universal models of rationality or deterministic applications of theology. Religious actors' interests originate in a specific place, time, and set of discourses; their behavior cannot be understood without understanding that context." For more on the constructivist approach to religion, see Menchik (2017).

[39] Indeed, "the social construction of reality" (Berger and Luckman 1991) is a foundational concept in the sociology of knowledge.

[40] The case concerned whether Hobby Lobby Inc. must comply with provisions in the Affordable Care Act, which covered birth control for company employees.

The case also provided an opportunity for the store owners and their socially conservative allies to amplify their view that the "morning-after pill" is a form of abortion that is forbidden in Christianity.

As in the Malaysian case, the rights-versus-rites frame tends to advance one or the other visions of liberalism (as a *shield from* religion, or as a *threat to* religion), while it fortifies the notion that religion is monolithic, fixed, and illiberal. Survey research conducted by Goidel et al. (2016) suggests that this sort of rhetorical positioning has a measurable effect on threat perception. The conservatives in their study who were more attentive to the news tended to believe that liberalism constituted a threat to religious liberty, and to Christianity itself. Although the study focused specifically on news consumption among socially conservative viewers, one can reasonably infer that the same television coverage may very well affirm the prejudice of an audience with a different political persuasion of the inverse proposition: that religion imperils liberalism, secularism, and equal rights.

There will always be voices that resist these binary constructions. In Malaysia, public intellectuals affirm that religion and liberal rights are not mutually exclusive, and that one can be both a committed liberal *and* a devout Muslim. However, the blare of binary polemics that engulf the media typically drowns these voices out. The lion's share of political messaging is constant, and that message is this: Malaysians need to choose once and for all whether religion or liberalism will reign supreme in the legal and political order. This binary constitutes religion as the opposite of liberalism, and vice-versa. Of course, mass publics do not passively absorb this dichotomous mindset wholesale. As in other settings, national-level polemics sit alongside the more complex social networks within which individuals are embedded.[41] Identity, belonging, and sense of political community develop through these everyday interactions, in the shadow of national-level political spectacle (Bowen 2003; Walsh 2004; Kendhammer 2016). The mundane reality of everyday social worlds runs parallel to the polarizing spectacle of the national stage.

A rights-versus-rites binary is increasingly evident in other national contexts, in different shades and to varying degrees. Rather than associate these tensions with the "problem" of religion, the variability of these constructions invites a deeper inquiry into the political and institutional contexts that feed their emergence. In pursuit of that end, this book moves from this more general theorizing to a context-rich study of the rights-versus-rites binary in Malaysian law, politics, and popular legal consciousness. The first step in this path is a more precise understanding of the legal and institutional frameworks that activate these constructions in Malaysia. Chapter 2 therefore moves to an empirical analysis, where I trace the legal construction of religious authority in Malaysia, from the colonial era to the present.

---

[41] It has long been noted that the cultural production of law takes place in the everyday social networks within which individuals are situated (Merry 1990; Ewick and Silbey 1998).

2

The Secular Roots of Islamic Law in Malaysia

"In a nation-state, the state is itself the only true repository of legal authority, the monopolization of which, by definition, it ever so zealously guards."

– Sherman Jackson (1996: xiv)

" . . . not every divergent understanding of law is sufficient to withstand the coercive power of the state."[1]

– Robert Cover (1983: 51)

Malaysia ranks sixth out of 198 countries worldwide in the degree of restrictions on the free practice of religion, surpassing even Saudi Arabia (Pew Research Center 2017). In another measure, the Government Involvement in Religion Index, only ten countries worldwide have a higher ranking than Malaysia.[2] Malaysian law requires Muslims to attend Friday prayer, to fast during Ramadan, and to abide by dietary restrictions all year long. Drinking, gambling, and "sexual deviance" are prohibited, as is interfaith marriage and conversion out of Islam.[3] But over and above these rules and regulations, it is the state's monopoly on religious interpretation that is the most striking feature of Malaysian law. Once recorded in the official Gazette, *fatwas* from state-appointed officials assume the force of law and public expression of alternate views is criminalized.[4] From this vantage point, Malaysia appears as a religious state,

---

[1] Republished with permission of *Harvard Law Review* from Cover, Robert M. 1983. "Foreword: Nomos and Narrative" *Harvard Law Review* 97: 4–68; permission conveyed through Copyright Clearance Center, Inc.

[2] This is the ranking for 2008 (the most recent year for which data is available in the Government Involvement in Religion Index at the time of publication). See http://www.religionandstate.org and Fox (2008).

[3] In the Federal Territories, the Syariah Criminal Offences Act criminalizes failure to perform Friday prayers (Article 14), breaking one's fast during Ramadan (Article 15), gambling (Article 18), drinking (Article 19), and "sexual deviance" (Articles 20–29). State-level enactments mirror most of these federal-level statutes. Enforcement of these laws varies widely depending on the type of offence.

[4] A *fatwa* (pl. *fatawa*) is a non-binding legal opinion provided by a qualified scholar of Islamic law in response to a question. As examined later in this study, however, the Malaysian state has institutionalized the *fatwa* in a manner that fundamentally subverts this principle. Once published in the official gazette, a *fatwa* acquires the force of law.

at least for the 60% of Malaysian Muslims who are subject to these laws. To be sure, the idea that the shariah courts apply religious law while the civil courts apply secular state law is a notion that is widely accepted in contemporary Malaysia, both among advocates for Islamic law and staunch secularists alike. In elite and popular discourse, it is difficult to escape the binary trope of a secular legal sphere juxtaposed beside (or against) an autonomous religious sphere. However, this binary elides the way that religion and religious authority are constituted by way of state law in the first place. The shariah courts did not drop from the heavens. Rather, they are creatures of state law and the codes that they apply are little more than what the state declares Islamic law to be. The state monopoly on religious interpretation and the imposition of select fragments of *fiqh* should not be taken as the straightforward "implementation" of Islamic law, or the adoption of an "Islamic" system of governance, or the achievement of an "Islamic state," as the government periodically claims.[5] There are no such ideal-types.[6] What Malaysia does offer is an instructive example of how efforts to regulate religion in this fashion come in tension with core epistemological commitments of Islamic legal theory.

In making this argument, I risk entering contested terrain in the field of Islamic legal studies. In recent years, one of the foremost authorities in the field, Wael Hallaq, has drawn fire for arguing that Islamic law and the modern state are fundamentally incompatible. Hallaq (2009; 2014) contends that the methodological and substantive pluralism of the Islamic legal tradition, along with its core internal logics, developed outside the context of the modern state and that these constitutive features cannot be sustained under the legal monism that is part and parcel of contemporary statecraft.[7] Other scholars, primarily historians, challenge these claims. They contend that proto-state institutions were not only central to the development of Islamic law well before the advent of the modern state, but also that rulers were always important constitutive agents in both the application and development of Islamic law (Baldwin 2017; Burak 2015; Ibrahim 2015; Stilt 2011). The debate between Hallaq and his critics may ultimately reflect a difference of focus and approach. Hallaq appears to privilege the idealized self-conception of jurists, as presented through their doctrine.[8] His critics, on the other hand, consider the political realities that often ran roughshod over the pure legal reasoning articulated by jurists. Whether the advent of the modern state precipitated an irreversible rupture in the Islamic legal tradition, as Hallaq contends, or whether rulers had

---

5   Another way to put it is that any claim to Islamic law, or an "Islamic" system of governance, or an "Islamic state" must contend with myriad competing claims for other formations of Islamic law. No single formation is the sole or exclusive instantiation of Islam or Islamic law.

6   See Abd al-Raziq (1925), Ali (2009), and An-Na'im (2008).

7   For lengthy critiques of Hallaq's work, see Fadel (2011) and March (2015).

8   Rumee Ahmed (2012: 154) describes the pure legal reasoning of jurists as the construction of a "subjunctive world." That is, an idealized vision of " . . . how the world can be, or perhaps how the world should be." Ayesha Chaudhry articulates a similar conception with the term "idealized cosmology" (2013: 11).

always played a central role in the development of the Islamic legal tradition as suggested by his critics, these questions are ultimately for historians to settle.[9] My objective is different. My aim in the forthcoming chapters is to examine *the politics of claims-making* around Islam and Islamic law in contemporary Malaysia by the government, the courts, interest groups, the religious establishment, and everyday citizens.

This goal entails still more risks and liabilities. I am sympathetic to Baudouin Dupret's view that "Islamic law is what people consider as Islamic law, nothing more, nothing less, and it is up to theologians, believers, and citizens, not social scientists, to decide whether something does conform or not to some 'grand tradition'" (2007: 79). I am also mindful of Dupret's insistence that social scientists do not occupy a position " . . . vis-à-vis the social that would allow them to 'reveal' to 'self-deceived people' the truth that is concealed from them because of their 'lack of critical distance', 'ignorance' and/or 'bad faith'" (2007: 79). Yet the fact remains that politics and religion are "mutually infused" (Camaroff 2009) in contemporary Malaysia. A detailed examination of this mutual infusion is therefore necessary if one wishes to better understand just about any aspect of Malaysian politics, including the strident debates around shariah versus civil court jurisdictions, the intensifying construction of binaries between Islam and liberal rights, the politics of ethnic and religious polarization, the prospects for women's rights in Muslim family law, perceptions of government legitimacy, and much more.

This chapter traces the legal construction of religious authority in the Malay Peninsula from the colonial era through to the present. I first offer a brief primer on Islamic legal theory, focusing on core features such as the locus of innovation, the place of human agency, internal mechanisms of change, and its pluralist epistemology. Against this backdrop, I examine the construction of religious authority by way of state law in contemporary Malaysia. Specifically, I investigate how state and federal authorities enacted select fragments of *fiqh* while jettisoning core epistemological commitments of *usul al-fiqh*.[10]

CORE PRINCIPLES IN THE ISLAMIC LEGAL TRADITION

One of the defining features of Islam is that there is no "church." That is, Islam has no centralized institutional authority to dictate a uniform doctrine as might be found, for example, in the Catholic Church.[11] For guidance, Muslims consult the textual sources of authority in Islam: The Qur'an, which Muslims believe is the word

---

[9]   I also recognize the possibility that other institutional configurations may be able to preserve the integrity of classical modes of reasoning. For an exploration of these possibilities, see Rabb (2013).

[10] *Usul al-fiqh* carries the literal meaning "the origins of the law" or "the roots of the law" but it can also be translated as "principles of understanding" or "Islamic legal theory" in that it constitutes the interpretive methodology undergirding Islamic jurisprudence.

[11] There are exceptions, such as the Ismailis, but they represent a tiny minority among the worldwide Muslim community.

of God, as revealed to the Prophet Muhammad in the seventh century, and the Sunnah, the normative example of the Prophet. The absence of a centralized institutional authority resulted in a pluralistic religio-legal tradition. In the first several centuries of the faith, schools of jurisprudence formed around leading religious scholars (*fuqaha'*). Each school of jurisprudence (*madhhab*) developed its own distinct set of methods for engaging the central textual sources of authority to guide the Muslim community. Techniques such as analogical reasoning (*qiyas*) and consensus (*ijma*), the consideration of the public interest (*maslaha*), and a variety of other legal concepts and tools were developed to constitute the interpretive methods of *usul al-fiqh*, from which Islamic jurisprudence is derived. The legal science that emerged was one of tremendous complexity, both within each *madhhab* and amongst them. Dozens of distinct schools of Islamic jurisprudence emerged in the early centuries of the faith. However, most died out or merged over time, eventually leaving four central schools of jurisprudence in Sunni Islam that have continued to this day: the Hanafi, Hanbali, Maliki, and Shafi'i.[12]

The engine of change within each school of jurisprudence was the private legal scholar, the *mujtahid*, who operated within the methodological framework of his or her *madhhab* to perform *ijtihad*, the disciplined effort to discern God's law. The central instrument of incremental legal change was the *fatwa*, a non-binding legal opinion offered by a *mujtahid*.[13] Because *fatwas* are typically issued in response to questions posed by individuals in specific social situations, *fatwas* responded to the diverse contexts of different Muslim communities.[14] In this sense, the evolution of Islamic jurisprudence was a bottom-up, not a top-down process (Masud, Messick, and Powers 1996: 4).

Differences among jurists inevitably produced vigorous doctrinal debates. As if to guard against the centripetal force of their disagreements, jurists valorized diversity of opinion (*ikhtilaf*) as a generative force in the search for God's truth. The proverb, "In juristic disagreement there lies a divine blessing" underlined this aspiration (Hallaq 2001: 241). To be sure, reality frequently diverged from this ideal. Historians will point to examples throughout history where jurists were harshly repressed, with the complicity of their fellow legal scholars. Nonetheless, *ikhtilaf* was idealized as a core normative ethos.

Diversity of opinion was also sustained through a conceptual distinction between *shari'a* (God's way) and *fiqh* (understanding). Pre-modern jurists did not use the specific terms "*shari'a*" and "*fiqh*" – these terms came about in the contemporary

---

[12] Ja'fari *fiqh* constitutes another branch of Islamic jurisprudence in Shi'a Islam. For the sake of simplicity, I focus only on Sunni Islam, which comprises approximately 85 percent of the worldwide Muslim population, including the Muslim population of Malaysia.

[13] The *fatwa* is often incorrectly translated as a religious "edict," but fatwas are merely non-binding legal opinions that do not, by themselves, carry the force of law.

[14] Less commonly, muftis could pose hypothetical questions, followed by a legal opinion on the matter. For more on the *fatwa* in Islamic law and society, including dozens of historical and contemporary examples, see Masud, Messick, and Powers (1996).

era – but their writings clearly demonstrate recognition of this *conceptual* distinction. Whereas jurists consider the *shari'a* as immutable, they acknowledge the diverse body of *fiqh* opinions as the product of human engagement with the textual sources of authority in Islam. In this dichotomy, God is infallible, but human effort to know God's Will with any degree of certainty is imperfect and fallible. The norm was so valorized in the writings of jurists that they concluded their legal opinions and discussions with the statement *"wa Allahu a'lam"* (and God knows best). The phrase was meant to acknowledge that no matter how sure one is of her or his analysis and argumentation, only God ultimately knows which conclusions are correct. The distinction between God's perfection and human fallibility asked of jurists to acknowledge that competing legal opinions from other scholars, or from other schools of jurisprudence, may also be correct. As Hallaq (2009: 27) relates, "for any eventuality or case, and for every particular set of facts, there are anywhere between two and a dozen opinions, if not more, each held by a different jurist... there is no single legal stipulation that has monopoly or exclusivity."

But what are lay Muslims to do with so many differing opinions on offer? Most jurists hold that lay Muslims are obliged to follow the fatwas of their chosen school of jurisprudence through the principle of *taqlid*, a term that means "to follow (someone)."[15] The principle recognizes the fact that lay Muslims do not have the requisite expertise to engage in *ijtihad*, leaving them dependent on the guidance of scholars who do.[16] Nonetheless, the conceptual distinction between the *shari'a* and *fiqh* helps delimit the relationship between experts in Islamic jurisprudence and lay Muslims. Because human understanding of God's Will is unavoidably fallible, the authority of a scholar can never be understood as absolute. A *fatwa* merely represents the legal opinion of a fallible scholar; it is not considered an infallible statement about the Will of God.

The distinction between the *shari'a* and *fiqh* also provides a rationale for change over time (Johansen 1999; Weiss 1992; Abou El Fadl 2001; Hallaq 2009). Whereas God's Way is considered immutable, *fiqh* is regarded as dynamic and responsive to the varying circumstances of the Muslim community across time and space.[17] According to Hallaq, "Muslim jurists were acutely aware of both the occurrence of, and the need for, change in the law, and they articulated this awareness through such maxims as 'the fatwa changes with changing times'... or through the explicit

---

[15] The specific *mathhab* that one follows is often a function of geography and one's local religious community. In some regions, there may be a dominant or "official" *mathhab*, while there may be several in other regions.

[16] Abou El Fadl (2001: 50–53) maintains that this religious authority is not unconditional and that it is incumbent on lay Muslims to evaluate a scholar's qualifications, sincerity, and reasoning to the best of their ability. If an individual believes that the reasoning of another scholar or even another school of jurisprudence is closer to the Will of God, he is obliged to follow his conscience, as he alone must ultimately answer to God.

[17] "Shari'ah as a moral abstract is immutable and unchangeable, but no Muslim jurist has ever claimed that *fiqh* enjoys the same revered status" (Abou El Fadl 2001: 76).

notion that the law is subject to modification according to 'the changing of the times or to the changing conditions of society.'"[18]

Another conceptual distinction, this time between *fiqh* and *siyasa*, is also worth noting.[19] Whereas *fiqh* is the diverse body of legal opinions produced by scholars primarily outside of the state, *siyasa* constituted the realm of policy, backed by coercive political authority. The *fiqh/siyasa* distinction is probably best understood as a longstanding doctrinal concern rather than an accurate description of law in action. The distinction is itself likely an artifact of how jurists wished to see themselves and their work (as independent from the machinations of power) rather than an accurate representation of realities on the ground. The *fiqh/siyasa* distinction is, in other words, part of the "idealized cosmology" (Chaudhry 2013: 11) developed by jurists.

In any case, more important than what Islamic legal theory had to say about pluralism and legal change were the practical realities of pre-modern governance. State capacity was limited in the pre-modern era. This began to change, however, with new technologies of governance. In the Ottoman Empire, legal codification and a variety of administrative reforms were introduced to repel rising European powers and incipient challenges from within the Empire. In other cases, such as that of Malaya, legal codification and state-building were intimately tied to colonial rule (Hussin 2016; Massoud 2013). Legal codification and administrative innovations enabled states to regulate their societies in a far more systematic and disciplined manner. To be sure, a growing body of scholarship suggests that proto-state institutions had already shaped the development and application of Islamic law well before the arrival of the modern state (Baldwin 2017; Burak 2015; Ibrahim 2015; Stilt 2011). But there was no administrative apparatus that applied uniform legal codes in the way that we now take for granted (Jackson 1996). The speed and extent of this transformation is evident in the rapid expansion of state power on the Malay Peninsula in the 19th and 20th centuries.

CODIFICATION AS THE DEATH OF PLURALISM

Although Islam spread through the Malay Peninsula beginning in the fourteenth century, the institutionalization and bureaucratization of Islamic law is a more recent development.[20] Religious and customary norms were primarily socially embedded at the local level in the pre-colonial era. Religious leaders were "those members of village communities who, for reasons of exceptional piety or other

---

[18] Hallaq 2001: 166.
[19] For more on the relationship between *fiqh* and *siyasa*, see Vogel (2000), Quraishi (2006), and Stilt (2011).
[20] According to Peletz, "despite the references to Islamic law that exist in fifteenth-century texts such as the *Undang-Undang Melaka*, there is little if any solid evidence to indicate widespread knowledge or implementation of such laws in the Malay Peninsula prior to the nineteenth century" (2002: 62).

ability, had been chosen by the community to act as imam of the local mosque, or the court imam . . . ."[21] The colonial period marked an important turning point for the institutionalization, centralization, and bureaucratization of religious authority in the Malay Peninsula.[22]

The British first gained control of port cities for trade and commerce in Penang (1786), Singapore (1819), and Malacca (1824).[23] Together, the three outposts formed the Straits Settlements, which were later ruled directly as a Crown colony beginning in 1867. Separately, Britain established protectorates in what would come to be known as the Federated Malay States of Perak, Negeri Sembilan, Pahang, and Selangor, and the Unfederated Malay States of Johor, Kedah, Kelantan, Perlis, and Terengganu. The British first established its system of "indirect rule" in Perak. There, the British recognized Raja Abdullah as the Sultan of Perak in return for an agreement that the advice of a British Resident "must be asked and acted upon on all questions other than those touching Malay religion and custom . . . ." (Maxwell and Gibson 1924: 28–29; See Hussin 2007; 2016 for additional context). The Treaty of Pangkor and analogous treaties left local rulers to oversee religious and customary law, while English common law governed all other aspects of commercial and criminal law. By the early twentieth century, the whole of the Malay Peninsula was brought under similar agreements, as Britain extended its control and local rulers accommodated to consolidate their power vis-à-vis local competitors (Hussin 2016).

With a free hand in the Straits Settlements (which were ruled directly), the British issued a "Muhammadan Marriage Ordinance" in 1880. Special courts for Muslim subjects were established as a subordinate part of the judicial system in 1900.[24] Jurisdiction of the Muslim courts was limited to family law matters, and decisions were subject to appeal before the High Courts, which functioned under British common law (Horowitz 1994: 256). With British assistance and encouragement, similar Muhammadan marriage enactments went into force in Perak (1885), Kedah (1913), Kelantan (1915), and most other states of British Malaya.[25] Additional laws organized court functions and specified select criminal offenses.[26] State-level religious councils (*Majlis Agama Islam*) and departments of religious affairs (*Jabatan Agama Islam*) were also established. According to Roff (1967: 72), these institutional

---

[21] "In the realm of religious belief, as in that of political organization, the Malay state as a rule lacked the resources necessary for centralization of authority" (Roff 1967: 67).

[22] See Roff (1967), Hooker (1984), Horowitz (1994), Hussin (2007), Lindsey and Steiner (2012).

[23] Britain gained control of Malacca by way of the Anglo-Dutch Treaty, which had divided the Malay Archipelago between Britain and the Netherlands.

[24] Straits Settlements Enactment 5 of 1880. The first iteration of this ordinance carried the spelling "Mahomedan" while later iterations used the spelling "Muhammadan."

[25] There were exceptions. Johore adopted a version of the Ottoman Mejelle in the early 20th century (Horowitz 1994: 255), which underlines the fact that the move towards codification was not simply a function of colonial rule, but was rather a function of state-building through this period more generally.

[26] For an example, see the Muhammadan Offenses Enactment of Selangor (1938).

transformations produced "an authoritarian form of religious administration much beyond anything known to the peninsula before."

> A direct effect of colonial rule was thus to encourage the concentration of doctrinal and administrative religious authority in the hands of a hierarchy of officials directly dependent on the sultans for their position and power .... By the second decade of the twentieth century Malaya was equipped with extensive machinery for governing Islam. (Roff 1967: 72–73)

The introduction of codified law, new legal concepts and categories, and English-style legal institutions all marked a significant departure from practices that had varied widely across the Malay Peninsula. The new legal regime was also incongruent with core epistemological assumptions of *usul al-fiqh*. The term "Anglo-Muslim law" is used to describe this peculiar melding of legal traditions. The law was "Anglo" in the sense that the concepts, categories, and modes of analysis followed English common law, and it was "Muslim" in the sense that it applied to Muslim subjects. As such, Anglo-Muslim law was an entirely different creature from classical Islamic law.[27] As Hooker explains, by the beginning of the twentieth century, "a classically-trained Islamic jurist would be at a complete loss with this Anglo-Muslim law" whereas "a common lawyer with no knowledge of Islam would be perfectly comfortable" (Hooker 2002: 218). Passages from religious texts were sometimes cited to support the rationale for particular court decisions, but the mode of legal analysis was English common law. Hooker explains, "'Islamic law' is really Anglo-Muslim law; that is, the law that the state makes applicable to Muslims" (2002: 218).

Islam was not the only religious tradition that was appropriated by the state in this fashion. Just as "Anglo-Muslim law" was applied to Muslim subjects, "Anglo-Hindu law" and "Chinese customary law" codes were developed for ethnic Chinese and ethnic Indian subjects.[28] The tremendous ethnic, linguistic, and religious diversity within each of these communities was flattened by these monolithic legal categories, at least for the purpose of state law.

"Muhammadan law" may have been an invention of colonialism, but a second wave of "Muslim law" enactments from the early 1950s to mid-1960s carried Anglo-Muslim law into the independence period. The Administration of Muslim Law Enactment of Selangor (1952) provided a unified code to govern all aspects of law that applied to Muslims, replacing earlier legislation that had been issued in a piecemeal fashion. The Enactment delineated the membership, functions, and powers of a *Majlis Ugama Islam dan Adat Istiadat Melayu* (Council of Religion and

---

[27] Hussin (2007: 777) explains that " ... the particular type of plurality that was achieved looked less like the coexistence of separate but equal elements of different legal systems within one structure than it resembled a peculiar legal Frankenstein creature – different functional elements pieced together to achieve a singular and unique purpose, the other parts of each system discarded by design."

[28] For more on Anglo-Hindu and Chinese customary law in British Malaya, see Hooker (1975: 158–181).

Malay Custom); regulations concerning marriage, divorce, and criminal offenses; and the functions and procedures of the courts. Similar enactments were adopted in Terengganu (1955), Pahang (1956), Malacca (1959), Penang (1959), Negeri Sembilan (1960), Kedah (1962), Perlis (1964), and Perak (1965).[29]

All of this is not to say that there were no other visions of Islam and Islamic law from this point forward. It is only to say that state institutions demonstrated an increasing capacity to define, authorize, and enforce Anglo-Muslim law over other formations.

NAMING AS A MEANS OF CLAIMING ISLAMIC LAW

In addition to codification and vastly increased specificity in the law, there was an important shift in the way that Anglo-Muslim law was presented to the public beginning in the 1970s. Until that time, Anglo-Muslim family law had been grounded in substantive aspects of custom and *fiqh*, but there was little pretense that the laws themselves constituted "shariah." For example, the 1957 Federal Constitution outlined a role of the states in administering "Muslim law" as did the state-level statutes that regulated family law. However, a constitutional amendment in 1976 replaced each iteration of "Muslim law" with "Islamic law."[30] Likewise, every mention of "Muslim courts" was amended[31] to read "Syariah courts."[32] The same semantic shift soon appeared in statutory law. The *Muslim* Family Law Act became the *Islamic* Family Law Act; the Administration of *Muslim* Law Act became the Administration of *Islamic* Law Act; the *Muslim* Criminal Law Offenses Act became the *Syariah* Criminal Offenses Act; the *Muslim* Criminal Procedure Act became the *Syariah* Criminal Procedure Act, and so on.[33]

Why is this important? In these amendments, the new terminology exchanged the *object of the law* (Muslims) for the purported *essence of the law* (as "Islamic"). This semantic shift is an example of what Erik Hobsbawm (1983) calls "the invention of tradition." The authenticity of the Malaysian "shariah" courts is premised on fidelity to the Islamic legal tradition. Yet, the Malaysian government constituted Islamic law

---

[29] Administration of Muslim Law Enactment of Terengganu (1955), Administration of Muslim Law Enactment of Pahang (1956), Administration of Muslim Law Enactment of Malacca (1959), Administration of Muslim Law Enactment of Penang (1959), Administration of Muslim Law Enactment of Negeri Sembilan (1960), Administration of Muslim Law Enactment of Kedah (1962), Administration of Muslim Law Enactment of Perlis (1964), Administration of Muslim Law Enactment of Perak (1965).

[30] As per Article 160A of the Federal Constitution, the official version of the Constitution is in English. Article 160B provides that the Yang di-Pertuan Agong can prescribe a Bahasa Malaysia version as authoritative, but Article 160B has not been utilized to date.

[31] Act A354, section 45, in force from August 27, 1976.

[32] In Malaysia, "shariah" is transliterated "syariah." For simplicity and reader familiarity, I use "shariah" except when citing a direct quotation, or when referring to federal acts and state enactments.

[33] I refer here to the Acts currently in force in the Federal Territories, but the same shift in terminology is evident in most state jurisdictions.

in ways that are in significant tension with the plural and open-ended orientation of *usul al-fiqh*. It should be remembered that the distinct form of Anglo-Muslim law is less than a century old. But every reference to state "fatwas" or the "shariah courts" serves to strengthen the state's claim to embrace the Islamic legal tradition. Indeed, the power of this semantic construction is underlined by the fact that even in a critique such as this, the author finds it difficult, if not impossible, to avoid using these symbolically laden terms. As Shahab Ahmed (2016: 107) explains: "How and when we use the word 'Islamic' is important because the act of naming is a meaningful act: the act of naming is an act of identification, designation, characterization, constitution, and valorization." When naming the shariah court system or examining court cases in subsequent chapters, I must use the terms "shariah high court," "fatwa committee," "state mufti," and so on. It is with the aid of semantic shifts and visual cues that the government presents the shariah courts as a faithful rendering of the Islamic legal tradition.[34] Indeed, they are presented as the *only* possible rendering of Islam, as underlined by the criminalization of differing views. Walton (2001) shows that "persuasive definitions" such as these have considerable power when they are "deployed to serve the interest of the definer."[35]

It is instructive that at the same moment the Malaysian state recast Anglo-Muslim law as "Islamic law," the government was getting out of the business of regulating religious/customary law for non-Muslims by way of the Marriage and Divorce Act of 1976. As previously noted, there had existed five separate statutes on marriage and customary law for ethnic Chinese, Hindus, and natives of Sabah and Sarawak. In place of this pluri-legal arrangement, family law for *all* non-Muslims was henceforth governed by a unified civil family law code. Only Anglo-Muslim family law (now "Islamic law") remained on a separate judicial track, rebranded as state level "shariah courts."[36]

This semantic shift was likely an effort to endow Muslim family law and Muslim courts with a more pronounced religious facade to burnish the government's religious credentials. The change in terminology came during a period when the *dakwah* movement was picking up considerable steam in Malaysian political life. The ruling UMNO faced constant criticism from PAS President Asri Muda to defend Malay economic, political, and cultural interests through the early 1970s.[37] The Malaysian Islamic Youth Movement (*Angkatan Belia Islam Malaysia* – more popularly known by its acronym, ABIM) also formed in August 1971, heralding a new era of grassroots opposition. UMNOs central political challenge was to defend itself

---

[34] My focus here is on terms such as "Islamic law" and "syariah courts," but the courts themselves are replete with visual symbols that are designed to achieve the same effect. For parallel examples in corporate settings, see Sloan-White (2017) on the corporate *sharia* elite.

[35] See also, Stevenson (1944) and Schiappa (2003).

[36] For more context on the formation of a unified, non-Muslim family law code, see Siraj (1994).

[37] PAS entered into the Alliance coalition in the 1974 elections but nonetheless continued to press for further Islamization within the ruling coalition.

against the constant charge that the government was not doing enough to advance Islam.

UMNO began to pursue its own Islamization program in the mid-1970s with the establishment of a Federal Religious Council, an Office of Islamic Affairs, and an Islamic Missionary Foundation (Noor 2004: 267).[38] Initiatives such as these only accelerated in the 1980s under the leadership of Mahathir Mohammad (1981–2003). A shrewd politician, Mahathir sought to co-opt the ascendant *dakwah* movement to harness the legitimizing power of Islamic symbolism and discourse (Nasr 2001; Liow 2009). During his twenty-two years of rule, the religious bureaucracy expanded at an unprecedented rate and Islamic law was institutionalized to an extent that would have been unimaginable in the pre-colonial era (Hamayatsu 2005). The National Council for Malaysian Islamic Affairs was enlarged and elevated into a division within the Prime Minister's office in 1985. It was then elevated and expanded once more in 1997, taking the current name, the Department of Islamic Development Malaysia (*Jabatan Kamajuan Islam Malaysia*), better known by its acronym JAKIM. New state institutions proliferated, such as the Institute of Islamic Understanding (*Institut Kefahaman Islam Malaysia*, IKIM) and the International Islamic University of Malaysia (IIUM). Primary and secondary education curricula were revised to include more material on Islamic civilization, and radio and television content followed suit (Camroux 1996; Barr and Govindasamy 2010). But it was in the field of law and legal institutions that the most consequential innovations were made.

THE STATE'S MONOPOLY ON ISLAMIC LAW

A plethora of new legislation was issued at the state and federal levels in the 1980s and 1990s that formalized substantive and procedural aspects of Anglo-Muslim law even more than the second wave of Muslim law enactments from the 1950s and 1960s.[39] The most recent iteration of family law enactments (those in force today) grew out of an effort to provide more consistency across state jurisdictions. The effort to forge a uniform family law ultimately failed, but state governments vastly increased the level of specificity in their Muslim family law codes in the process.[40]

The magnitude of this shift is apparent in the word count of the relevant section of the Islamic Family Law Act (1984), which replaced the Selangor Administration of Muslim Law Enactment (1952) in the newly created Federal Territories.[41] The 1952

---

[38] The Islamic Missionary Foundation is charged with promoting Islam at home and abroad.

[39] I focus on the acts in force in the Federal Territories, for the sake of brevity and because state-level enactments are modeled on federal-level acts.

[40] The effort to forge a uniform family law was an attempt to provide more consistency across state jurisdictions to prevent forum shopping on issues such as divorce and registration of polygamous marriages.

[41] The Federal Territory of Kuala Lumpur constituted a new, federal-level jurisdiction beginning in 1974. Prior to its incorporation as a federal territory in 1974, Kuala Lumpur was part of the State of

Selangor Enactment carried 3,400 words in the section dealing with family law, while the 1984 Islamic Family Law Act carried more than 20,000 words – nearly a six-fold increase. The main aspect accounting for the difference in length is that the earlier Selangor Enactment had left many provisions to be determined " … in accordance with Muslim law" while the Islamic Family Law Act and parallel state enactments provided far more specificity on what "Muslim law" entailed. More than ever, judges were required to simply apply legal code and abstain from independent inquiry in pursuit of what "Muslim law" might entail. The vastly increased specificity in Muslim family law and the formalization of shariah court functions suggests that judges began to enjoy less discretion. Indeed, Peletz's (2015) anthropological account of the same court across three decades confirms that these sweeping legal and institutional reforms had profound effects on the day-to-day operation of the shariah courts.[42]

Activists welcomed many of the provisions in the 1984 Islamic Family Law Act as progressive advances for women's rights (Zainah Anwar 2008). But they protested subsequent amendments that made it more difficult for women to secure divorce, placed women in a weaker position in the division of matrimonial assets, and provided women with fewer rights in terms of child custody and maintenance (Badlishah 2003; Zainah Anwar and Rumminger 2007).[43] These provisions were in tension with Article 8 (1) of the Federal Constitution, which states "All persons are equal before the law and entitled to the equal protection of the law." However, Article 8 (5) (A) clarifies that "This Article does not invalidate or prohibit any provision regulating personal law." Because of this constitutional bracketing, women are unable to challenge the constitutionality of these provisions.

It should be emphasized that none of these stipulations are unambiguously "Islamic." Indeed, women's rights activists field powerful arguments from within the framework of Islamic law for why these provisions can and must be understood as betraying the core values of justice and equality in Islam. Yet, with the semantic

---

Selangor and was therefore governed by the Muslim Law Enactment of Selangor. The 2003 Selangor Islamic Family Law Enactment follows the Act for the Federal Territories almost verbatim.

[42] As late as the 1980s, the Muslim courts had demonstrated "a pronounced concern with consensus, reconciliation, and compromise (*muafakat, persesuaian, persetujuan*) … " Peletz goes on to explain that "The Islamic magistrate does, of course, adjudicate the cases brought before him, but before doing so the magistrate and members of his staff try to settle cases through the less formal and less binding processes of mediation and arbitration" (Peletz 2002: 85). The location of this court in Rembau, Negeri Sembilan, suggests that these changes affected the shariah court system not only in urban centers, but in its entirety.

[43] Specifically, Article 13 required a woman to have her guardian's consent to marry (regardless of her age) while men had no similar requirement. Article 59 denied a wife her right to maintenance or alimony if she "unreasonably refuses to obey the lawful wishes or commands of her husband." Articles 47–55 made it easy for a husband to divorce his wife, while women faced lengthy court procedures when they did not have their husband's consent. Article 84 granted custody to the mother until the child reaches the age of seven (for boys) or nine (for girls), at which time custody reverts to the father. Moreover, Article 83 detailed conditions under which a mother could lose her limited custody due to reasons of irresponsibility, whereas no such conditions were stipulated for fathers.

shifts from "Muslim law" to "Islamic law," and "Muslim court" to "Syariah court," the law was endowed with a new religious facade.

Around the same time as these reforms, the training of shariah court judges and lawyers followed suit. The curriculum focused on the mastery of legal codes and their proper application, rather than the ability to engage in classical modes of reasoning.[44] The International Islamic University of Malaysia (IIUM) was the first to establish a formal, one-year training and certification program for shariah court judges in 1986. But rather than bringing scholars with expertise in *usul al-fiqh*, courses were taught by retired civil court judges with no background in Islamic legal theory (Horowitz 1994: 261). More programs were established in the years that followed, but the focus on codes and their proper application remained the primary emphasis for those staffing the shariah courts.[45]

The new Islamic Family Law Act and parallel state-level enactments were only the tip of the iceberg. The most striking features of the Malaysian legal system is the extent to which state and federal authorities claim a monopoly on religious interpretation. The Administration of Islamic Law Act and parallel state-level enactments impose a monopoly on religious interpretation. The Islamic Religious Council (*Majlis Agama Islam*), the Office of the Mufti, and the Islamic Legal Consultative Committee wield absolute authority in this regard.[46] Yet, surprisingly, those who staff these bodies are not required to have formal training in Islamic jurisprudence.[47] Only six of the twenty-one members of the Islamic Religious Council are required to be "persons learned in Islamic studies."[48] Similarly, although the Islamic Legal Consultative Committee is charged with assisting the Mufti in issuing *fatwas*, committee members are not required to have formal training in Islamic law.[49]

---

[44] This transformation in the curriculum and training in Islamic law is a familiar story elsewhere. See Cardinal (2005).

[45] For a treatment of the training and education of shariah court judges and lawyers in Malaysia, see Whiting (2012) and Zin (2012).

[46] Articles 4–31 of the Administration of Islamic Law Act empower the Islamic Religious Council of the Federal Territories (*Majlis Agama Islam Wilayah Persekutuan*). This Council is composed mostly of officials who are appointed by the Yang di-Pertuan Agong who is elected from among the nine hereditary state rulers. The office of Mufti is similarly appointed by the Supreme Head of State in consultation with the Islamic Religious Council (Article 32). Finally, an Islamic Legal Consultative Committee is charged with assisting the Mufti in issuing *fatwas* in Article 37.

[47] Article 10 states that "The Majlis shall consist of the following members: (a) a Chairman; (b) a Deputy Chairman; (c) the Chief Secretary to the Government or his representative; (d) the Attorney General or his representative; (e) the Inspector-General of Police or his representative; (f) the Mufti; (g) the Commissioner of the City of Kuala Lumpur; and (h) fifteen other members, at least five of whom shall be persons learned in Islamic studies."

[48] The criteria for what constitutes a person "learned in Islamic studies" are not specified, but it is doubtful that formal training in classical jurisprudential method (*usul al-fiqh*) is part of this requirement.

[49] The Islamic Legal Consultative Committee consists of "(a) the Mufti, as Chairman; (b) the Deputy Mufti; (c) two members of the Majlis nominated by the Majlis; (d) not less than two fit and proper

Even the office of the Mufti merely specifies that officeholders should be "fit and proper persons," without further explanation.[50]

Despite these vague requirements, the powers provided to these state religious authorities are extraordinary. Most significantly, the Mufti is empowered to issue *fatwas* that, upon publication, are "binding on every Muslim resident in the Federal Territories."[51] Accordingly, *fatwas* in the contemporary Malaysian context do not serve as nonbinding opinions from religious scholars as in classical Islamic jurisprudence; rather, they carry the force of law and are backed by the full power of the Malaysian state.[52] Moreover, the Administration of Islamic Law Act allows this lawmaking function to bypass legislative institutions such as the Parliament.[53] Other elements of transparency and democratic deliberation are also excluded by explicit design. For example, Article 28 of the Act declares, "The proceedings of the Majlis shall be kept secret and no member or servant thereof shall disclose or divulge to any person, other than the Yang di-Pertuan Agong [Supreme Head of State] or the Minister, and any member of the Majlis, any matter that has arisen at any meeting unless he is expressly authorized by the Majlis." In other words, the Administration of Islamic Law Act subverts not only basic principles of Islamic legal theory, but also the foundational principles of liberal democracy that are enshrined in the 1957 Constitution, by denying public access to the decision-making process that leads to the establishment of laws.

The Shariah Criminal Offences Act (1997) further consolidates the monopoly on religious interpretation established in the Administration of Islamic Law Act. Article 9 criminalizes defiance of religious authorities:

> Any person who acts in contempt of religious authority or defies, disobeys or disputes the orders or directions of the Yang di-Pertuan Agong as the Head of the religion of Islam, the Majlis or the Mufti, expressed or given by way of *fatwa*, shall be guilty of an offence and shall on conviction be liable to a fine not exceeding three thousand ringgit or to imprisonment for a term not exceeding two years or to both.

Article 12 criminalizes the communication of an opinion or view contrary to a *fatwa*:

> Any person who gives, propagates or disseminates any opinion concerning Islamic teachings, Islamic Law or any issue, contrary to any *fatwa* for the time being in force in the Federal Territories shall be guilty of an offence and shall on conviction be liable to a fine not exceeding three thousand ringgit or to imprisonment for a term not exceeding two years or to both.

---

persons to be appointed by the Majlis; and (e) an officer of the Islamic Religious Department of the Federal Territories to be appointed by the Majlis, who shall be the Secretary."

[50] Article 32.   [51] Article 34.

[52] Article 34 goes on to state "[a] fatwa shall be recognized by all Courts in the Federal Territories as authoritative of all matters laid down therein."

[53] The Malaysian Parliament passed the Administration of Islamic Law Act into law, implying that this elected body maintains an oversight function. Practically speaking, however, fatwas acquire legal force without public scrutiny or periodic review by Parliament.

Article 13 criminalizes the distribution or possession of a view contrary to Islamic laws issued by religious authorities:

> (1) Any person who (a) prints, publishes, produces, records, distributes or in any other manner disseminates any book, pamphlet, document or any form of recording containing anything which is contrary to Islamic Law; or (b) has in his possession any such book, pamphlet, document or recording, shall be guilty of an offence and shall on conviction be liable to a fine not exceeding three thousand ringgit or to imprisonment for a term not exceeding two years or to both.

This state monopoly is also advanced through the structure of the shariah court system itself, which is meant to achieve uniformity in legal application. The Administration of Islamic Law Act and parallel state-level enactments establish a hierarchy in the shariah court judiciary akin to the institutional structure that one would find in common law and civil law systems.[54] Articles 40 through 57 of the Administration of Islamic Law Act establish Shariah Subordinate Courts, a Shariah High Court, and a Shariah Appeal Court. While the concept of appeal is not entirely alien to the Islamic legal tradition, there is little precedent for hierarchical judicial structures prior to the emergence of the modern state (Powers 1992). This innovation is far from trivial given that hierarchy in judicial institutions is designed to achieve a political logic: appellate court structures secure legal uniformity and "the downward flow of command" (Shapiro 1980: 643; Shapiro 1981: 51–52). This is precisely the opposite dynamic of that which we observe in the Islamic legal tradition, where jurisprudence evolved in a bottom-up and pluralistic manner, rather than top-down and uniform (Masud, Messick, and Powers 1996: 4).

It is not only the structure of the shariah court system that resembles the English common law model. Procedural codes also follow suit. The Shariah Criminal Procedure Act (1997) and the Shariah Civil Procedure Act (1997) borrow extensively from the framework of the civil courts in Malaysia. The drafting committee copied the codes of procedure wholesale, making only minor changes where needed. Placed side by side, one can see the extraordinary similarity between the documents, with whole sections copied verbatim. Abdul Hamid Mohamad, a legal official who eventually rose to Chief Justice of the Federal Court, was on the drafting committees for the various federal and state shariah procedures acts and enactments in the 1980s and 1990s. He candidly described the codification of shariah procedure as follows:

> We decided to take the existing laws that were currently in use in the common law courts as the basis to work on, remove or substitute the objectionable parts, add whatever needed to be added, make them Shari'ah-compliance [sic] and have them enacted as laws. In fact, the process and that "methodology," if it can be so called, continue until today.

---

[54] State-level administration of Islamic law enactments largely mirrors the Administration of Islamic Law Act in force in the Federal Territories. For simplicity, I refer only to the federal act.

The provisions of the Shari'ah criminal and civil procedure enactments/act are, to a large extent, the same as those used in the common law courts. A graduate in law from any common law country reading the "Shari'ah" law of procedure in Malaysia would find that he already knows at least 80% of them . . . a common law lawyer reading them for the first time will find that he is reading something familiar, section by section, even word for word. Yet they are "Islamic law." (Mohamad 2008: 1–2, 10)[55]

Abdul Hamid Mohamad and others involved in the codification of shariah court procedures did not have formal education in Islamic jurisprudence or Islamic legal theory. Abdul Hamid's degree was from the National University of Singapore where he studied common law, yet he was centrally involved in the entire process of institutionalizing the shariah courts. Ironically, the "Islamization" of law and legal institutions in Malaysia was not a project of the traditional *'ulama*. Rather, it was a project of state officials like Abdul Hamid Mohamad, who lacked formal training or in-depth knowledge of Islamic legal theory.[56] The relative lack of training and familiarity with *usul al-fiqh* may be one reason why these officials pursued such reforms with the conviction that they were advancing the position of Islam in the legal system.

In addition to this binding monopoly on the interpretation of Islamic law, the Malaysian government built a significant infrastructure for delivering its state-sanctioned understanding of Islam. Witness that fifty-six deviant sects (including Shia Islam) have been outlawed. In the Federal Territories, the Administration of Islamic Law Act also establishes a monopoly on the administration of mosques, including the trusteeship and maintenance of all existing mosques (Articles 72 and 74), the erection of new mosques (Article 73), and the appointment and discipline of local imams (Articles 76–83).[57] More than this, federal and state agencies dictate the content of Friday sermons *(khutab)*.[58] Imams, already on the government payroll and licensed by the state, are also monitored and disciplined if they veer too far from state-proscribed mandates.[59] Combined with the extensive reach of the state in other areas, such as public education, television and radio programming, and quasi-independent institutions such as IKIM (Institute for Islamic

---

[55] Abdul Hamid Mohamad related the same details in a personal interview on November 17, 2009.

[56] More on Abdul Hamid Mohamad's background can be found in his autobiography (Abdul Hamid Mohamad 2016).

[57] For similar dynamics in other Muslim-majority countries, see Moustafa (2000) and Wiktorowicz (2001).

[58] (Sing. *Khutbah*, pl. *khutab*). *Khutab* are written by the Department of Islamic Development Malaysia (*Jabatan Kemajuan Islam Malaysia*—JAKIM). Parallel agencies (such as *Jabatan Agama Islam Negeri Selangor* —JAIS) provide additional *khutab* for each state respectively. JAKIM *khutab* are archived at http://www.islam.gov.my/e-khutbah (last accessed 8/1/2016). Earlier, JAKIM archived *khutbah* going back to 2003 at http://www.islam.gov.my/khutbah-online (last accessed April 3, 2015) but this link has since been removed. For an analysis of the content of these *khutab*, see Mohd Al Adib Samuri and Hopkins (2017).

[59] For example, see *Malaysiakini*, August 3, 2012. "Jais monitoring 38 'hot mosques' following protest."

Understanding), the state plays a prominent role in shaping popular understand-ings of Islam.[60]

STATE POWER, SECULARISM, AND THE POLITICS OF ISLAMIC LAW

This chapter opened with the observation that Malaysia ranks among the top countries worldwide in the degree of state regulation of religion. From this vantage point, Malaysia appears to be the antithesis of a secular state and the realization of a religious state, at least for the sixty percent of Malaysian Muslims who are subject to such rules and regulations. Aspects of religion and governance are clearly inter-twined in Malaysia, but the Malaysian case illustrates how the simple dichotomy of "secular" versus "religious" can obfuscate more than it reveals. As recent work shows (e.g., Asad 2003; Agrama 2011; Dressler and Mandair 2011), the secular/religious binary takes its own starting point for granted and overlooks the ways that *both* categories are constructed as mirror opposites along with the expanding regulatory capacity of the modern state.

This secular/religious dichotomy provides a particularly poor schema through which to understand state incorporation of Islamic law. Perhaps most obviously, the conventional labels of "religious" and "secular" impose a binary with zero-sum properties. At any given point, the religious and the secular are imagined to be in an uneasy truce, a state of simmering tension, or an all-out struggle for supremacy. An advance for one is a loss for the other. Indeed, the two most common narratives of Islam and politics in contemporary Malaysia depict an otherwise secular state capitulating to pressure and adopting Islamic law, or, alternately, proactively and instrumentally harnessing Islamic law for political advantage.[61] While both readings capture important dynamics in the competition over religious authority, these sorts of arguments tend to present Islamic law along a zero-sum continuum. At any given moment Malaysia is understood as being somewhere on a continuum between a "secular" and "religious" state. Media frames and popular political discourse cycle through the same tropes ad nauseam, incessantly asking the anxious question of whether Malaysia is, will become, or was ever meant to be a "secular state" or an "Islamic state."[62] This is not to deny the fact that Malaysians have divergent visions for the future of their country. And this is not to minimize the very real consequences that these political struggles have for individual rights, deliberative democracy, and a host of other important issues. It is only to say that the secular/religious schema too often assumes a unidimensional and ahistorical conception of Islamic law and, therefore, implicitly accepts the state's claim to Islamic law at face value. Anxiety

---

[60] These efforts are likely an important reason why most "everyday Malaysians" tend to understand Islamic law as being uniform and fixed, rather than pluralistic and responsive to local conditions. For survey results on these and related issues, see Moustafa (2013a).

[61] These arguments are well documented in Liow (2009).

[62] Agrama (2012) identifies precisely the same anxieties in his important book on secularism in Egypt.

over "how much" Islamic law is incorporated as state law too often assumes that the content is consistent with Islamic legal theory in the first place.

As select fragments of *fiqh* are constituted in state law, no space is left for the interpretive method that undergirds Islamic jurisprudence. These institutional configurations collapse important conceptual distinctions between the *shariah* (God's way) and *fiqh* (human understanding), facilitating the state's claim to "speak in God's name" (Abou El Fadl 2001). By monopolizing interpretation, codifying select fragments of *fiqh*, and deploying those laws through state institutions, the Malaysian state is "judging in God's name" (Moustafa 2014a). The religious councils, the shariah courts, and the entire administrative apparatus are Islamic in name, but they are modeled on the Malaysian civil courts. A deep paradox is at play: the legitimacy of the religious administration rests on the emotive power of Islamic symbolism, but its principal mode of organization and operation is fundamentally rooted in the Weberian state. What is commonly taken for Islamic law in Malaysia is simply what the state declares Islamic law to be. Seen in this light, the intense controversies around shariah versus civil court jurisdictions (examined in Chapters 4–6) should not be taken as the product of an essential or inevitable conflict between Islam (or Islamic law) and liberal rights, but rather as a tension between two parallel tracks of state law.

3

Islam and Liberal Rights in the Federal Constitution

Constitutions are foundational documents. They are meant to organize institutions of governance, entrench fundamental rights, and serve as important expressions of national identity. Agreement on these foundational principles is considered crucial among experts in constitutional design. But even in the best of circumstances, when compromise is forthcoming at the time of drafting, any constitutional text will serve as both an object and an instrument in future political struggles. Conflict is inevitable because the aims and objectives of political actors evolve over time, and because constitutional provisions are often left vague or discordant to overcome divergent interests in the constitution-writing process (Lerner 2011). This chapter provides the historical context for understanding the origins of the major provisions in the Federal Constitution concerning religion and liberal rights. I examine the political context of British Malaya with a focus on the key players and the competing interests that became entrenched in the new constitutional order.[1] This "constitutional ethnography" is essential for understanding (a) the legal construction of race and religion in British Malaya, (b) the dual constitutional provisions for liberal rights and Anglo-Muslim law and, (c) the formation of separate jurisdictions for Muslims and non-Muslims in areas of personal status and family law. In subsequent chapters, I examine how each of these legal features fuels the judicialization of religion.

THE LEGAL CONSTRUCTION OF RACE AND RELIGION IN BRITISH MALAYA

As a major crossroads for centuries, the Malay Peninsula has a long history of ethnic diversity and cross-fertilization. Parts of the Peninsula, particularly those coastal areas with the most exposure to trade routes, were already multiethnic by the time the British arrived. But economic forces from the middle of the nineteenth century accelerated the rate of demographic change. British commercial interests recognized the tremendous potential for tin production. With the assistance of Malay rulers and ethnic Chinese business interests, laborers were brought from China by

---

[1] For a comparative study of constitution writing and religion, see Bâli and Lerner (2017).

the hundreds of thousands to work in tin mines. Likewise, with the rubber industry booming by the turn of the twentieth century, British commercial interests turned to South Asia for laborers to work on vast rubber plantations. The bulk of Indian migrants were Tamil laborers, but smaller numbers of non-labor migrants had already been brought from Ceylon and South India to work for the colonial administration. Still more Indian lawyers, doctors, and merchants immigrated, resulting in a mix of highly educated professionals and desperately poor laborers.

While most accounts of immigration to the Malay Peninsula focus on the influx of Chinese and Indian workers, it is important to note that, by 1931, as many as 244,000 of the 594,000 Malays in the former protectorates were either first-generation arrivals from the Netherlands, East Indies, or descendants of Indonesian migrants who had arrived after 1891 (Andaya and Andaya 2001: 184).[2] And just as Chinese and Indian migrants were a mix of various linguistic groups, "Malay" migrants were similarly diverse. Contemporary Malaysia is overwhelmingly a nation of immigrants.

Colonial policy tended to overlook the tremendous ethnic and linguistic diversity internal to each of these groupings. Each "race"[3] was treated as a homogeneous block, and census categories were merged over time, producing new legal and social identities (Hirschman 1986, 1987). As in other times and places, the legal construction of racial boundaries served economic and political objectives (Mamdani 2012; Mawani 2009; Merry 2000). A case in point is the now-taken-for-granted term "Malay," which was socially, politically, and legally constituted through specific policies of colonial governance, such as land law (Shamsul A. B. 2001; Milner 1998). The first legal definition of Malay came by way of the Malay Reservations Act,[4] which defined a Malay as "a person belonging to any Malayan race who habitually

---

[2] Immigration from Indonesia and elsewhere continues to the present day. Critics of the Malaysian government claim that these immigrants are extended citizenship to boost the proportion of Malay/Muslims vis-à-vis other ethnic and religious communities. For more background on one aspect of these claims, see Royal Commission of Enquiry on Immigrants in Sabah (2014).

[3] The term "race" may raise eyebrows among some readers. It is used here for analytical rather than normative purposes to mark a distinct shift in the way that difference was encoded in state law beginning in the colonial period as a means to justify the social and economic hierarchies that were part and parcel of the colonial project. Bashi (1998) and Gomez (2010) explain the analytical utility of the term "race" with the observation that "both race and ethnicity are about socially constructed group difference in society [but] race is always about hierarchical social difference, whereas ethnicity may be non-hierarchical, depending on the social context" (Gomez 2010: 490–491). The term "race" thus captures a power dimension that tends to fall out of the picture in discussions of "ethnicity." In using the term, it is important to be clear that I subscribe to the three components of the constructionist view of race outlined by Gomez: (1) a biological basis for race is rejected; (2) race is viewed as a social construct that changes along with political, economic, and other contexts; and, (3) "although race is socially constructed . . . [it] has real consequences."

[4] The Malay Reservations Act of 1913 applied in the Federated Malay States and was followed by comparable enactments in Kelantan (1930), Kedah (1931), Perlis (1935), Johore (1936), and Terengganu (1941). The Act was preceded by the Selangor Land Code of 1891, which required that "the original customary land holder must be Mohammedan" and prohibited the land from being sold or mortgaged to non-Muslims. The Selangor Land Code illustrates one of the earliest examples of the conflation of race and religion by the British (Andaya and Andaya 2001: 183).

speaks . . . any Malayan language and professes the Moslem religion" (Voules 1921: 506). The original purpose of the Reservations Act was to set land aside for traditional agricultural pursuits, first among them rice cultivation. The Act was made in the name of preserving Malay interests and "way of life," but the reality had more to do with limiting the expansion of ethnic Chinese business interests, barring Malays from rubber production, and preserving adequate food supplies in the colony. While the official and unofficial bases for the legal definition of "Malay" were context-specific and ultimately short-lived, the legal category remained virtually intact until today, as enshrined in Article 160 (2) of the present-day Federal Constitution.

Racial designations became increasingly important for access to government jobs and education. As always, the political context is crucial. By the turn of the twentieth century, ethnic Chinese and ethnic Indian communities comprised nearly half the total population of British Malaya. It was also clear that the vast bulk of the Malay community had missed out on the economic boom. The British sought to make good (at least symbolically) on their stated policy of protecting the interests of the Malays through targeted initiatives. The Malay College was established in 1905 to provide English education to the children of Malay elites, and a Malay Administrative Service was created around the same time to assist the Malayan Civil Service (Means 1972: 34). Non-Malays were barred from these institutions regardless of any qualifications that they might have had. These race-based concessions were designed to address Malay grievances and bolster the position of the Malay elite as a strategic ally to the British vis-à-vis the increasingly large and dynamic ethnic Chinese community.[5]

Even with these concessions, Malay nationalists believed that their community faced an existential threat. It is not difficult to understand why. In the Federated Malay States, the ethnic Chinese community tripled in size (from 163,422 to 433,244) in the two decades from 1891 to 1911, while the ethnic Indian community increased more than eight times (from 20,154 to 172,465) in the same period (Puthucheary 1978: 8). The 1911 census records Malays as comprising only 51 percent of the total population, and this figure declined further to 49.2 percent in the 1931 census (Noor 2004: 18). An Aliens Ordinance was issued by the colonial administration to regulate the entry of new workers beginning in 1933, but the Malay share of the population remained less than half of the total population (49.5 percent) by the time of the 1947 census. The ethnic Malay community was frightfully concerned that, with independence, they would be a vulnerable minority, subject to domination by the ethnic Chinese and (to a far lesser extent) ethnic Indian communities.

---

[5] Increasing numbers of Malay elites in the civil service also helped to relieve administrative pressures on the colonial administration.

THE FORMATION OF RACE-BASED POLITICAL PARTIES

Following the Second World War, Britain began to prepare Malaya for eventual independence. A "Malayan Union Plan" was issued in 1945, in the form of a White Paper. It proposed a unitary state, including the Federated Malay States, the Unfederated Malay States, Penang, and Melaka. Under the Plan, the Sultans would retain their positions but lose their formal sovereignty. Citizenship would be extended to all residents of Malaya and citizens would enjoy equal rights, with no preferential treatment by race. Varying responses to the Malayan Union Plan exposed the complex and competing interests of the ethnic Malay, Chinese, and Indian elite, as well as complex class and ideological dimensions within each group.[6] Fearful that the Malay community would be overwhelmed by the economic might of the Chinese community under the terms of the plan, Malay nationalists mobilized in opposition. Out of this effort emerged the United Malays National Organization (*Pertubuhan Kebangsaan Melayu Bersatu*), more popularly known by its acronym, UMNO. The Malayan Union Plan was swiftly defeated, and UMNO was transformed into a formidable political party. Later that year, the Malayan Indian Congress (MIC) was founded, followed by the Malayan Chinese Association (MCA), which was established mainly as a counterweight to the (Chinese) Malayan Communist Party. These three race-based parties would soon dominate in the independence period.

In lieu of the Malayan Union, British officials negotiated an interim agreement with UMNO leaders and with the Sultans. The result was the Federation of Malaya Agreement of 1948, which cut against the spirit of the Malayan Union Plan on virtually every count. Requirements for citizenship were made more restrictive, the sovereignty of the Sultans was preserved, and a federal structure was established with powers reserved for the states (Andaya and Andaya 2001: 268). The Federation of Malaya Agreement also required that the British High Commissioner "safeguard the special position of the Malays and the legitimate interests of the other communities" (Clause 19 (1) (d)). Accordingly, the colonial administration continued to allocate civil service positions exclusively to Malays.[7] Scholarships, special business permits, and licenses were also reserved for Malay business and tradespersons (Huang-Thio 1964).

Despite strong cross-pressures, UMNO, the MCA, and the MIC had sufficient mutual interest to cooperate as a coalition ("The Alliance") in the 1955 election.[8] The Alliance sidestepped communal differences and focused their campaign on the immediate goal of independence. Their cooperation paid off. The Alliance won

---

[6] For a detailed account of the elite-pacted authoritarian institutions that were crafted in response to pressures from below, see Slater (2010: 75–93). Also, see Andaya and Andaya (2001: 264–267).

[7] One-fifth of civil service positions were allotted to non-Malays beginning in 1953. For more detail, see Puthucheary (1978).

[8] UMNO and the MCA had previously won 226 of 268 municipal and town council seats between 1952 and 1954. Their victory at the local level demonstrated that cooperation was both possible and fruitful (Andaya and Andaya 2001: 275–276; Noor 2004: 79).

a stunning 81 percent of the popular vote and all but one of 52 constituencies (Andaya and Andaya 2001: 276). In the process, they had discovered a winning formula: Each of the component parties was race-based, and each spoke in the name of its respective community. Inter-communal differences were managed through behind-the-scenes bargaining and compromise. The promise of continued success at the ballot box proved a sufficient incentive for the race-based parties to continue to work together. This delicate balancing act soon constituted a fundamental feature of Malaysian politics: Race-based parties generate political mileage by playing to their communal base, yet brinkmanship requires constant backroom political management, lest differences spin out of control. The strong Alliance mandate in the 1955 elections was an encouraging sign that political elites could overcome significant inter-communal differences. But the most profound challenge facing the Alliance was agreeing on the basic contours of an independence constitution. Thorny issues such as the status of Malay privileges and the requirements of citizenship had been stumbling blocks in the past. To secure independence, the Alliance needed to work constructively with the Reid Commission, which was charged with drafting the Independence Constitution. The final shape of the Independence Constitution, including clauses on Islamic law and liberal rights, reflected the compromises that were struck to bridge the competing interests of the major stakeholders.

EQUAL CITIZENSHIP VS. RACE-BASED PRIVILEGES IN THE MALAYAN CONSTITUTION

One of the most significant bargains in the new constitution concerned citizenship for ethnic Chinese and ethnic Indian migrants. The Federation of Malaya Agreement extended citizenship only to those who declared permanent settlement, could establish that they were residents for fifteen of the previous twenty-five years, and had competence in English or the Malay language.[9] By these criteria, Andaya and Andaya (2001) estimate that less than 10 percent of ethnic Chinese qualified for automatic citizenship (268). A more relaxed citizenship requirement was therefore among the most important objectives for the ethnic Chinese and ethnic Indian communities. In a departure from the Federation of Malaya Agreement, the Independence Constitution extended citizenship to all those who were born in the Federation or who satisfied certain other requirements.[10] The number of non-Malay citizens soared as a result of this

---

[9] The name "Federation of Malaya" was retained until 1963 when Sabah, Sarawak, and Singapore (for two years only) joined in political union. For more comprehensive accounts of the political maneuvers, lobbying, and compromise that occurred in the drafting of the Federal Constitution, see Fernando (2002). For more on Article 3 specifically, see Fernando (2006) and Stilt (2015).

[10] For a precise description of the requirements of citizenship, see the Second Schedule of the Federal Constitution.

concession.[11] In return, Malay special privileges were affirmed in the new Constitution.[12] Article 153 reproduced the wording of the Federation of Malaya Agreement almost verbatim, declaring "It shall be the responsibility of the Yang di Pertuan Agong [the Supreme Head of State] to safeguard the special position of the Malays and the legitimate interests of other communities . . . ."[13] The text simply replaced the British High Commissioner with the Supreme Head of State as the authority entrusted with safeguarding Malay rights.[14] Article 153 details these privileges, which include quotas for Malay entry into the civil service (clause 2), quotas for Malay business licenses and permits (clauses 6 and 8), special scholarships and educational facilities for Malay students (clause 2), and quotas for Malay students at universities (clause 8a, added in 1971). Additional provisions entrenched other privileges. Article 89, for example, carried over the colonial policy of allocating tracts of land for the exclusive ownership and use of Malays.

The provision of public resources along racial lines required a legal definition of "Malay." Once again, colonial-era frameworks provided a ready model for adoption. Article 160 (2) of the Constitution defines a Malay as "a person who professes the religion of Islam, habitually speaks the Malay language, [and] conforms to Malay custom . . . ." This definition was virtually identical to the legal provisions in the Malay Reservations Act of 1913, where colonial authorities had defined a Malay as "a person belonging to any Malayan race who habitually speaks . . . any Malayan language and professes the Moslem religion." As a result, the legal conflation between Malay and Islam was carried over and entrenched in the Independence Constitution.

ISLAM AS THE RELIGION OF THE FEDERATION

Another key passage in the Constitution is Article 3 (1). It reads, "Islam is the religion of the Federation; but other religions may be practiced in peace and harmony in any part of the Federation." It is no surprise that UMNO pressed for a religion clause as

---

[11]   New citizens were required to affirm their exclusive loyalty to the Federation through a written oath, stating "I absolutely and entirely renounce and abjure all loyalty to any country or State outside the Federation, and I do swear that I will be a true, loyal and faithful citizen of the Federation, and will give due obedience to all lawfully constituted authorities in the Federation." The constitution was amended in 1962 to require allegiance to "His Majesty the Yang di-Pertuan Agong" rather than "all lawfully constituted authorities in the Federation." This amendment points to the ways in which some aspects of the constitutional bargain were subsequently altered.

[12]   "UMNO's final acceptance of this provision was only obtained in exchange for a guarantee of Malay Privileges" (Andaya and Andaya 2001: 276).

[13]   The Constitution would later be amended to include the "natives of any of the States of Sabah and Sarawak."

[14]   Article 153 also requires the Supreme Head of State to protect "the special interests of other communities," but details on how competing interests should be balanced were not specified. These mechanisms were almost certainly vague by design.

an expression of Malay identity. Malays were equated with Islam by way of state law as far back as the Malay Reservation Act of 1913. According to state law and popular convention, to be Malay was to be Muslim. This conflation of race with religion in the popular imagination is most clearly demonstrated by the term used to describe conversion itself. An individual who converts to Islam is said to have "masuk Melayu" (entered or become Malay). For UMNO, a religion clause would serve as an expression of state identity that was synonymous with race.

What is remarkable about the inclusion of Article 3 (1) in the Independence Constitution is that UMNO had gained the consent of its partners in the Alliance, the Malayan Chinese Association (MCA) and the Malayan Indian Congress (MIC). This cooperation partly reflected UMNO's dominant position within the Alliance. But equally, the support of the MCA and the MIC was part of a complex political bargain struck between political elites in the critical years leading up to independence. The Alliance submitted a joint memorandum to the Reid Commission requesting that, "The religion of Malaysia shall be Islam." The memorandum further specified that "the observance of this principle shall not impose any disability on non-Muslim nationals professing and practising their own religions, and shall not imply that the State is not a secular State" (Fernando 2006: 253). No doubt, this proviso was necessary to secure agreement from the MCA and the MIC, the non-Muslim, non-Malay component parties of the Alliance.

Ironically, resistance to a religion clause came from those figures who were meant to be the guardians of Islam: the Sultans. As it turns out, the Sultans were concerned that a religion clause would impinge on their mandate as the religious leaders of their respective states. This political posture was a direct legacy of colonial bargains, going back to the Treaty of Pangkor where the Sultans were granted jurisdiction over matters of religion and custom while relinquishing the rest of their authority (see Chapter 2). The fact that the Sultans opposed a religion clause, while the non-Muslim MCA and MIC were willing to oblige, further suggests that the inclusion of Article 3 had little to do with religion qua religion, and more to do with the complicated bargain being negotiated.

The Reid Commission initially rejected the Alliance proposal, based on objections that had come from the Sultans. However, the tide changed through UMNO's persistence, lobbying from within the Reid Commission by Justice Abdul Hamid (who had proved to be a vociferous advocate for a religion clause), and substantive compromises among stakeholders.[15] The Sultans ultimately agreed to

---

[15] For details on how these negotiations evolved, see Stilt (2015) and Fernando (2002; 2006). Interestingly, in his formal appeal to include a religion of the state clause, Justice Abdul Hamid pointed to the many other countries that had already adopted similar clauses: "Not less than 15 countries of the world have a provision of this type entrenched in their constitutions. Among the Christian countries, which have such a provision in their Constitutions, are Ireland (Art. 6), Norway (Art. 1), Denmark (Art. 3), Spain (Art. 6), Argentina (Art. 2), Bolivia (Art 3), Panama (Art. 1), and Paraguay (Art. 3). Among the Muslim countries are Afghanistan (Art. 1), Iran (Art. 1), Iraq (Art. 13), Jordan (Art. 2), Saudi Arabia (Art. 7), and Syria (Art. 3) . . . . If in these countries a religion has been

a constitutional provision stating that Islam is the religion of the federation in return for their own constitutionally entrenched right to administer Anglo-Muslim law at the state level. Article 3 of the Constitution was finally drafted to read, "Islam is the religion of the Federation; but other religions may be practised in peace and harmony in any part of the Federation." In addition to the second part of the clause safeguarding the practice of other religions, additional provisions were meant to ensure that Article 3 would not infringe on the rights of non-Muslims. Clause 4 of Article 3 guarantees, "Nothing in this Article derogates from any other provision of this Constitution." Article 8 (1) declares "all persons are equal before the law and entitled to equal protection of the law." Article 8 (2) expands upon this guarantee by specifying ". . . there shall be no discrimination against citizens on the ground only of religion, race, descent, place of birth or gender in any law . . . ." Article 11 directly addresses freedom of religion by further guaranteeing that "Every person has the right to profess and practice his religion . . . ." These specifications were no doubt meant to underline the commitment that Article 3 would not deprive citizens of fundamental liberties provided for in the Constitution. Despite these various guarantees, the vague phrase "religion of the Federation" would become the subject of contention decades later.

Ironically, all the provisions that were meant to secure fundamental rights would eventually become instruments and objects of litigation. Even within the same constitutional provisions, we can identify axes of legal tension. For example, Article 8 (1) declares "all persons are equal before the law and entitled to the equal protection of the law." Clause 5 of the same article carries the additional proviso that "[t]his Article does not invalidate or prohibit any provision regulating personal law . . . ." Thus, the Anglo-Muslim, Anglo-Hindu, and Chinese customary law regimes – all of which were discriminatory against women – were exempt from the Constitution's commitment to guarantee equal protection under the law.[16] Similarly, Article 11, which addresses freedom of religion, provides that, "*Every person* has the right to profess and practice his religion . . . ." However, the third clause of the same article states that "*every religious group* has the right to manage its own religious affairs . . . ." Article 11 thus provides for individual rights (the right of the individual to practice in accordance with his or her religious conviction) while it gestures to collective rights (the right of each religious community to manage its religious affairs). This celebration of rights on paper did not anticipate the significant legal tensions that this framework would produce between conflicting visions of individual and communal rights to "freedom of religion." Compromise among the

declared to be the religion of the State and that declaration has not been found to have caused hardships to anybody, no harm will ensue if such a declaration is included in the Constitution of Malaya." Report of the Federation of Malaya Constitutional Commission 1957 (London: Her Majesty's Stationery Office) Colonial No. 330.

[16] As previously noted, there had existed five separate family law statutes until all of those for non-Muslims were unified into a single legal framework by the Law Reform (Marriage and Divorce) Act of 1976.

drafters of the Constitution only sowed the seeds for protracted legal battles decades later.[17]

SUBSTANTIVE PROVISIONS OF ANGLO-MUSLIM LAW

Leaving aside the contested symbolism of Article 3, more clearly defined arrangements for the administration of Anglo-Muslim law are specified elsewhere in the Constitution. The Ninth Schedule establishes the basic institutional foundation, by delineating the powers of the states vis-à-vis the federal government. The states were granted jurisdiction over:

> Muslim law and personal and family law of persons professing the Muslim religion, including the Muslim law relating to succession, testate and intestate, betrothal, marriage, divorce, dower, maintenance, legitimacy, guardianship ... mosques or any Muslim public place of worship, creation and punishment of offences by persons professing the Muslim religion against precepts of that religion, except in regard to matters included in the Federal List; the constitution, organization and procedure of Muslim courts, which shall have jurisdiction only over person professing the Muslim religion and in respect only of any of the matters included in this paragraph, but shall not have jurisdiction in respect of offences except in so far as conferred by federal law; the control of propagating doctrines and beliefs among persons professing the Muslim religion; the determination of matters of Muslim law and doctrine and Malay custom ...[18]

The administration of religion is a state-level enterprise because of the separate treaties that the British had forged with local rulers. The Sultans had managed to preserve their role as the heads of religion within the federal structure of the Federation of Malaya Agreement of 1948, and later they managed to entrench those powers in the Independence Constitution.[19] A comparison of these consecutive legal frameworks reveals a high degree of path dependence. The bifurcated legal system that first emerged in the state of Perak in 1874, as a product of the Treaty of Pangkor (later replicated in other Malay protectorates), came to be entrenched in the Federation of Malaya Agreement. Later still, similar wording was carried over into the Independence Constitution (now the Federal Constitution). In this bifurcated legal system, the federal courts came to administer all matters of civil, criminal, and administrative law, whereas state jurisdiction was limited to issues of personal status law within the Muslim community, including such matters as marriage, divorce, child custody, religious status.

---

[17] Indeed, these disharmonies are what fuel the construction of constitutional identity (Jacobsohn 2010).
[18] This is the original wording from The Ninth Schedule, List II (1), of the Independence Constitution of 1957. Some of this language changed through constitutional amendments, as detailed later. See *Malayan Constitutional Documents*, published by the Government Printer, Kuala Lumpur (1958).
[19] Federation of Malaya Agreement, Article 5.

SHARIAH COURT VERSUS CIVIL COURT JURISDICTION

One of the distinct institutional legacies of the colonial period was the formation of Muslim courts (later renamed "shariah" courts) that applied Muslim law (later rebranded "shariah" law). Shariah court decisions were subject to review by the civil courts. However, the government amended Article 121 in 1988. A new clause specified that the High Courts "shall have no jurisdiction in respect of any matter within the jurisdiction of the Syariah courts." The new provision, Article 121 (1A), was meant to demarcate a clear division between the functions of the civil courts and the duties of the shariah courts. Muslims would henceforth be subject to the exclusive jurisdiction of the shariah courts in matters of religion. In practice, however, dozens of high-profile cases presented difficult legal conundrums (Chapter 4). These cases generated enormous political controversy and became important focal points for civil society mobilization (Chapter 5). The spectacle ultimately shaped popular understandings of Islam and its place in Malaysian politics and society (Chapter 6, 7). Because Article 121 (1A) plays a central role in this litigation, it is useful to provide context on the origins of the amendment itself.

Before the 1988 constitutional amendment, the civil courts exercised jurisdiction in matters related to the shariah courts, but only on occasion. For example, in *Myriam v. Mohamed Ariff*, a Muslim woman initiated a civil suit to challenge her ex-husband's custody of their two children.[20] In *Boto v. Jaafar*, another Muslim woman sued her ex-husband in a civil court for equal division of matrimonial assets rather than settle for three months of maintenance, according to the provisions that applied in the Muslim courts.[21] But these sorts of cases were less frequent than one might expect.[22] Generally speaking, the civil courts adjudicated family law cases between Muslims only when there was a solid legal basis.[23] Even then, it appears that the civil courts overturned shariah court decisions only with reluctance.[24] Figure 3.1 illustrates the total number of High Court decisions that concerned Islam between 1936 and 2014. One notes that there were very few High Court rulings similar to *Myriam v. Mohamed Ariff* or *Boto v. Jaafar*. In other words, these decisions were the rare exceptions, not the rule. In fact, before the adoption of Article 121 (1A), High Court decisions mentioning Islam were

---

[20] *Myriam v. Mohamed Ariff* [1971] 1 MLJ 265.

[21] *Boto' Binti Taha v. Jaafar Bin Muhamed* [1985] 2 MLJ 98.

[22] Additional examples include *Nafsiah v. Abdul Majid* [1969] 2 MLJ 174; *Roberts v. Ummi Kalthom* [1966] 1 MLJ 163.

[23] For example, in exercising jurisdiction in *Myriam v. Mohamed Ariff*, the presiding judge cited a provision of the Selangor Administration of Muslim Law Enactment (1952) that allowed the civil court review of shariah court decisions. Article 45 (6) of the Selangor Administration of Muslim Law Enactment of 1952 stated, "Nothing in this Enactment contained shall affect the jurisdiction of any civil court and, in the event of any difference or conflict arising between the decision of a court of the *Kathi Besar* or a *Kathi* and the decision of a civil court acting within its jurisdiction, the decision of the civil court shall prevail."

[24] In *Boto v. Jaafar*, the presiding judge cites the "celebrated" writing of Islamic law advocate Professor Ahmad Ibrahim. This was very likely an effort to legitimize its review of a shariah court decision.

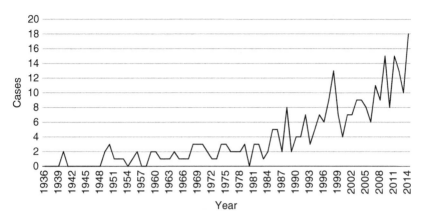

FIGURE 3.1: Reported Civil Court Decisions Referencing Islam, by Year
Source: Data compiled from the *Malayan Law Journal* and the *Current Law Journal*.[25]

fewer than two per year on average, and the total number of decisions touching on Islam never surpassed five in one year. It is one of the great ironies that High Court decisions touching on Islam increased significantly only *after* the passage of Article 121 (1A), for reasons examined later.

Nonetheless, a handful of activists, academics, and government officials advocated for the adoption of a constitutional amendment that would prevent the federal civil courts from overturning state-level shariah court decisions. The most important advocate for such a change was Ahmad Mohamed Ibrahim (1916–1999) who was the most prominent early advocate for an increased role of Islamic law in the Malaysian legal system. It is useful to know something of Ahmad Ibrahim's formative years to understand his approach to Islam in the Malaysian legal order. Ibrahim was born in Singapore and studied law in the United Kingdom. Upon returning to Singapore, Ibrahim served as a chief lawyer in the infamous Maria Hertogh (Natrah) child custody case.[26] The case precipitated riots when the colonial administration of Singapore ruled that a girl who had been adopted into a Muslim family must be returned to her Dutch biological parents.[27] For nationalists at the time, the Natrah case symbolized the colonial administration's complete disregard for Islam. Ibrahim was thirty-four years of age at the time, and his work on the case is said to have had a profound effect on his outlook. When he immigrated to Malaysia in 1969, he became an early and outspoken advocate for a more expansive role for Muslim law

[25] This data was generated by running the search terms "Islam" or "Muslim" in the *Malayan Law Journal* and the *Current Law Journal*, followed by the secondary search term "religion" within the search results. Decisions were then reviewed to exclude false positives. The data is meant to provide a general notion of the volume of High Court decisions that mention Islam over time.

[26] Colonial Singapore was part of British Malaya, but it was administered separately as a Crown colony.

[27] *Adrianus Petrus Hertogh and Anor v. Amina Binte Mohamed and Ors.* [1951] 1 MLJ 12; *Amina Binte Mohamed v. HE Consul-General for the Netherlands* [1950] 1 MLJ 214.

and the formalization of Muslim court functions vis-à-vis the civil courts. As a professor of law at the University of Malaya and later as the Dean of the Faculty of Law at the International Islamic University of Malaysia (IIUM), Ibrahim advocated the introduction of a constitutional amendment that would safeguard the jurisdiction of the shariah courts vis-à-vis the federal civil courts. He wrote of the instances in which the civil courts had overturned shariah court decisions, citing them as evidence of the need to expand and defend the role of the shariah courts in the Malaysian legal system.

In Ahmad Ibrahim's account, the government formed a committee headed by Tan Sri Syed Nasir Ismail to examine "the unsatisfactory position of the shariah courts ... and suggest measures to be taken to raise their status and position" (Ibrahim 2000: 136). The committee stressed the need to improve the physical infrastructure of the shariah courts, improve the training of judges, and raise the stature of the shariah courts vis-à-vis the civil courts. One of several committee recommendations for raising the stature of the shariah courts was to oust the civil courts from shariah court jurisdiction by way of a constitutional amendment. Mahathir Mohammed endorsed the proposal and, in 1988, introduced a constitutional amendment declaring that the High Courts of the Federation "shall have no jurisdiction in any respect of any matter within the jurisdiction of the shariah courts." Opening debate in the *Dewan Rakyat*, Mahathir explained that this amendment was necessary to protect the jurisdiction of the shariah courts vis-à-vis the federal civil courts:

> One thing that has brought about dissatisfaction among the Islamic community in this country is the situation whereby any civil court is able to change or cancel a decision made by the shariah court. For example, an incident happened before where a person who was unhappy with the decision of the shariah court regarding child custody brought her charges to the High Court and won a different decision. The Government feels that a situation like this affects the sovereignty of the shariah court and the execution of shariah law among the Muslims of this country. It is very important to secure the sovereignty of the shariah court to decide on matters involving its jurisdiction, what is more if the matter involves shariah law. Therefore, it is suggested that a new clause be added to Article 121 – clause (1A), which will state that the courts mentioned in the Article do not have any jurisdiction over any item of law under the control of the shariah court.[28]

For the record, no primary source evidence from the period supports Mahathir's contention that civil court decisions had produced "a feeling of dissatisfaction among Muslims in the country." The civil courts rarely overturned shariah court rulings and, in the rare cases when they did, these decisions were *not* covered extensively in the press. A review of Malay language newspaper coverage revealed that, among the four cases most often cited by Ahmad Ibrahim as examples of civil

---

[28] Minutes of the *Dewan Rakyat*, March 17, 1988, page 1364.

court interference, the newspapers covered none of them.[29] The discussion did not go far beyond the small circle of legal professionals who had promoted Article 121 (1A) to elevate the symbolic stature of the shariah courts vis-à-vis the federal civil courts.

Given the profound impact of Article 121 (1A) on Malaysian law and politics, the brevity of parliamentary debate is striking. The discussion was short partly because seven leading Democratic Action Party (DAP) members (including Lim Kit Siang and Karpal Singh) were being held in detention under the Internal Security Act in the aftermath of Operation Lalang. Discussion of Article 121 (1A) was also overshadowed by the debate on a second constitutional amendment, introduced simultaneously, that weakened the independence of the federal courts vis-à-vis the executive.[30]

One of the few reservations in the parliamentary debate came from Chua Jui Meng of the MCA. He posed the hypothetical question: "If a non-Muslim is falsely accused in the shariah courts, will he be able to appeal to the High Court?"[31] Chua's question proved prescient years later, albeit not in the exact scenario that he posed in Parliament. However, such concerns were quickly brushed aside, and the amendment passed with the support of 142 Members of Parliament.[32] Having passed the *Dewan Rakyat*, the constitutional amendment made its way to the upper house of Parliament, where there were even fewer opposition figures. Deputy Prime Minister Abdul Ghafar bin Baba introduced the amendment in the *Dewan Negara* with the same reasoning that Mahathir had provided previously:

> This amendment is suggested because in the past if people were not satisfied with a decision given by the shariah court, they were able to bring the same case to the High Court with the intention of procuring a different decision. This situation has brought about a feeling of dissatisfaction among Muslims in this country and has affected the sovereignty of the shariah courts. In the government's opinion, the civil court should not question the matters under the jurisdiction of the shariah court anymore, more so because the issues that arise in such cases involve Islamic law.

---

[29] The four cases that were most often cited by Ahmad Ibrahim as examples of civil court interference are *Myriam v. Mohamed Ariff* [1971] 1 MLJ 265; *Boto'Binti Taha v. Jaafar Bin Muhamed* [1985] 2 MLJ 98; *Nafsiah v. Abdul Majid* [1969] 2 MLJ 174; and *Roberts v. Ummi Kalthom* [1966] 1 MLJ 163. The most prominent Malay-language newspapers were examined for several weeks following each of these court decisions to understand the extent of media coverage or lack thereof.

[30] Both amendments came at a time when Mahathir Mohammad was fighting for his political life. In June 1987, UMNO had an internal party election in which Mahathir retained leadership of the party by a slim majority of 761 to 718 votes. A legal challenge to the election results, combined with several court decisions against the executive, precipitated a purge of the Chief Justice of the Supreme Court, Tun Salleh Abas, and two other Supreme Court justices. As we will see in the next chapter, weakened judicial independence made the civil courts more vulnerable to pressure when the contested jurisdictions became a politically salient topic. For more on the 1988 judicial crisis, see the official inquiry commissioned by the Malaysian Bar Council (2008).

[31] Minutes of the *Dewan Rakyat*, March 17, 1988, p. 1386.

[32] 18 Members of Parliament opposed the bill, 17 of whom were DAP members.

In these matters, shariah court judges are competent. This amendment is in line with the government's aspiration of raising the position and sovereignty of our shariah courts.[33]

Several UMNO loyalists voiced their emphatic support. Tuan Haji Hamid Araby bin Haji Md. Salih summed up the praise for the amendment:

Following what was said by several of my colleagues, the position of the shariah courts will rise with this amendment. In the past, the shariah courts were made a laughing stock because people who did not succeed in the shariah court could bring their case to the civil court and change the shariah court decision. This is a huge mockery to Islam, our official religion. Praise God, our leaders today have come to realize that the shariah court's position must be raised to be on par with the magistrate court and others. Thank goodness this amendment is made.[34]

Despite the colorful praise for the amendment and dogmatic assertions of shariah court dignity, there was surprisingly little press coverage of Article 121 (1A). It is hard to know what to make of this, as one would expect UMNO politicians to trumpet their Islamic credentials in the popular press in the same manner that they had in Parliament. However, it seems that the introduction of Article 121 (1A) was overshadowed by the more immediate spectacle of Mahathir asserting executive dominance over the judiciary.[35] Newspaper coverage focused on Article 121 (1), which weakened judicial independence, but not clause 1A. Thus, clause 1A was adopted with little debate or popular awareness outside of a small number of lawmakers, legal scholars, and practitioners. Two decades later, the Article 121 (1A) cases became the primary focal point of tension concerning the "religious" vs. "secular" identity of the Malaysian state.

---

[33] Minutes of the *Dewan Negara*, April 4, 1988, p. 43.
[34] Minutes of the *Dewan Negara*, April 4, 1988, p. 103.
[35] For an example of this coverage, see "Pindaan Perjelas Kuasa Hakim," *Berita Harian*, March 18, 1988.

4

The Judicialization of Religion

This chapter turns to the judicialization of religion in Malaysia.[1] The central argument presented here is that the drivers of judicialization have little to do with religion itself (as a practice of faith) and everything to do with the regulation of religion (as a state project). The burning questions, controversies, and conundrums that are adjudicated by Malaysian courts are nearly always a byproduct of state regulation. I suggest that the judicialization of religion is most acute in contexts that are comparable to Malaysia, where: (a) religion is tightly regulated, (b) different legal regimes are applied to different (legally constituted) communities, (c) constitutional commitments are made to both religion and liberal rights, and (d) courts are relatively empowered with broad public access.[2]

As the reader will recall, the Malaysian state regulates Islam more than almost any other country. The Federal Constitution provides for separate family and personal status laws for Muslims and non-Muslims. This bifurcated legal system hardwires complex institutional dilemmas. This is not only because the shariah courts entrench an illiberal vision of Islam that is in tension with state commitments to liberal rights, but also because courts are put in a position where they must "see like a state" (Scott 1998) and categorize individuals in order to apply different personal status and family law regimes. These legal institutions are meant to operate independent of one another, but in the context of Malaysia's complex, multi-religious society, situations arise where legal entanglements are unavoidable. These quandaries destabilize the legal system and fuel the construction of a "rights-versus-rites" binary. They also open opportunities for activists – both self-ascribed Islamists and secularists – to engage in strategic litigation to challenge the status quo and assert broad claims about Islam, liberal rights, and the role of the state.

---

[1] The judicialization of religion was defined in the Introduction as a circumstance wherein courts increasingly adjudicate questions and controversies over religion.

[2] This chapter is not meant to provide an exhaustive inventory of necessary or sufficient conditions that drive the judicialization of religion. Instead, it is meant to offer a contextualized case study of these mechanisms at work in Malaysia. This is first and foremost a theory-building endeavor, not a theory-testing exercise.

The most significant flashpoint concerning shariah versus civil court jurisdiction is Article 121 (1A) of the Federal Constitution. The Article states that the High Courts of the Federation "shall have no jurisdiction in respect of any matter within the jurisdiction of the Syariah courts." As noted in Chapter 3, the government introduced the clause in a 1988 constitutional amendment, despite the fact that the civil courts had rarely intervened in shariah court matters. The amendment was meant to clarify the distinct competence of the shariah courts. In practice the clause produced legal difficulties from virtually the moment it came into force. What follows is an analysis of the entire universe of Article 121 (1A) cases, grouped by the three different types of conundrums that emerged.[3]

BURYING THE DEAD

The first type of legal conundrum to emerge from Article 121 (1A) concerned the burial rites/rights when the official religious status of the deceased is contested. The first such reported case decided by the High Court was *Ng Wan Chan v. Federal Territories Islamic Religious Council*.[4] In this case, a widow found herself in the position of having to fight for the right to bury her husband following his death in 1991. Ng Wan Chan knew her husband as a practicing Buddhist. However, upon his death, the Federal Territories Islamic Religious Council claimed that he had officially converted to Islam in 1973 and he therefore required a proper Muslim burial. This case was one of many in which Islamic religious councils claimed the right to bury the dead when there was an official record of conversion to Islam. These situations stir particularly intense emotions when there are questions about whether the deceased had registered as a Muslim under duress, for material benefit, or in anticipation of marriage to a Muslim at some earlier stage in life. When these "body snatching" situations emerge, the family will often attempt to negotiate with the religious authorities and seek permission to pay their respects and to mourn briefly before the body is taken away for a Muslim burial. In some cases, non-Muslim prayers may be permitted. In other cases, they are not, and family members can only look on and mourn privately. In still other situations, families will contest the authenticity of the conversion and litigate for the right to bury their family member in keeping with their religious rites. Ng Wan Chan opted to litigate. A prominent lawyer-activist cum politician, Karpal Singh, served as her attorney.

Karpal Singh attempted to block the Federal Territories Islamic Religious Council in the High Court, but the Islamic Religious Council challenged the

---

[3]   Case selection in Chapters 4 and 5 is not anecdotal, but exhaustive of all Article 121 (1A) cases that were reported in the *Current Law Journal* and the *Malayan Law Journal*.

[4]   *Ng Wan Chan v. Majlis Ugama Islam Wilayah Persekutuan & Anor* [1991] 3 MLJ 487. It should be noted that only a select number of High Court decisions were published in the *Malayan Law Journal* and the *Current Law Journal,* the leading outlets at the time. There may have been other Article 121 (1A) decisions prior to *Ng Wan Chan,* but this is the first such published decision.

jurisdiction of the civil courts to intervene. The Islamic Religious Council contended that Article 121 (1A) gave the shariah courts exclusive jurisdiction to determine the religious status of the deceased. The High Court rejected the Council's challenge and reasoned that the shariah courts only had jurisdiction to consider issues that were expressly conferred by state law in accordance with the Federal Constitution.[5] The High Court proceeded to consider the factual merits of the case and delivered its judgment, declaring that "the deceased was a Buddhist at the time of his death." and "his widow, the plaintiff, is entitled to the remains of the deceased."[6]

The High Court soon faced a similar question in *Dalip Kaur*, a case that shaped all subsequent jurisprudence on the matter.[7] In this case, a young Sikh man, Gurdev Singh, had converted to Islam. Evidence suggested that he had a Muslim girlfriend at the time, and the High Court inferred that Gurdev had converted to marry her (as marriage is not permissible between non-Muslims and Muslims) but he died before the wedding. His mother, Dalip Kaur, wished to bury her son in accordance with Sikh rites. With representation by Karpal Singh, she claimed that her son had converted back to his original Sikh faith before his death. She provided documentation of rebaptism from a Sikh temple along with his signature on a deed poll.[8] She also presented supporting evidence that her son was not a practicing Muslim: he had attended Sikh religious services, he had continued to eat pork, and he had remained uncircumcised. However, the High Court received expert testimony that rejected the baptism and determined that the signature on the deed poll was forged. Considering this testimony, the High Court ruled that Gurdev Singh must not be buried in accordance with Sikh rites and that his remains must be withheld from his mother. The High Court decision was penned by Abdul Hamid Mohamad, who was a judicial commissioner on the High Court at the time. He would eventually rise to become the Chief Justice of the Federal Court.

Dalip Kaur appealed to the Supreme Court concerning the more general question of what constitutes conversion out of Islam, considering the fact that there was no explicit provision in the Kedah Administration of Islamic Law Enactment.[9] The Supreme Court remitted the case back to the High Court with instructions to refer a series of queries to the Fatwa Committee of Kedah.[10] The Court sought to

---

[5] The High Court declared, "If state law does not confer on the syariah court any jurisdiction to deal with any matter stated in the State List, the syariah court is precluded from dealing with the matter. Jurisdiction cannot be derived by implication." *Ng Wan Chan v. Majlis Ugama Islam Wilayah Persekutuan & Anor* [1991] 3 MLJ at 489.

[6] *Ng Wan Chan v. Majlis Ugama Islam Wilayah Persekutuan & Anor* [1991] 3 MLJ 174 at 178.

[7] *Dalip Kaur v. Pegawai Polis Daerah, Balai Polis Daerah, Bukit Mertajam & Anor* [1992] 1 MLJ 1.

[8] A deed poll is a legal statement to express an active intention.

[9] Malaysia's highest appellate court was named the Supreme Court between 1985 and 1994. Before and after those dates, it is referred to as the Federal Court of Malaysia.

[10] This was done via the High Court, as provided in Section 37 (4) of the Administration of Muslim Law Enactment of Kedah. It provides that "If in any Civil Court any question of Muslim law falls for decision, and such Court requests the opinion of the Majlis on such question, the question shall be

clarify the actions that constitute a renunciation of faith in Islamic law. The questions submitted to the Fatwa Committee and the answers that were received are as follows:[11]

Q: If a Muslim declares through a deed poll that he rejects Islam, has he in fact left Islam?

A: [Yes] if a Muslim declares through a deed poll that he rejects Islam, he has left Islam (He is an apostate).

Q: If a Muslim prays at a Sikh temple following Sikh worship rituals, has he left Islam?

A: [Yes] A Muslim who prays at a Sikh temple following Sikh worship rituals has also left Islam (He is an apostate).

Q: If a Muslim carries out a ceremony to embrace Sikhism, has he left Islam?

A: [Yes] A Muslim who carries out a ceremony to embrace Sikhism has left Islam (he is an apostate). However, to determine whether or not someone has left Islam (committed apostasy), it is necessary to be convicted by a shariah court and be sentenced for apostasy first. If there is no shariah court conviction and sentence, that person is still a Muslim.

Q: If a Muslim eats pork, has he left Islam?

A: [No] A Muslim who eats pork has not left Islam.

Q: If a non-Muslim converts to Islam but is uncircumcised and remains as such until death, does he die as a non-Muslim, simply because he is uncircumcised?

A: A person who converts to Islam who is not circumcised is a legitimate Muslim.

[Therefore] In the opinion of the Kedah Islamic Council Fatwa Committee, which convened on 27 October 1991, Gurdev Singh a/l Guruvak Singh, Identity Card: A 1028701 is a Muslim because he professed his faith in Islam by saying the two clauses of the affirmations of faith in front of the Kadi of Kulim District, Kedah on the 1st of June 1991 as stated in the pledge form for new converts to Islam, number 5/91, and he remains Muslim because there is no judgment from any Shariah Court in Kedah that convicted him of having left Islam.[12]

The Fatwa Committee distinguished between acts that constitute apostasy in their understanding of *religious doctrine* on the one hand, and the procedure for determining an individual's official religious status in a *legal and regulatory* sense on the other.[13] The Fatwa Committee determined that Gurdev Singh had taken actions

---

referred to the Fetua [sic] committee which shall . . . give its opinion thereon and certify such opinion to the requesting court."

[11] The judges and litigants collectively agreed on the questions to be posed to the fatwa committee.

[12] *Dalip Kaur v. Pegawai Polis Daerah, Balai Polis Daerah, Bukit Mertajam & Anor* [1992] 1 MLJ 1 at 6.

[13] There are differing views on apostasy within the Islamic legal tradition. For further contextualization in the Islamic legal tradition and in contemporary Malaysia, see Saeed and Saeed (2004).

that constituted apostasy in a religious sense, but affirmed that his official status remained unchanged without a decision from a shariah court, the appropriate body for handling such matters. Thus, while Singh may have left Islam in practice, his official status is Muslim. In other words, the decision articulates a specific *fiqh* position regarding apostasy and yet immediately sidelines whatever religious doctrine might have to say in deference to administrative practices of the state.[14]

Before proceeding further, it is important to recall that members of the Fatwa Committee, an officially constituted state body, are *not* required to have formal training in Islamic law, nor are they required to have any training in the common law. The sole requirement for membership on the Fatwa Committee is that members be "fit and proper Muslims."[15] It is perhaps no wonder that the Fatwa Committee introduced such a glaring lacuna into the law, which required compliance with an administrative procedure that does not exist. Nonetheless, the decision of the Fatwa Committee was considered an authoritative pronouncement of *the* Islamic position regarding apostasy. Having reviewed the "fatwa," the Supreme Court affirmed the High Court decision.

A dissenting opinion noted the problematic aspects of the decision. Among the three-judge panel, Justice Hashim Yeop Sani observed, "the new [clause] 1A of Article 121 of the Constitution effective from 10 June 1988 has taken away the jurisdiction of the civil courts in respect of matters within the jurisdiction of the syariah courts."[16] However, the amendment "does not take away the jurisdiction of the civil court to interpret any written laws of the states enacted for the administration of Muslim law." With this delicate entry, the Justice waded deeper into the legal morass, noting that the Kedah Administration of Muslim Law Enactment did not provide Muslims with an avenue through which to change their official religious status.[17] He highlighted the failure of the state to provide a solution. Justice Hashim also noted that a provision in the Administration of Muslim Law Enactment had afforded Muslims an avenue to convert out of Islam in the neighboring state of Perak, but that the provision was repealed in 1975. He recommended that "clear

---

14   The fatwa was peculiar in more ways than one. The Committee regarded the conversion as a criminal offense, yet there was no legal avenue for the shariah court to prosecute an apostasy offense under the Kedah Administration of Muslim Law Enactment. The Kedah Enactment detailed several criminal offenses in Articles 142–169, but there were no provisions concerning apostasy. An attorney familiar with the case reflected on the changing legal context as one possible reason for the apparent contradiction: "I think the Fatwa Committee used the terms 'convict' and 'sentence' loosely. The usage of the Malay words, such as 'sabit' and 'hukum,' was not firmly fixed in 1991, since the language of the courts were largely still in English. It may well be that the Fatwa Committee merely meant a decision of a court, rather than a punitive measure" (Interview with the author November 26, 2016). If accurate, this transmutation underlines the general argument that the increasing regulation of religion and the increased fixity of these terms introduced new lacunas into the law.

15   Administration of Muslim Law Enactment Kedah (1962), section 36.

16   Justice Hashim Yeop Sani was, at the time, the Chief Judge of the High Court in Peninsular Malaysia, and the 3rd highest office bearer in the Judiciary.

17   Gurdev Singh converted to Islam in Kedah, making the Administration of Muslim Law Enactment of Kedah the relevant legal framework.

provisions should be incorporated in all the state Enactments to avoid difficulties of interpretation by the civil courts." For his part, Justice Mohamed Yusoff adopted a narrower perspective. Rather than acknowledge the lacunas in the law, Justice Yusoff simply stated:

> Such a serious issue would, to my mind, need consideration by eminent jurists who are properly qualified in the field of Islamic jurisprudence. On this view it is imperative that the determination of the question in issue requires substantial consideration of the Islamic law by relevant jurists qualified to do so. The only forum qualified to do so is the syariah court.

Justice Hashim Yeop Sani's dissenting opinion had identified a significant problem in the law, but the Court declared that the parties were bound by their agreement to accept the Fatwa Committee's determination that, " ... the deceased was a Muslim as he had been duly converted to Islam and there was no decision of a syariah court which decided that he had renounced or left the Islamic faith." Dalip Kaur lost the appeal and, with it, her right to bury her son in accordance with Sikh rites.[18] The court decision had a lasting impact on civil court jurisprudence for decades to come. While Justice Hashim Yeop Sani had identified a critical lacuna in the law, it was Justice Mohamed Yusoff's statement that became the standard refrain of civil court judges in future decisions.

FREEDOM OF RELIGION

The next landmark case also went all the way to the apex court, which was by then renamed the Federal Court. *Soon Singh v. Malaysian Islamic Welfare Organization of Kedah* involved a Sikh man who had converted to Islam as a minor but later reverted to his original Sikh faith in a religious ceremony.[19] Unlike the previous cases that concerned the religious status of the dead, Soon Singh was flesh and blood Malaysian, pleading for official recognition of his religious conversion out of Islam.

At the time of his reversion back to his original Sikh faith, Malaysians like Soon Singh were able to secure official recognition of conversion out of Islam by affirming a statutory declaration before a commissioner of oaths and registering a new name in

---

[18] In another case, the Court of Appeal further restricted the purview of the shariah courts to cases in which they had *exclusive* jurisdiction. When an offense could be tried under both the Shariah Criminal Offenses Act and the Malaysian Penal Code, the case could go to the Civil Courts. See *Sukma Darmawan Sasmitaat Madja v. Ketua Pengarah Penjara Malaysia & Anor.* [1999] 1 MLJ 226. The substance of this case is also worthy of comment. Sukma Darmawan was alleged to have had sexual relations with Anwar Ibrahim. The case was part of a series of prosecutions against Ibrahim after he was removed from his position as Deputy Prime Minister. The prosecutions were widely discredited but, at that moment, also intersected with the emerging case law around Article 121 (1A).

[19] *Soon Singh v. Pertubuhan Kebajikan Islam Malaysia (PERKIM) Kedah & Anor* [1994] 1MLJ 690; [1999] 1 MLJ 489.

the civil court registry through a deed poll.²⁰ With this documentation, an individual could then apply for a new identity card reflecting the name change, which signified one's new religious status.²¹ However, Singh encountered difficulties when he sought a declaration of his new religious status from the High Court in Kuala Lumpur. The Kedah Islamic Affairs Department challenged the High Court's jurisdiction in light of the newly adopted constitutional amendment, Article 121 (1A). The High Court agreed that the new amendment prevented it from certifying Soon Singh's new faith. The Court drew upon the "fatwa" from *Dalip Kaur v. Pegawai Polis Daerah, Balai Polis Daerah, Bukit Mertajam & Anor* and ceded jurisdiction on that basis. The court decision stated:

> It is clear from the fatwa that a Muslim who renounced the Islamic faith by a deed poll or who went through a baptism ceremony to reconvert to Sikhism continues to remain in Islam until a declaration has been made in a syariah court that he is a "murtad" [apostate]. Therefore, in accordance with the fatwa, the plaintiff is still a Muslim. He should go to a syariah court for the declaration. Whether or not his conversion is invalid is also a matter for the syariah court to determine in accordance with hukum syarak and the civil courts have no jurisdiction.

Singh appealed, pointing out that there were no express provisions in the Kedah Administration of Muslim Law Enactment that conferred jurisdiction on the shariah courts. However, the Islamic Affairs Department invoked Article 121 (1A) again. The Supreme Court affirmed the decision and adopted a new doctrine of implied jurisdiction. The new doctrine effectively ceded jurisdiction to the shariah courts on all cases concerning conversion out of Islam. The Court held that "jurisdiction of the syariah courts to deal with conversions out of Islam, although not expressly provided for in some State Enactments, can be read into those enactments by implication derived from the provisions concerning conversion into Islam."²² Similar cases that followed conformed to the same logic. The civil courts would no longer certify conversion out of Islam, ceding their jurisdiction to the shariah courts.²³

---

²⁰ A statutory declaration is a sworn statement made outside of pending legal proceedings. A deed poll is a legal statement to express an active intention.

²¹ Ahmed, *Islam in Malaysia*, 10–11.

²² The decision was quite convoluted in that it did not point directly to the state powers detailed in Schedule 9, List Two, of the Federal Constitution. Rather, it referred to other Article 121 (1A) decisions that had examined state enactments for evidence of jurisdiction. The court then reasoned that since state enactments regulated conversion into Islam, they must, by implication, also provide state shariah courts with jurisdiction over cases dealing with conversion out of Islam.

²³ Soon Singh can be contrasted with a slightly earlier decision, that of *Teoh Eng Huat v. The Kadhi, Pasir Mas, Kelantan & Anor* [1990] 2 MLJ 300. In that case, a 17-year-old Chinese Buddhist, Susie Teoh Bee Kue, eloped with her Muslim boyfriend and converted to Islam. Susie's father raised a case contesting her conversion on the basis of the Guardianship Act of 1961. The High Court recognized Susie's conversion to Islam, but the Supreme Court considered the argument that Susie could not lawfully change her religious designation without the permission of her father. The Supreme Court eventually overturned the High Court ruling that had recognized her conversion to Islam. However, Susie had reached the age of majority by the time of the Supreme Court ruling, rendering the decision

The decision papered over the fact that most state enactments provide no viable avenue for official conversion out of Islam, with some states treating requests for official change of religion as criminal offenses. Six of Malaysia's thirteen states (Perlis, Kedah, Penang, Selangor, Johor, and Sarawak) and the Federal Territories do not criminalize conversion out of Islam, but nor do they specify a legal mechanism for the official recognition of religious conversion. Five more states (Perak, Pahang, Terengganu, Malacca, and Sabah) criminalize conversion out of Islam with punishments that include fines and imprisonment (and whipping in the case of Pahang).[24] In three more states (Sabah, Kelantan, and Malacca), a judge may order mandatory counseling at a "faith rehabilitation center" for periods ranging from six to thirty-six months. Negeri Sembilan is the *only* state that provides a formal avenue for official conversion out of Islam, but the process is lengthy, and it requires mandatory counseling.[25] As a result, the shariah courts received only 686 petitions for change of official religious status out of Islam between 2000 and 2010. Of these, the courts approved only 135 petitions – or less than fourteen approvals per year, nationwide.[26] Most, if not all, of these 135 individuals had converted to Islam for marriage but then reverted to their previous faith. This small number of conversions over the course of the decade suggests that official conversion out of Islam is – for all practical purposes – virtually impossible.

Nonetheless, the civil courts remained aloof. Such indifference was painfully clear in cases like *Md Hakim Lee v. Majlis Agama Islam Wilayah Persekutuan.* A former Buddhist who had converted to Islam, Md Hakim Lee sought to revert his official religious status to Buddhism.[27] Lee pleaded that Article 11 of the Federal Constitution guaranteed his right to change his religious status. The case provided the civil courts with the first opportunity to consider Article 121 (1A) in light of a constitutional provision guaranteeing religious freedom. The Federal Territories Islamic Religious Council challenged the jurisdiction of the civil courts to hear the case. Justice Abdul Kadir Sulaiman agreed with the Council, declaring that "the language of art 121 (1A) ... is clear and without any ambiguity." He explained that shariah court jurisdiction was not limited to matters explicitly provided for in the Administration of Islamic Law Act. Henceforth, shariah court jurisdiction included *any matter* listed in Schedule Nine of the Federal Constitution concerning states' rights. When Md Hakim Lee's attorneys argued that such a strict interpretation of

"academic" in the words of the Court. What is notable about the Susie Teoh case is that the civil court system exercised jurisdiction on the matter.

[24] For example, the Terengganu Administration of Islamic Law Enactment of 1996 provides that "any Muslim who attempts to renounce the religion of Islam or declares himself to be non-Muslim, shall on conviction be liable to a fine not exceeding three thousand ringgit or to imprisonment for a term not exceeding one year or both."

[25] I rely on Mohamed Adil (2007a; 2007b).

[26] These figures were announced by the Islamic Affairs Minister in the Prime Minister's Department and reported in *Malaysiakini*, June 14, 2011. Figures for different periods are provided in Adil (2007, 2008).

[27] *Md Hakim Lee v. Majlis Agama Islam Wilayah Persekutuan, Kuala Lumpur* [1998] 1 MLJ 681.

Article 121 (1A) harmed his right to freedom of religion, Justice Abdul Kadir Sulaiman explained that "the issue is not one of whether a litigant can get his remedies, but one of jurisdiction of the Courts to adjudicate … The fact that the plaintiff may not have his remedy in the syariah court would not make the jurisdiction exercisable by the civil court."[28] This refrain was heard time and again in cases that followed.

Lina Joy v. Federal Territories Islamic Religious Council

One of the most controversial cases that attracted national and international attention was that of Lina Joy, an ethnic Malay woman who sought official recognition of her conversion to Christianity so that she could marry her non-Muslim partner. In 1997, she applied to change the name on her National Registration Identity Card from Azlina bte Jailani (a Muslim name) to Lina Lelani (a non-Muslim name). While there is no official route to marriage between Muslims and non-Muslims in Malaysia, changing one's name was a way for star-crossed lovers to circumvent the letter of the law and register a marriage with the state. However, the administrative unit charged with processing the name change, the National Registration Department (NRD), rejected Azlina's paperwork. They did not explain why. Azlina then filed a second request, this time to change her legal name to "Lina Joy."[29] The National Registration Department approved this second application, but Joy's replacement identity card now stated her official religious affiliation: "Islam." The statement of her official religious status was the result of a new administrative procedure that was designed to close the loophole that had enabled Muslims to effectively sidestep the state's regulation of religion by way of a name change. Joy filed a third application, this time to remove the word "Islam" from her identity card, but the NRD refused to accept her application without certification from a shariah court that she was no longer a Muslim. However, there was no formal legal avenue for official recognition of conversion through the shariah court administration in the Federal Territories. Lina Joy's attorney, Benjamin Dawson, explained that Joy was sent from law office to law office, but lawyers shied away from the case due to sensitivities around conversion out of Islam for ethnic Malays in particular.[30] Dawson took the case and helped Joy initiate a lawsuit against the National Registration Department and the Federal Territories Islamic Religious Council.[31] They pointed to Article 11 (1) of the Malaysian Constitution, which states, "Every person has the right to profess and practice his religion …." They argued that Joy had no obligation to seek certification from a third party and that Article 11 gave Joy

---

[28]   *Md Hakim Lee v. Majlis Agama Islam Wilayah Persekutuan, Kuala Lumpur* [1998] 1 MLJ at 684, 687.
[29]   She explained in both applications that she had converted to Christianity and that she intended to marry a Christian man. It is likely that this statement raised alarms among those in the NRD.
[30]   Personal interview, November 23, 2012.
[31]   *Lina Joy v. Majlis Agama Islam Wilayah Persekutuan & Anor* [2004] 2 MLJ 119.

alone the freedom to declare her religion.[32] Counsel for the government argued that the High Court should dismiss the petition because apostasy was a legal matter within the exclusive jurisdiction of the shariah courts.

The High Court agreed but, unlike earlier cases such as *Md Hakim Lee v. Majlis Agama Islam*, where the courts had sidestepped constitutional protections on freedom of religion, Justice Faiza Tamby Chik addressed Article 11 directly. He explained that Joy's fundamental freedoms were not violated because the actual intent of Article 11 is to protect the freedom of *religious communities* to practice their faith free of interference, rather than for *individuals* to profess and practice the religion of their choice. To support this interpretation, Justice Faiza pointed to other clauses in Article 11 of the Federal Constitution, including Clause 3, which states: "Every religious group has the right ... to manage its own religious affairs ...", as well as to Article 3(1) of the Federal Constitution, which proclaims that "Islam is the religion of the Federation; but other religions may be practiced in peace and harmony." The actual meaning of freedom of religion, Justice Faiza argued, is that religious groups should be left to regulate their internal matters without outside interference:

> When a Muslim wishes to renounce/leave the religion of Islam, his other rights and obligations as a Muslim will also be jeopardized and this is an affair of Muslim [sic] falling under the first defendant's jurisdiction .... Even though the first part [of Article 11] provides that every person has the right to profess and practice his religion, this does not mean that the plaintiff can hide behind this provision without first settling the issue of renunciation of her religion (Islam) with the religious authority which has the right to manage its own religious affairs under art 11 (3) (a) of the FC.[33]

Justice Faiza reasoned that Article 11(3) protects *religious communities* to practice their faith free of interference, including the ability to regulate matters of entry *and* exit from the faith. Those guarantees must supersede the ability of *individuals* to drift among different religious affiliations to suit whimsical desires under the guise of Article 11 (1). Departing from such an interpretation would threaten "public order."[34]

It is worth noting that Justice Faiza made extensive use of Islamist scholarship to support his reasoning. Extended quotations were offered from Professor Ahmad Ibrahim, the most prominent early advocate of an expanded role for Islamic law

[32]　Joy's attorneys challenged the constitutionality of Article 2 of the Administration of Islamic Law (Federal Territories) Act of 1993 and related state enactments. They also claimed that the Shariah Criminal Offences Act of 1997 and related State Enactments were not applicable to the plaintiff, who was now a Christian.

[33]　*Lina Joy v. Majlis Agama Islam Wilayah Persekutuan & Anor* [2004] 2 MLJ at 126.

[34]　"I am of the opinion that this threaten [sic] public order and this cannot have been the intention of the legislature when drafting the FC and the 1993 Act." *Lina Joy v. Majlis Agama Islam Wilayah Persekutuan & Anor* [2004] 2 MLJ at 126.

in the Malaysian legal system, as well as more recent writings from Muhammad Imam and others. The High Court decision makes broad claims about the meaning of Article 3, with implications for all facets of social and political life. According to the decision, " ... the position of Islam in art 3(1) is that Islam is the main and dominant religion in the Federation. Being the main and dominant religion, the Federation has a duty to protect, defend and promote the religion of Islam." Islamist lawyers had found a ready ally in Justice Faiza. Although he did not rise to the upper reaches of the Malaysian judiciary, Justice Faiza's legal reasoning played an important role in shaping two of the most important cases concerning shariah court jurisdiction: *Lina Joy v. Majlis Agama Islam*, which shaped all religious freedom cases thereafter, and *Shamala v. Jeyaganesh*, a crucial child custody/conversion case (discussed later in this chapter).

Having lost the battle in the High Court, Lina Joy's legal team shifted strategy and focused on the administrative question of whether the Director General of the National Registration Department had overstepped his authority by requiring certification of Joy's religious conversion by a shariah court.[35] In a split decision, Justice Abdul Aziz Mohamad and Justice Arifin Zakaria took the position that whether a person had renounced Islam is "a question of Islamic law that was not within the jurisdiction of the NRD and that the NRD was not equipped or qualified to decide."[36] The dissenting judgment from Justice Gopal Sri Ram took the position that "an order or certificate from the Syariah Court was not a relevant document for the processing of the appellant's application. It was not a document prescribed by the 1990 Regulations." Justice Sri Ram concluded that "[w]here a public decision-maker takes extraneous matters into account, his or her decision is null and void and of no effect."[37]

Having lost in the Court of Appeal, Joy and her attorneys had one final opportunity in the highest appellate court, the Federal Court of Malaysia. Joy's legal team focused again on two central questions: 1) whether the NRD was empowered by law to impose the requirement that the applicant provide certification of apostasy from a shariah court, and, 2) whether the implied jurisdiction theory developed in *Soon Singh* and *Md Hakim Lee* should prevail over the express jurisdiction theory expounded in *Ng Wan Chan* and *Lim Chan Seng*. Watching briefs were held by NGOs on both sides of the case. The Bar Council, HAKAM, and the Malaysian Consultative Council of Buddhism, Christianity, Hinduism, and Sikhism held watching briefs on behalf of Lina Joy, while conservative Muslim organizations holding watching briefs included ABIM, the Muslim Lawyers Association, and the Shariah Lawyers Association of Malaysia.

---

[35] It is not clear why the legal team abandoned the more robust legal challenge that was taken up in the High Court.

[36] *Lina Joy v. Majlis Agama Islam Wilayah Persekutuan & Ors* [2005] 6 MLJ 193.

[37] *Lina Joy v. Majlis Agama Islam Wilayah Persekutuan & Ors* [2005] 6 MLJ 193 at 194.

In a 2–1 split decision, the 53-page decision reproduced the same fault lines that were present in the Court of Appeal.[38] Chief Justice Ahmad Fairuz and Justice Alauddin found the NRD's actions reasonable and further that the *Soon Singh* decision was sound. In a decision with far-reaching effect, they concluded that "art 11(1) should not be argued as a provision that provides unrestricted right of freedom [and] the right to profess and practise a religion should always be subject to the principles and practices prescribed by the said religion."[39]

The dissenting judgment from Justice Richard Malanjum pointed once again to the glaring lacuna in the law: "The insistence by NRD for a certificate of apostasy from the Federal Territory Syariah Court or any Islamic Authority was not only illegal but unreasonable. This was because under the applicable law, the Syariah Court in the Federal Territory has no statutory power to adjudicate on the issue of apostasy."[40] Justice Malanjum explained that, in such a situation, the Federal Court has a constitutional duty to protect fundamental rights, regardless of Article 121 (1A):

> Since constitutional issues are involved especially on the question of fundamental rights as enshrined in the Constitution, it is of critical importance that the civil superior courts should not decline jurisdiction by merely citing Art 121 (1A). The Article only protects the Shariah Court in matters within their jurisdiction, which does not include interpretation of the provisions of the Constitution. Hence, when jurisdictional issues arise civil courts are not required to abdicate their constitutional function. Legislation criminalizing apostasy or limiting the scope of fundamental liberties . . . are constitutional issues in nature, which only the civil courts have jurisdiction to determine.

By making individual liberties subject to specific regulations on apostasy, the majority decision in *Lina Joy v. Federal Territories Islamic Religious Council* exacerbated the difficulties at the heart of all prior conversion cases.

The Lina Joy case was also unique in one regard: Joy was an ethnic Malay, whereas prior conversion cases concerned non-ethnic Malays who had converted to Islam (typically for marriage) and who subsequently sought to revert to their prior religious status. Lina Joy's case thus exposed a "racial" dimension to religious freedom cases. In its decision, the High Court pointed to Article 160 of the Federal Constitution, which defines Malay as "a person who professes the religion of Islam, habitually speaks the Malay language, [and] conforms to Malay custom . . . ." Citing Article 160, the High Court explained that Lina Joy's racial (and therefore religious) status carried legal consequences that could not be abandoned:

> In her affidavit affirmed on 8 May 2000, the plaintiff stated that her father is a Malay. His name is Jailani bin Shariff. All his life, the father has been professing and practising [sic] the Islamic religion. So is the mother. Her name is Kalthum bte

---

[38] *Lina Joy lwn Majlis Agama Islam Wilayah Persekutuan dan lain-lain* [2007] 4 MLJ 585.

[39] *Lina Joy lwn Majlis Agama Islam Wilayah Persekutuan dan lain-lain* [2007] 4 MLJ: 618–619.

[40] *Lina Joy lwn Majlis Agama Islam Wilayah Persekutuan dan lain-lain* [2007] 4 MLJ: 597–598.

Omar, a Malay. Both of the parents are still professing and practising [sic] the Islamic religion. And being Malays they habitually speaks [sic] the Malay language and conform to Malay custom. The plaintiff also stated that she is raised, and grew up in a household of Islamic belief although her belief in Islam is shallow. In exh C, she stated that her original name is Azlina bte Jailani as is stated in her I/C No 7220456. I therefore conclude that the plaintiff is a Malay. By art 160 of the FC, the plaintiff is a Malay and therefore as long as she is a Malay by that definition she cannot renounce her Islamic religion at all. *As a Malay, the plaintiff remains in the Islamic faith until her dying days* [emphasis added].[41]

The decision provides a clear illustration of how law and the social imaginary conflate Malay racial and religious identity in contemporary Malaysia. In fact, it is worth noting that the majority opinion in *Lina Joy* was written in Bahasa Malaysia and not in English, as is conventional practice. This departure from standard convention was surely meant to deliver the message that matters concerning Islam and Malay identity are first and foremost Malay issues, as opposed to Malaysian issues.

Lina Joy v. Federal Territories Islamic Religious Council illustrates how the extensive regulation of religion and race gives rise to festering legal conundrums. But rather than working to untangle these legal conundrums by deregulating the religious sphere, the government moved in the opposite direction. Additional regulations were introduced to shore up religious and racial compartmentalization. Before 2001, Malaysian identity cards did not state an individual's religious status. Religious affiliation was imputed from one's name. Malaysians could change their official name and for most purposes, including marriage, they were assumed to be non-Muslim. This possibility ended when the government began to list religion on national identity cards. An amendment to the regulations guiding the National Registration Department (NRD) in 2001 also required that applicants submit documentation from a shariah court or a state department of religious affairs to change their official religion.[42] Although it is impossible to know with certainty, it is likely that these regulations changed as a direct result of Lina Joy's attempt to marry a non-Muslim man by changing her name.[43]

The (Near) Impossibility of Shariah Court Conversion

The majority decision in *Lina Joy v. Federal Territories Islamic Religious Council* presumes that the shariah courts provide a viable avenue for securing recognition of conversion out of Islam. As noted earlier, however, official recognition of conversion is practically impossible to obtain. The few shariah court judges who were willing to

---

[41] *Lina Joy v. Majlis Agama Islam Wilayah Persekutuan & Anor* [2004] 2 MLJ at 144.

[42] P.U. (A) 70/2000 came into force retroactively on October 1, 1999; National Registration Regulations, 1990 (amended 2001).

[43] The timing of the rule change and their retroactive effect suggests that this is the case.

"certify" an individual's non-Muslim status grew more hesitant to accommodate after the extraordinary public spectacle that emerged in *Lina Joy v. Federal Territories Islamic Religious Council*.[44] The case of Rashidah bt Mohamad Myodin illustrates the roadblocks that Malaysian Muslims face when they attempt to change their official religious status from Muslim to non-Muslim.[45] The case further shows how rigid legal categories are unable to cope with the complex social realities of Malaysia's multiethnic and multi-religious society.

Rashidah bt Mohamad Myodin was registered as a Muslim at birth, but a Hindu foster parent adopted her at the age of three. Rashidah was therefore raised Hindu even though she was officially Muslim. She eventually filed an application with the Shariah Court of Kuala Lumpur for a formal declaration that she was not a Muslim.[46] In its proceedings, the Shariah Court acknowledged that Rashidah had never practiced Islam. However, the judge rejected her application because the Administration of Islamic Law Act for the Federal Territories does not provide a legal mechanism for officially certifying that an individual is not a Muslim. This lacuna was precisely the conundrum that Justice Richard Malanjum identified in his dissenting opinion in *Lina Joy v. Federal Territories Islamic Religious Council*, as had other judges before him. Although the civil courts ceded jurisdiction to the shariah courts in personal status matters for individuals registered as Muslim, the shariah courts were an administrative dead-end for those seeking to change their official religious status. Individuals like Rashidah bt Mohamad Myodin and Lina Joy faced a lacuna in the law, with no remedy in either the federal civil courts or in the shariah courts.[47]

Zaina Abidin bin Hamid v. Kerajaan Malaysia and Ors

The case of *Zaina Abidin bin Hamid* highlights the fact that this legal lacuna can impact entire families across generations.[48] This story begins in the 1950s when an ethnic Indian Hindu man by the name of Maniam converted to Islam to marry an ethnic Indian Muslim woman. This was a "paper conversion." In other words, while Maniam was now officially Muslim and he took the official Muslim name Hamid, he continued to practice Hinduism. Maniam and his wife raised their son, Zaina Abidin bin Hamid, in accordance with the Hindu faith. In 1973, their son changed his legal name by deed poll to Balachandran so that he might be recognized as

---

[44] This was explained by lawyers Latheefa Koya and Ravi Nekoo, both of whom worked on legal aid cases through the Kuala Lumpur Legal Aid Centre. Interview with the author, June 29, 2009.

[45] Application 14200–002-2003 with the Shariah Court of Kuala Lumpur. I rely on Mohamed Adil (2007a) for the details of this case.

[46] It is instructive that the Kuala Lumpur Shariah Court is the same court that Lina Joy would have approached for a certificate of apostasy if she had attempted to pursue that avenue.

[47] For another example, see *Balbir bin Abdullah lwn. Mahadzir bin Mohd Nor, Jurnal Hukum*, v. 27 (1) at 53.

[48] *Zaina Abidin bin Hamid @ S. Maniam and Ors v. Kerajaan Malaysia and Ors* [2009] 6 MLJ 863.

Hindu.[49] Balachandran later married a Hindu woman under the Law Reform (Marriage and Divorce) Act and they had three children. The 1989 Selangor Administration of Islamic Law Enactment (revised in 2003) defines a Muslim as someone who is *born to a Muslim*. Because Balachandran was the son of a Muslim, the State of Selangor therefore considered Balachandran a Muslim. Moreover, his three children were also officially Muslim. This adds up to three generations of practicing Hindus, all of whom are officially registered as Muslim, thus making them beholden to the rules and regulations that apply to Muslims in Malaysia. This status was especially crippling to Balachandran's children, who would only be able to marry Muslims. The legal quandary of the Balachandran family put the absurdity of Malaysia's tightly regulated religious system into high relief. These practicing Hindus could only marry – *wait for it* – Muslims! To add to the irony, this result is precisely the opposite of what the state regulation of religion had aimed to accomplish in Malaysia.

Balachandran and his three children were represented by K Shanmuga and Fahri Azzat, two of the top attorneys litigating freedom of religion cases. As part of their strategy, the attorneys focused the attention of the court on what it means to "profess" a faith in Article 11 (1) of the Federal Constitution. They argued that any state regulation that ties an individual's religious status to anything other than their professed faith is inconsistent with the Federal Constitution. The High Court struck out the entire case as an abuse of process on the grounds that settled law provided the civil courts with no jurisdiction to hear such matters, leaving it to the shariah court system to decide. The legal team appealed.[50] The Court of Appeal agreed that there had been an error. It set aside the High Court decision and remitted the case back to the High Court to be heard on its merits. To date, the plight of the Balachandran family remains unresolved.

Given case law on the matter, the chances that the Balachandran family will prevail are slim at best. The reader will recall that between 2000 and 2010, shariah courts nationwide had approved only 135 petitions for the official recognition of conversion out of Islam.[51] I managed to interview one of the only attorneys who had successfully shepherded a case through the Kuala Lumpur Shariah court administration. As one of the very few cases where a "letter of release" was obtained from a shariah court, it is worth reviewing. In this case, an ethnic Indian Hindu woman and an ethnic Indian Muslim man had married in accordance with Hindu religious rites in the mid-1970s, but the wedding had not been registered.[52] The couple had

---

[49]   The reader will recall that this avenue was possible in the 1970s.

[50]   At this point, Edmund Bon Tai joined the case representing the MCCBCHST. Meanwhile, the Government of Malaysia was represented by the Attorney General's Chambers, while the Selangor State Legal Adviser represented the Government of Selangor.

[51]   These figures were announced by the Islamic Affairs Minister in the Prime Minister's Department and reported in *Malaysiakini*, June 14, 2011.

[52]   These are the facts of the case as presented in the statutory declaration presented to the Kuala Lumpur Shariah Court. The names and specific details are not provided to preserve anonymity.

several children, each of whom was given a Muslim name. However, the children were practicing Hindus and they never practiced Islam. Each child filed statutory declarations to this effect and they appeared in the shariah court where they managed to convince the presiding shariah court judge that they were not and had never been practicing Muslims. The was an extremely rare decision and one that was only possible before the spectacle that emerged around the Article 121 (1A) cases in 2004.

Siti Fatimah Tan Abdullah: The Exception that Proves the Rule

Penang Religious Council v. Siti Fatimah Tan Abdullah represents another of the very few cases where a registered Muslim successfully changed her official religious status. The case is instructive because it is the exception that proves the rule. Siti Fatimah Tan Abdullah was a Buddhist who converted to Islam to marry an Iranian man. After Siti Fatimah Tan Abdullah's husband had left her, she petitioned the shariah court for a formal declaration that she was no longer Muslim.[53] The shariah court obliged, but the Penang Islamic Religious Council appealed the judgment to the Shariah Court of Appeal. Capitalizing on the lacuna in the Administration of Islam Enactment, the Islamic Religious Council argued that the shariah court did not have the power to declare Siti Fatimah a non-Muslim. The Shariah Court of Appeal examined the technical minutia of the Administration of the Religion of Islam Enactment for the State of Penang, including the intent of the specific language deployed in Articles 61 (3) (b) (x) and 107. The Shariah Court of Appeal agreed with the Religious Council's objection that the Enactment did not allow Muslims to renounce Islam: "[F]or those who had thus become Muslims, they could not be declared as non-Muslims under this section .... clothing the Syariah Court with jurisdiction to grant leave to anyone to abandon the religion of Islam is abhorrent and repugnant to the principles of Hukum Syarak."[54] However, the Shariah Court of Appeal affirmed that Siti Fatimah was not a Muslim on the basis that she had, in fact, *never* been a Muslim. "The evidence showed that the respondent had professed Islam only for the purpose of her marriage, had never performed the practices of Islam and had engaged in idol-worshipping even after her conversion to Islam."[55] The Shariah Court of Appeal concluded that "the respondent's declaration of faith herein did not constitute a valid conversion into Islam as per the requirements [and] since the respondent's conversion process was flawed, she could no longer be taken as a Muslim. She must remain a Buddhist and could not, therefore, be accused of apostasy."[56] The case confirmed that there was no avenue for Muslims to legally convert out of Islam in the state of Penang. Only if the original conversion to Islam was found to be faulty could one be declared non-Muslim under

---

[53] *Majlis Agama Islam Pulau Pinang lwn. Siti Fatimah Tan Abdullah* [2009] 1 CLJ (Sya) 162.
[54] [2009] 1 CLJ (Sya) at 166.   [55] [2009] 1 CLJ (Sya) at 166.   [56] [2009] 1 CLJ (Sya) at 166–7.

the Administration of Islam Enactment. In other words, the case was the exception that proved the rule.

The cases examined up to this point concern individuals who were officially registered as Muslim but who sought legal recognition of conversion. Nearly all of them remained in a quandary as the result of Malaysia's hyper-regulated religious sphere and the unwillingness of the civil courts to consider their plight. These individuals faced long ordeals in court. But others had it much worse, as in the case of a woman who went by the name Priyathaseny.

Priyathaseny v. Department of Islamic Religious Affairs Perak

Priyathaseny v. Perak Department of Islamic Religious Affairs concerns an ethnic Malay Muslim woman who converted to Hinduism in 1998 to marry an ethnic Indian of Hindu faith.[57] Because changing one's official religious status is impossible for ethnic Malays and there is no legal path for a Muslim to marry a non-Muslim, Zuraidah bte Hassan changed her name to Priyathaseny, a Hindu name. The couple performed a Hindu marriage ceremony, but they did not register the marriage with the state authorities. After giving birth to her first child and while pregnant with her second, Priyathaseny was arrested and charged with deriding the religion of Islam and cohabitation outside of lawful Muslim wedlock under the Administration of Islamic Law Enactment and the Shariah Criminal Enactment of Perak (1992). The Enactment provides that "Any Muslim who declares himself to be a non-Muslim so as to avoid any action being taken against him under this Enactment or any other law in force is guilty of an offence and shall, on conviction, be liable to a fine not exceeding five thousand ringgit or to imprisonment for a term not exceeding three years or to both." Despite Priyathaseny's conversion ceremony, her change of name, and her Hindu wedding ceremony, the state nonetheless considered her Muslim. While in custody, Priyathaseny pleaded guilty on the advice of a shariah court lawyer. She was fined RM 5,000 (approximately $1,300) and detained for three days. During this period, her husband converted to Islam under the threat that Priyathaseny would be jailed if he did not.

Upon their release, the couple initiated litigation in the civil courts. Priyathaseny sought a declaration that the charges against her were null and void because she did not profess Islam. They also sought the reregistration of her husband as a Hindu on the grounds that his conversion was made under duress. Finally, Priyathaseny challenged the constitutionality of certain aspects of the Administration of Islamic Law and Shariah Criminal Enactments based on Article 11 of the Federal Constitution, guaranteeing freedom of religion. The Department of Religious Affairs challenged the civil court's jurisdiction based on Article 121 (1A).

---

[57] *Priyathaseny & Ors v. Pegawai Penguatkuasa Agama Jabatan Hal Ehwal Agama Islam Perak & Ors* [2003] 2 CLJ 221.

In response to this preliminary objection, her attorney Shanmuga Kanesalingam reasoned that a shariah court was not the appropriate forum because the case concerned constitutional questions, not under the purview of the shariah courts. Leaving the matter to the shariah courts would not provide relief, and it would put the family in jeopardy by making them subject to further criminal charges. Shanmuga explained that:

> To send this case to Syariah Court would be to give the Syariah Court powers over persons who do not profess Islam in Malaysia [which is] a country comprising people professing and practicing so many different religions. This cannot be right, particularly as the Federal Constitution expressly provides that the Syariah Courts shall have jurisdiction "only" over persons "professing the religion of Islam."[58]

The presiding High Court Justice sided with the preliminary objection fielded by the Department of Islamic Religious Affairs and refused to review the Administration of Islamic Law and Shariah Criminal Enactments. The judge referred to previous Article 121 (1A) jurisprudence and declared: "I am now guided by and bound by the pronouncement of our apex court in *Soon Singh* that the jurisdiction of this court is now ousted from determining the merits of this application. The central issue is clearly out of the bound of jurisdiction of the civil court as it is clearly a matter that can only be determined by the Syariah authorities."[59]

Why were the civil courts ceding broad authority to the shariah courts? Liberal lawyers maintained that the original intent of Article 121 (1A) was to prevent the civil courts from overturning shariah court decisions that lay within the shariah court's express jurisdiction. Liberal lawyers contend that, when properly read, Article 121 (1A) should not preclude the civil courts from retaining jurisdiction over cases where fundamental rights are at stake.[60] Doing so abandons a primary role of the federal judiciary. A basic problem, liberal rights lawyers explained, is that judges had been made increasingly vulnerable to political pressures after the government weakened judicial independence in 1988. This vulnerability is especially acute when the courts adjudicate "sensitive issues" such as the position of the shariah courts vis-à-vis the civil courts and anything touching on religion. In this view, the willingness of the civil courts to cede authority to the shariah courts is the product of political pressures rather than the specific constitutional text embodied in Article 121 (1A). This interpretation fits the political context of a much more recent case concerning the religious status of Azmi Mohamad Azam.

---

[58] *Priyathaseny & Ors v. Pegawai Penguatkuasa Agama Jabatan Hal Ehwal Agama Islam Perak & Ors* [2003] 2 CLJ at 226.

[59] *Priyathaseny & Ors v. Pegawai Penguatkuasa Agama Jabatan Hal Ehwal Agama Islam Perak & Ors* [2003] 2 CLJ at 227. The Court of Appeal later overturned the decision in 2009 and remitted the case back to the High Court for consideration on its merits. However, lawyers did not secure a resolution to the original plea. As a result, the case remains in a state of legal limbo.

[60] Interviews with Shanmuga Kanesalingam (July 9, 2009) and Malik Imtiaz Sarwar (November 5, 2009).

Azmi Mohamad Azam v. Director of Jabatan Agama Islam Sarawak

Azmi Mohamad Azam, also known as Roneey Rebit, litigated to change his official religious status from Muslim to Christian in 2015.[61] Roneey's parents had converted to Islam in 1983 when Roneey was just ten years old, and they changed his official religious status along with their own. Roneey's official name became Azmi bin Mohamad Azam @ Roneey.[62] As an adult, Roneey embraced Christianity and had himself baptized in 1999. In 2014, he attempted to secure formal state recognition of his conversion from the state. With his baptism certificate in hand, Roneey requested a new identity card recording a new, non-Muslim name from the National Registration Department (NRD). The NRD informed Roneey that to make such a change, they required a "letter of release from Islam" and a shariah court order.[63] Roneey attempted to comply. He approached the Islamic Affairs Department, but they told Roneey that they could not help without a shariah court order.[64] Facing this run-around with no clear path to official recognition of his conversion, Roneey raised a case in the High Court of Sarawak. After reviewing the facts of the case and the relevant case law, the High Court determined that Roneey's official religious status should be Christian. The Court ordered the NRD to record his new name and to change his official religious status on his identity card and in the National Registry. Roneey managed to win official recognition of his conversion, a feat that so many others before him had failed to secure.

There are two notable aspects of the High Court decision. The first is that Roneey's ethnic background appears to have been a determinative factor. In several passages, the court highlights the fact that Roneey is "a Bidayuh by race" and that he had been brought up in a Christian Bidayuh community.[65] Interestingly, the Court juxtaposes this context with that of the Lina Joy case, presumably to draw a distinction between the two cases to provide a rationale for the official recognition of Roneey's conversion. The High Court explains that "In Lina Joy case [sic] the appellant was a Malay woman brought up as a Muslim."[66] By contrast, "the applicant in the present case is a Bidayuh by race and brought up in a Christian Bidayuh community since birth. The choice of Islam religion [sic] was decided for him by his parents . . . ."[67] Part of the difficulty in *Lina*

---

[61] *Azmi Mohamad Azam v. Director of Jabatan Agama Islam Sarawak & Ors* [2016] 6 CJL 562.
[62] Much of the press coverage reported his name as "Rooney," but the court decision records his name correctly, as "Roneey."
[63] *Azmi Mohamad Azam v. Director of Jabatan Agama Islam Sarawak & Ors* [2016] 6 CJL at 565.
[64] The reader will recall that this is precisely the situation that Lina Joy faced, only she had refused to request the letter from a shariah court, knowing full well that others before her reached the same impasse.
[65] The Bidayuh are an indigenous group in Southern Sarawak.
[66] *Azmi Mohamad Azam v. Director of Jabatan Agama Islam Sarawak & Ors* [2016] 6 CJL at 571. Of course, Lina Joy had no choice about the official faith that she was brought up in, but this parallel was not addressed by the court.
[67] Ibid, 571.

Joy v. Majlis Agama Islam, it will be recalled, is the fact that Islam and the Malay "race" are bound together as a single legal category in Article 160 of the Federal Constitution – one of many legacies of the colonial-era legal regime. Moreover, Malay ethnic identity is conflated with Islam in popular legal consciousness. It appears that the High Court was attempting to identify a rationale for breaking with the precedent set in *Lina Joy v. Majlis Agama Islam* and citing Roneey's "race" was one way to do this. Another distinction articulated by the Court is that Roneey " ... has never practiced the Islamic faith."[68] The logic of the ruling is thus reminiscent of the Shariah Court of Appeal decision in *Penang Islamic Religious Council v. Siti Fatimah Tan Abdullah*.[69] In that judgment, the Shariah Court of Appeal had established that Siti Fatimah Tan Abdullah was not Muslim because she had, in fact, *never* been Muslim.

Nonetheless, *Azmi v. Director of Jabatan Agama Islam* is a potential game-changer for future case law. The High Court emphasized the importance of *belief* for determining an individual's religious status, as opposed to some external criteria that is regulated by the state and imposed on individuals. The High Court decision declared that:

> the freedom of religion gives individuals the liberty to worship their Creator in the way they think and are more agreeable with. In order to give life and meaning to "constitutional freedom of religion", the exercise of that freedom should not be impeded by subjecting the applicant to the decision of a Syariah Court. He does not need a Syariah Court Order to release him from Islam religion because the right to choose his religion lies with the applicant himself and not the religious body. The rights to religious freedom are the natural rights of mankind and thus, only the applicant alone can exercise that right. In other words, the exercise of constitutional religious freedom is out of bound/jurisdiction of a Syariah Court and the applicant can approach the civil court for a declaration that he is a Christian.

The Court based its decision in Article 11 (1) which provides that "Every person has the right to profess and practice his religion ... ." Equally important, the Court pointed to the Ninth Schedule of the Federal Constitution, which determines state power over the administration of religion. Here, the Court reproduced the text of the Ninth Schedule, highlighting in bold that the shariah courts, " ... **shall have jurisdiction only over persons professing the religion of Islam**."[70] The decision goes on to explain, "Given that the Syariah Court shall have jurisdiction only over persons **professing** the religion of Islam, it is therefore helpful at this juncture to ascertain the meaning of 'professing' or 'profess.'" Next,

---

[68]   Whether the claim is true or not will never be known, as the only legal rationale that has worked in terms of securing official conversion out of Islam has been the claim the individual had never practiced Islam.

[69]   *Majlis Agama Islam Pulau Pinang lwn. Siti Fatimah Tan Abdullah* [2009] 1 CLJ (Sya) 162.

[70]   *Azmi Mohamad Azam v. Director of Jabatan Agama Islam Sarawak & Ors* [2016] 6 CJL at 574 (emphasis in the original).

the decision turns to the meaning of "profess" and its implications for the case at hand:

> *Longman Dictionary of Contemporary English* defined "profess" as "a statement of your belief, opinion, or feeling." From the definition aforesaid, it conveys the meaning that to profess a religion is making a public statement about the religion you believe in. Thus, a person professing the religion of Islam is a person who has made a public declaration, affirmed his faith in or his allegiance to Islam.
>
> It is a fact that the Islam religion [sic] was chosen and decided for the applicant (a minor) by his mother when she converted to be a Muslim; his conversion was not by reason that he professed the religion of Islam. To put it in another way, the conversion of the applicant to Muslim faith was not on his own volition by affirming, declaring his faith in or allegiance to Islam religion but by virtue of his mother's conversion when he was a minor aged ten years old and his mother has determined his religion. In my view, since the applicant, who is a Bidayuh by birth, had not in the first place professed his faith in Islam but his conversion followed that of his mother as he was a minor at the material time, logic dictates that he cannot be considered as a person professing that particular faith. That the applicant has not lived like a person professing Islam is seen in his averment that he was raised and brought up in the Bidayuh Christian community.
>
> In my view, by reason that the applicant's conversion in the first place was not based on his professing Islam but by virtue of his mother's conversion and by his mother's choice for him, now that the applicant is a major, he is at liberty not only to exercise his constitutional religious right to choose his religion, he can come to this court to enforce his choice to be reflected in his identity card, i.e., his name and religion.
>
> In the light of the above the third respondent has not acted fairly towards the applicant by insisting on a letter of release from Islam and a court order to effect [sic] the amendments applied for by the applicant.
>
> For the reasons aforesaid, I allow the judicial review and make the following declarations:
>
> (a) that the applicant is a Christian;
> (b) that the third respondent do change the applicant's name from Azmi b Mohamad Azam Shah @ Roneey to Roneey anak Rebit;
> (c) that the third respondent do drop the applicant's religion Islam in his identity card and/or the records and/or particulars of the applicant's religion held at the National Registry to that of Christian.[71]

The court did not address the question of whether an adult who professes Islam can subsequently profess a different faith and change her or his official religious status. Nor does it address the situation of a Malay Muslim professing a different faith. However, the attention to the meaning of the word "profess" carries potentially significant implications for future case law.

---

[71] *Azmi Mohamad Azam v. Director of Jabatan Agama Islam Sarawak & Ors* [2016] 6 CJL at 575.

Subsequent developments underline the political backdrop for these legal conundrums. After the High Court ruling, the National Registration Department
initiated an appeal, but quickly backtracked and withdrew the case. Newspapers
reported that the Chief Minister of Sarawak, Adenan Satem, secured an agreement
from Prime Minister Najib that the NRD would not pursue the appeal. A deal had
apparently been cut to guard the position of the *Barisan Nasional* component party
in the May 7, 2016, Sarawak State elections. Given that Christians make up the
largest religious community in Sarawak, the political calculus of Najib's intervention in the NRD appeal was hard to miss. Whether future litigation around freedom
of religion will continue to focus on the word "profess" is yet to be seen. Given the
trajectory of civil court jurisprudence over the past decade, it is doubtful that the
focus on belief will stick. What the Roneey case suggests is that political context is
a defining feature in shaping the outcome.

CHILD CUSTODY AND CONVERSION

Another thorny question concerned child custody and the religious status of children when one parent converts to Islam, but not the other. An early example of this
was *Tan Sung Mooi v. Too Miew Kim*, in which a couple had married in accordance
with Chinese customary rites in 1964 and filed for divorce in 1991.[72] When Tan Sung
Mooi submitted an application for maintenance and division of matrimonial assets,
her husband's legal team protested that the High Court was not the proper legal
forum to hear the case considering Too Miew Kim's conversion to Islam. The matter
went to the Supreme Court, which decided that the civil courts must exercise
jurisdiction because the Law Reform (Marriage and Divorce) Act 1976 (which was
applicable only to non-Muslims) had applied to the parties as non-Muslims at the
time of the divorce. After examining the legal technicalities, the Court ruled that
"It would be a grave injustice to non-Muslim spouses and children whose only
remedy would be in the Civil Courts if the High Court no longer has jurisdiction
since the Syariah Courts do not have jurisdiction over non-Muslims." The Supreme
Court confirmed, "[T]he respondent's legal obligations under a non-Muslim marriage cannot be extinguished or avoided by his conversion to Islam."[73] *Tan Sung
Mooi v. Too Miew Kim* was resolved with little fanfare because such cases were not
yet in the public spotlight. Future cases would be far more contentious, particularly
when the official religious status of the children was in dispute.

Chang Ah Mee v. Islamic Religious Affairs Department was an early case involving
child custody.[74] In this case, a non-Muslim couple had been married for three years
when the husband, Khoo Tak Jin, converted to Islam and changed his daughter's
official religious status without his wife's consent. Chang Ah Mee turned to the civil

---

[72] *Tan Sung Mooi v. Too Miew Kim* [1994] 3 CLJ 708.
[73] *Tan Sung Mooi v. Too Miew Kim* [1994] 3 CLJ at 709.
[74] *Chang Ah Mee v. Jabatan Hal Ehwal Agama Islam & Ors.* [2003] 1 CLJ 458.

courts to have her daughter's conversion nullified on account of the Sabah Administration of Islamic Law Enactment, which requires the consent of the "parents" of an infant for purposes of conversion [emphasis added]. The Department of Islamic Religious Affairs countered that Article 12 (4) of the Federal Constitution states, " ... the religion of a person under the age of eighteen years shall be decided by his parent or guardian." The Department of Islamic Religious Affairs argued that because the text of the Constitution specified "parent" (in the singular form), *either* the father or the mother should have the right to initiate a religious conversion without the consent of the other spouse. The High Court ruled "there is no merit in the argument" because the Constitution "does not discriminate against the sexes." Therefore, the term "parent" in Article 12 (4) "must necessarily mean both the father and the mother. To allow just the father or just the mother to choose the religion would invariably mean depriving the other of the constitutional rights under art. 12 (4)."[75] The High Court ruled the conversion null and void. What is notable about this case is that the Department of Islamic Religious Affairs did not invoke Article 121 (1A) to challenge the jurisdiction of the civil courts to hear the case.[76] It is unclear why lawyers did not invoke the Article, but it appears to have helped the court to exercise jurisdiction. This is the only instance – until the Indira Gandhi decision – in which a court had declared the conversion of a child in such circumstances to be null and void. Had the Department of Islamic Religious Affairs challenged the jurisdiction of the civil courts, Chang Ah Mee likely would have been unable to recover her rights. The critical importance of Article 121 (1A) was evident in the custody/conversion cases that soon followed.

Nedunchelian v. Nurshafiqah presented a similar child conversion/custody situation. In this instance, it was a mother who had changed the official religious status of her four children without her husband's consent.[77] Drawing on the reasoning in *Chang Ah Mee v. Department of Islamic Religious Affairs*, the father contested the conversions of the children on the grounds that Article 12 (4) must be understood to require the consent of both parents. However, the defendant's lawyer invoked Article 121 (1A). The High Court agreed and affirmed that "it is settled law that the Civil Courts have no jurisdiction ... as established by a plethora of cases."[78] The High Court reviewed the previous case law on the matter, including the principle established in *Md Hakim Lee* that "the issue is not one of whether a litigant can get his remedies but one of jurisdiction ... The fact that the plaintiff may not have his remedy in the Syariah Court would not make the jurisdiction exercisable by the civil court." The Court also differed with the understanding of Article 12 (4)

[75] *Chang Ah Mee v. Jabatan Hal Ehwal Agama Islam & Ors.* [2003] 1 CLJ at 459.
[76] That is, the report of the decision gave no mention of Article 121 (1A). Nonetheless, the Court held in its decision that "The issue as to the legality of the conversion has nothing to do with religion but with the interpretation of the provisions of the Enactment ..." [2003] 1 CLJ at 458.
[77] *Nedunchelian V Uthiradam v. Nurshafiqah Mah Singai Annals & Ors* [2005] 2 CLJ 306.
[78] *Nedunchelian V Uthiradam v. Nurshafiqah Mah Singai Annals & Ors* [2005] 2 CLJ at 310.

established in *Chang Ah Mee v. Department of Islamic Religious Affairs*. Whereas the *Chang Ah Mee* decision found that the intent of Article 12 (4) required the consent of both parents, *Nedunchelian v. Nurshafiqah* arrived at the opposite conclusion. The Court noted that Article 160b of the Constitution specifies that the Bahasa Malaysia version of the Federal Constitution is the authoritative text. That version of the Federal Constitution carries the term "ibu bapa," which the court interpreted as constituting the right of a single parent, as opposed to extending that right to both parents "kedua ibu bapa."[79] The husband lost his appeal and the custody of his children.

Of all the child custody/conversion cases, the one that commanded the most nationwide attention was *Shamala v. Jeyanganesh*.[80] Shamala Sathiyaseelan and Jeyaganesh Mogarajah, both Hindus, were married in 1998 under the Marriage and Divorce Act, which governs family law for non-Muslims. Four years later, Jeyanganesh left his wife, converted to Islam, and subsequently changed the official religious status of their two children (ages two and four) to Islam without his wife's knowledge or consent. Shamala took the children to her parents' home and filed a petition to secure their custody. She obtained an interim custody order from the civil courts, the appropriate legal body for adjudicating family law issues among non-Muslims. However, her husband secured a temporary custody order of his own, from a shariah court, on the grounds that he and his children were now Muslim and therefore under the jurisdiction of the shariah courts in matters of family law. The two custody orders came to opposite conclusions over who had the right to child custody.

In the High Court proceedings that ensued, Shamala sought a court order declaring the conversions of the children null and void. Shamala's attorney drew on the decision in *Chang Ah Mee v. Department of Islamic Religious Affairs* and called attention to the language of the Guardianship of Infants Act, which provides that "the rights and authority of mother and father shall be equal." However, Justice Faiza Tamby Chik, the same judge who had issued the High Court decision in *Lina Joy v. Majlis Agama Islam*, backed the interpretation of Article 12 (4) of the Constitution provided in *Nedunchelian v. Nurshafiqah*. He denied Shamala's petition to nullify the conversions and held that:

> by virtue of art. 121 (1A) of the Federal Constitution, the Shariah Court is the qualified forum to determine the status of the two minors. Only the Shariah Court has the legal expertise in hukum syarak to determine whether the conversion of the two minors is valid or not. Only the Shariah Court has the competency and expertise to determine the said issue.[81]

---

[79] This is despite the fact that the Federal Constitution was drafted in English. An amendment making the Bahasa Malaysia translation the authoritative version once it is decreed as such by the Agong – Malaysia's constitutional monarch – has not yet taken effect, since no such decree has been made to date.

[80] *Shamala a/p Sathiyaseelan v. Dr. Jeyaganesh a/l C Mogarajah* [2004] 2 MLJ 648

[81] *Shamala a/p Sathiyaseelan v. Dr. Jeyaganesh a/l C Mogarajah* [2004] 2 MLJ at 649.

The ruling put Shamala in a no-win situation. She had no remedy in the civil courts, nor did she have legal standing in the shariah courts because she was not Muslim. Even if she had wished to approach the shariah courts for relief, it was not an avenue that was available to her. Fearing that her husband would deny her joint custody, Shamala fled to Australia with the children and lodged an appeal with the Federal Court. The Federal Court dismissed her appeal, without considering the constitutional questions at stake, on the grounds that Shamala was in contempt of the court for denying Jeyaganesh visitation rights.[82] As Chapter 5 documents, *Shamala v. Jeyaganesh* was the first case that became a focal point for NGO mobilization.

In another case that mirrored many of these circumstances, *Subashini v. Saravanan* concerned a Hindu couple who had been married for four years when, in 2006, the husband (Saravanan) left his wife and converted to Islam. As in previous cases, Saravanan changed the religious status of their child, who was three years old at the time. Saravanan's wife (Subashini) was subsequently served with papers from the Registrar of the Syariah High Court, Kuala Lumpur, notifying her that Saravanan had initiated proceedings to claim custody of their child. Subashini applied for an injunction to restrain her ex-husband from continuing with any proceedings in the shariah court and she filed a petition for divorce in the civil courts.[83] Subashini's lawyers, Haris Ibrahim and Shanmuga Kanesalingam, insisted that the proper legal forum to hear issues related to the breakdown of a civil marriage must be the High Court. Further, they contended that the shariah court should have no jurisdiction over the matter because Subashini was not a person professing the religion of Islam. Conversely, Saravanan's attorney, Mohamed Haniff Khatri, claimed that the civil court had no authority to issue an injunction that is binding on the shariah courts. Khatri contended that from the moment of his conversion, Saravanan enjoyed standing in the shariah courts in personal status matters and that it was, in fact, the only legal avenue available to him. The High Court agreed with Khatri's reasoning and denied Subashini's request for a civil court injunction.[84] According to the Court, Saravanan was "subject to the jurisdiction of the Syariah Court which has exclusive jurisdiction over persons professing the religion of Islam." *Subashini v. Saravanan* pointed to yet another failure of the civil courts to remedy disputes over jurisdiction.

Husband and wife both filed appeals. Subashini's legal team (now an all-star cast with the addition of prominent human rights lawyer Malik Imtiaz) eventually won the right to approach the Federal Court, which gave a decision in late 2007.[85]

---

[82] *Shamala Sathiyaseelan v. Jeyaganesh Mogarajah & Anor* [2011] 2 MLJ 281

[83] *Subashini a/p Rajasingam v. Saravanan a/l Thangathoray* [2007] 2 MLJ 798.

[84] However, the High Court provided Subashini with an interim injunction pending appeal.

[85] This may appear to be in contradiction with the High Court's observation that Saravanan did not enjoy standing in the civil courts, but his appeal concerned constitutional questions, not personal status issues.

In a lengthy and complex decision spanning eighty-six pages, the Federal Court ruled in a 2–1 split decision. The decision reasoned that "by contracting the civil marriage, the husband and wife were bound by the Marriage Reform Act in respect to divorce and custody of the children of the marriage, and thus, the civil court continued to have jurisdiction over him, notwithstanding his conversion to Islam."[86] The Federal Court also exercised jurisdiction on the grounds that, although Subashini did not enjoy legal standing in the shariah court under Article 46 (2) (b) of the Administration of Islamic Law Act, Saravanan had legal standing in the civil courts (albeit only as a respondent). In this regard, *Subashini v. Saravanan* set an important precedent and addressed one of the key failings of *Shamala v. Jeyaganesh*. However, the Court affirmed the finding in *Nedunchelian v. Nurshafiqah* and *Shamala v. Jeyaganesh* that one parent could initiate the conversion of a child without the consent of the spouse. The Federal Court explained that it could not overrule a validly obtained order of a shariah court because such an action would constitute "interference by the High Court of the husband's exercise of his right as a Muslim to pursue his remedies in the Syariah High Court." The upshot of the decision was that the civil courts retained jurisdiction in custody cases between Muslim converts and their non-Muslim spouses, yet other questions concerning civil and shariah court jurisdiction remained unresolved.

These unresolved questions came to the fore yet again in *Indira Gandhi v. Muhammad Ridzuan Abdullah*. The circumstances of the case mirrored *Shamala v. Jeyaganesh* and *Subashini v. Saravanan* almost one to one. Patmanathan a/l Krishnan converted to Islam, assuming the name of Muhammad Ridzuan Abdullah in March of 2009. The next month, Ridzuan changed the official religious status of his three children without the knowledge or consent of his wife. Ridzuan then secured a permanent custody order for the three children from the shariah court. Indira's attorneys launched two lawsuits in the Ipoh High Court, the first to challenge the conversions and the second to secure custody of the children. Muhammad Ridzuan's attorneys urged the High Court to follow the precedent set in *Subashini v. Saravanan* that a child's official religious status could be changed by only one parent alone and that the civil courts have no jurisdiction to review the matter once the children are registered as Muslim. Indira's attorneys countered that the shariah courts must not have exclusive jurisdiction because, as a non-Muslim, Indira does not have legal standing in the Shariah High Court. They pointed to the decision in *Tan Sung Mooi v. Too Miew Kim*, where the Supreme Court ruled that conversion to another religion did not extinguish one's legal obligations under one's former religious status. They also highlighted the apparent double-standard that converts *out* of Islam are always subject to the duties of one's prior personal status law, as was the case in *Kamariah binti Ali v. Kelantan State Government*.

---

[86]   *Subashini a/p Rajasingam v. Saravanan a/l Thangathoray and other appeals* [2008] 2 MLJ 147.

Justice Dato' Wan Afrah Binti Dato' Paduka Wan Ibrahim exercised civil court jurisdiction in the application regarding custody, reproducing the reasoning in *Tan Sung Mooi*. The decision maintained that "it would be a grave injustice to non-Muslim spouses and children whose only remedy would be in the Civil Courts if the High Court no longer has jurisdiction since the Syariah Courts do not have jurisdiction over non-Muslims." The High Court conferred custody of the children to Indira. However, the children were still registered as Muslims, and Ridzuan had physical possession of the youngest child, whom he refused to return. The application to challenge the conversion was eventually heard in 2013, and another High Court Justice, Lee Swee Seng, annulled the conversions and ruled unilateral conversion of a child to be unconstitutional. The next year, the Ipoh High Court cited Ridzuan for contempt of the 2010 custody decision and ordered that he be arrested if the youngest child was not returned within the week. When Ridzuan failed to meet this deadline, the High Court ordered the police to find the child. What followed was a game of cat and mouse, with a barrage of legal actions from the High Court, the Court of Appeal, and the Federal Court concerning whether the police were legally obliged to execute the civil court warrant for arrest in light of the still contested legal positions over conflicting custody orders. In April 2016, the Federal Court held that both the syariah *and* civil court orders regarding custody were binding on the police, and the Court refused a recovery order under the Child Act 2001. However, the Federal Court held that the police were duty bound to assist the civil courts in the contempt proceedings against Ridzuan and issued an order of mandamus against the Inspector General of Police. By the end of 2015, there was also a 2–1 decision by the Court of Appeal upholding unilateral child conversions. The decision found that any matter of religion lay solely within the purview of the shariah courts. In May 2016, Indira Gandhi was granted leave to challenge the Court of Appeal ruling in Federal Court. The appeal was heard over three days in November 2016. The result of litigation was still pending at the time of writing.

* * *

These three types of cases – concerning the official religious status of the dead, religious freedom for the living, and battles over child custody/conversion – marked a fault line down the middle of the Malaysian judiciary. Rather than clarify matters of jurisdiction, Article 121 (1A) exacerbated legal ambiguities and produced new legal tensions. Ironically, the clause put the civil courts in a position of hearing *more* claims concerning religion, not fewer. Before the introduction of Article 121 (1A) in 1988, fewer than two High Court decisions touched on Islam per year on average (see Figure 3.1). After the amendment, the number of reported decisions mentioning Islam surpassed an average of eight per year, reaching an all-time high of eighteen reported decisions in 2014. In other words, Article 121 (1A) seems to have produced exactly the sorts of jurisdictional tensions and ambiguities that it was supposed to resolve. To be clear, this data is not presented as evidence of increasing civil court interference with shariah court jurisdiction, as many conservatives claim. Rather, these legal dilemmas were a product of the formalization of the shariah judicial system, the tightening state regulations on religion, and the introduction of Article 121 (1A). As the legal system was made increasingly rigid, boundary maintenance between the federal civil courts and the state shariah courts was judicialized. The fact that one jurisdiction is meant to implement "Islamic law" and the other "secular law" made this jurisdictional fault line ripe for ideological polarization.

To be sure, there were a variety of motives among those who raised Article 121 (1A) objections to civil court jurisdiction. For some litigants, Article 121 (1A) provided a means to achieve strategic advantage in a domestic squabble.[87] This was often the situation in custody/conversion cases, where conversion to Islam (or the threat thereof) provides leverage in divorce settlements.[88] In other circumstances, such as the freedom of religion and "body-snatching" cases, it is the religious bureaucracy and state lawyers that invoked Article 121 (1A) to affirm their role as gatekeepers for the religious community. For others, Article 121 (1A) provides an instrument to expand the ambit of the shariah courts and the position of Islam in the constitutional order. It is this last set of actors – those with an ideological agenda – to which we will return in Chapter 7. In the meantime, Chapter 5 turns to examine of how political activists mobilized on either side of an emergent "rights-versus-rites" binary to construct a political spectacle in the court of public opinion. As we shall see, the Article 121 (1A) cases became the center of a heated national debate around the place of Islam in Malaysia's legal and political order.

---

[87] In all the reported cases, the husbands contended that their conversions were sincere.

[88] An attorney familiar with many of these cases explained that anecdotal evidence suggest that wives are threatened by their husbands that if they do not agree to a divorce, or to certain disadvantageous terms of a divorce, they will lose control of their children by way of unilateral conversion.

5

Constructing the Political Spectacle

Liberal Rights versus Religion in the Court of Public Opinion

In polarizing public opinion, enemies paradoxically cooperate with each other, though the cooperation may be unintentional.

– Murray Edelman (1988: 69)

This chapter shifts from the court of law to the court of public opinion, where activists, politicians, and NGOs mobilized to frame the significance of the Article 121 (1A) cases for the future of Malaysia. Each case with contested civil/shariah court jurisdiction was important in a legal sense, but their radiating effects were more important still. Each case provided fodder for the media, and new opportunities for civil society mobilization. The cases became the focal points for contestation over a great number of issues, including the appropriate place for Islam in the legal and political order, the secular versus religious foundations of the state, the rights of non-Muslim and non-Malay communities, individual rights and duties rights in Islam, and perennial questions around religious authority – that is, who has the right to speak for Islam. In addition to triggering new normative debates and exacerbating longstanding grievances, the cases galvanized collective action and spurred the formation of entirely new NGOs on both sides of an emergent rights-versus-rites binary.

   It is not difficult to understand why these cases provoked grave concerns among liberal Muslims and non-Muslims. For these constituencies, each successive court decision suggested that the civil courts were beginning to cede jurisdiction to the shariah courts when cases touched on Islam, even when it meant trampling on the fundamental rights enshrined in the Federal Constitution, and even when non-Muslims were involved. Within the broad context of the *dakwah* movement over the preceding three decades, liberal rights activists understood these court decisions as a failure of this last bastion of secular law. However, the same court cases evoked fears among religious conservatives. For this constituency, each case was understood not as "creeping Islamization," but as an attack on the autonomy of the shariah courts and, indeed, on Islam itself. For example, in the debate surrounding *Lina Joy v. Majlis Agama Islam Wilayah Persekutuan*, conservatives focused less on Lina Joy's individual right to choose her faith, and more on the implications that an adverse ruling might have on the ability of the Muslim community to manage its religious affairs in multi-religious Malaysia. Conservatives reasoned that if the civil courts affirmed Joy's individual right to freedom of religion, it would constitute a breakdown in the autonomy of the shariah courts and a breach in the barrier that they understood Article 121 (1A) to guarantee.

Conservative activists were quick to contend that liberal rights instruments are premised on individual autonomy, which renders them unable to accommodate communal understandings of rights anytime they are in tension with individual rights claims. This line of reasoning came through loud and clear in meetings with prominent Muslim NGO leaders, including the President of *Jamaah Islah Malaysia* (JIM), Zaid Kamaruddin, and the President of *Angkatan Belia Islam Malaysia* (ABIM), Yusri Mohamad.[1] Similarly, Islamic Party of Malaysia Member of Parliament, Dzulkifli Ahmad lamented the fact that liberal rights activists only view the Article 121 (1A) cases from an individual rights perspective and that they do not acknowledge that such a framework challenges the ability of the Muslim community to govern itself free of outside interference.[2] For Dzulkifli and others, individual rights talk has universal aspirations that are inherently expansionist. Adverse court decisions involving Article 121 (1A) risk "abolishing and dismantling the Shariah Court" (2007: 153). Just as liberal rights discourse is laden with fear that individual rights face an imminent threat at the hands of religion, a deep anxiety set in among those who wished to protect the collective rights of the Muslim community.

Of course, an understanding of the Muslim community as a bearer of rights obfuscates the way that religious community and religious authority is constituted in Malaysia by way of state law in the first place (Chapter 2). The legal dilemmas concerning the authority and jurisdiction of the shariah courts are *not* the result of an essential tension between Islam and individual rights. Rather, they are the product of the state's specific formalization of two distinct fields of state law (Chapter 3). Nonetheless, most Malaysians understand these legal tensions as evidence of an inherent incompatibility between Islam and liberal rights in a more general sense. Political activists embraced a rights-versus-rites binary construction and fostered this (mis)understanding. These activists recognized that although legal battles are fought in the court of law, more important ideological struggles are won or lost in the court of public opinion (Moustafa 2013b). Marc Galanter suggests that "a single judicial action may radiate different messages to different audiences" (1983: 126). This is especially true when judicial actions are explained, framed, and amplified by competing groups of political actors.

---

[1] Interview with Zaid Kamaruddin (Kuala Lumpur, June 25, 2009) and Yusri Mohamad (Gombak, June 30, 2009).

[2] This view was summed up in the title of Dzulkifli Ahmad's book on the topic, *Blind Spot* (2007).

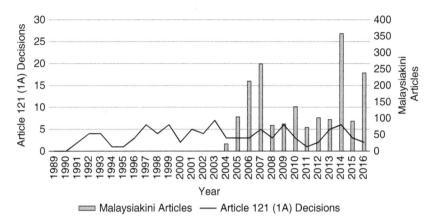

FIGURE 5.1: Reported Article 121 (1A) Decisions and *Malaysiakini* Coverage, by Year[3]
Source: Data compiled from *Malaysiakini,* the *Malayan Law Journal,* and the *Current Law Journal.*

BEFORE THE STORM

The central role of political activists in raising the political salience of these cases is apparent when one examines the timing and onset of public debate. Figure 5.1 illustrates the High Court decisions in which Article 121 (1A) claims were addressed. The long string of cases with contested civil/shariah court jurisdiction began soon after the constitutional amendment of Article 121 (1A) in 1988. However, the cases received virtually no press coverage for the first sixteen years that Article 121 (1A) was in force. For an illustrative example, consider the most important Article 121 (1A) decision of the 1990s, the Supreme Court decision in *Soon Singh v. PERKIM. Soon Singh v. PERKIM* was barely noted in the press, with a brief mention on page ten of the *New Straits Times.* Similarly, *Berita Harian* ran the story once. Likewise, *Utusan Malaysia* gave mention to *Soon Singh* in three stories prior to 2004. Finally, *Malaysiakini* carried no coverage of Article 121 (1A) cases until 2004. Why did it take so long for these cases to reach the media spotlight? And what precipitated such a stark change in 2004? There are several underlying contextual developments as well as key triggers that brought the cases to the forefront of public consciousness.

Certainly, one important enabling development was the swiftly changing media environment. The print media had been relatively docile through the 1990s as the result of strict government controls.[4] But the rapid proliferation of

---

[3] Data for Figure 5.1 was generated with the search term "121 (1A)" in the LexisNexis archive of the *Malayan Law Journal* and the *Malayan Law Journal Unreporteds* [sic]. In some instances, separate disputes were merged into the same court decision. In other instances, different aspects of the same case were settled in separate court decisions and cases with appellate decisions were counted more than once. For these reasons, Figure 5.1 provides an approximate notion of the increasing volume of civil court decisions that invoke, expound upon, or respond to Article 121 (1A) claims.

[4] A central instrument of government control is the Printing Presses and Publications Act of 1984, which applies to all print media including newspapers, books, and pamphlets. The Act was first introduced by

digital media operating free of government regulation changed this situation.[5] The independent online news outfit *Malaysiakini* launched in 1999. Within two years of operation, it claimed 210,000 daily readers. By 2008, *Malaysiakini* had become the most frequently visited website in Malaysia, with 1.6 million unique visitors each month. The rapid expansion of blogs and social media provided further avenues for political discussion in increasingly strident tones. The Internet became the principle means for dozens of new, non-governmental organizations to reach the public and shape political discourse. With one of the highest Internet penetration rates globally (and the highest of any Muslim-majority country through this period) Malaysians increasingly took their political frustrations to the keyboard.[6]

Malaysian civil society groups had also become more numerous, organized, and active by the late 1990s (Weiss 2006). Organizations speaking for different faith traditions were the first on the scene. The Malaysian Islamic Youth Movement (*Angkatan Belia Islam Malaysia* – more commonly known by its acronym, ABIM) formed in August 1971. The Malaysian Consultative Council of Buddhism, Christianity, Hinduism, Sikhism, and Taoism (MCCBCHST)[7] formed in 1982 because of rising anxieties in the non-Muslim community.[8] *Jamaah Islah Malaysia* (JIM) joined the scene in 1990, along with dozens of others representing different faith communities in Malaysia. Women's rights groups also formed, the most prominent among them Sisters in Islam (1988), the All Women's Action Society (1985), the Women's Aid Organization (1982), and the Women's Center for Change (1985). Human rights groups included SUARAM (1989). The heady days of the *reformasi* movement emboldened citizens to join civil society groups and to become more directly engaged in political life. In short, political consciousness was on the rise at the turn of the millennium.

---

the British in 1948 but was amended several times over to augment government control. Section three of the Act provides the Internal Security Minister absolute discretion to grant and revoke licenses, which are typically provided for only one year at a time and are subject to renewal. The government exercises these powers vis-à-vis newspapers on occasion, such as when it closed *The Star* and *Sin Chew Jit Poh* in 1987, in Operation Lalang. As in other countries, the most debilitating effect of the Act is that it encourages self-censorship in the media. At the opening of the millennium, before the explosion of digital media, Malaysia was ranked at a dismal 110 of 139 countries in the Press Freedom Index (Reporters without Borders 2002).

5   Online media have not been subject to the Printing Presses and Publications Act, although the government periodically suggests that this may change.

6   The sharp increase in online outlets also spurred more assertive reporting in the print media.

7   MCCBCHST was initially the MCCBCHS. Representatives from the Taoist community formally joined the organization later, when it became the Malaysian Consultative Council of Buddhism, Christianity, Hinduism, Sikhism, and Taoism (MCCBCHST).

8   An unpublished MCCBCHS document explains that the changing political context "gave rise for concern to the leaders of the non-Muslim religions and they saw that as a positive opportunity to come together to promote matters of mutual interests and defend against common threats . . . " MCCBCHS, "The First Ten Years."

The political spectacle that captured public attention like no other was the "Islamic state debate" that was heating up between the ruling party, UMNO (United Malays National Organization) and their religious-oriented rival, PAS (Islamic Party of Malaysia). As examined in Chapter 2, UMNO had gone to great lengths to formalize shariah court functions to harness the legitimating power of Islamic symbolism and discourse. But PAS worked hard to undercut the credibility of this project by constantly charging that UMNO had not done enough to advance "real" Islam. The stakes of the debate increased when PAS gained control of state legislatures in Kelantan in the 1990 election, Terengganu in the 1999 election, and a significant share of seats in the national parliament in both elections. Claiming to be the true champion of Islam, PAS raised the heat when it passed *hudud* enactments in Kelantan and Terengganu in 1993 and 2002. The enactments could not be implemented without federal government (i.e., UMNO) action and therefore served as a powerful wedge issue for PAS to claim stronger Islamic credentials than UMNO.[9]

Not to be outdone, Mahathir Mohammad declared that Malaysia was *already* an Islamic state on September 29, 2001. His statement precipitated a fierce round of one-upmanship between the ruling UMNO and PAS. For the next decade, political activists of all stripes debated whether Malaysia was meant to be an Islamic state. The debate often centered on Article 3 of the Federal Constitution. However, the meaning and intention of the phrase "Islam is the religion of the Federation" was anything but clear. Secularists took the position that this clause was added to the Independence Constitution only at the end of the drafting process and that it was only intended for ceremonial purposes. Secularists reminded the public that the Alliance had requested that Islam be the religion of the Federation with the important proviso that "observance of this principle ... shall not imply that the State is not a secular State."[10] Islamists, on the other hand, pushed a more expansive interpretation of Article 3. They pointed to the extensive provisions that are detailed in Schedule 9, List II of the Federal Constitution as evidence to support their claim. In 2003, PAS issued its most explicit statement on its vision of an Islamic state. The "Islamic State Document" was meant "to clarify the concept of a true Islamic state as opposed to a 'pseudo Islamic state.'"[11] The "Islamic state debate" was in full bloom with activists, politicians, and laypersons debating what an Islamic state might mean in practical terms for Malaysia's multi-religious society. Such was the political context when the Article 121 (1A) cases entered popular legal consciousness.

---

[9] According to Ninth Schedule (List 1) of the Federal Constitution, the ordinances fall within federal, not state powers.

[10] Alliance Memorandum to the Reid Constitutional Commission, as quoted in Fernando (2006: 253).

[11] For the text of the PAS Islamic State Document, see Tan and Lee (2008).

THE TRIGGER

The immediate trigger that brought the Article 121 (1A) cases into national consciousness was *Shamala v. Jeyaganesh*. As the reader will recall from the Introduction, Shamala Sathiyaseelan and Jeyaganesh Mogarajah were plunged into crisis in 2002 when Jeyaganesh converted to Islam and subsequently changed the official religious status of their two children, ages two and four, without his wife's knowledge or consent. The civil courts had ruled on similar cases in the past – but this case suddenly captured the national headlines.

An important difference in *Shamala v. Jeyaganesh* was that Shamala's attorney, Ravi Nekoo, made a concerted effort to attract public attention – an effort that was buoyed by the rapidly changing environment of civil society activism and digital media. Ravi was an active member of the legal aid community, and he was well networked with a variety of rights organizations in Kuala Lumpur. When Ravi discovered that *Shamala v. Jeyaganesh* was not a typical custody case, he turned to the most prominent women's rights groups in Kuala Lumpur: The Women's Aid Organization, the All Women Action Movement, the Women's Center for Change, Sisters in Islam, and the Women Lawyers' Association. He also turned to religious organizations, most notably the Hindu Sangam, the Catholic Lawyers Society, and the Malaysian Consultative Council of Buddhism, Christianity, Hinduism, Sikhism, and Taoism (MCCBCHST). These groups took an immediate interest in the case, and they quickly gained formal observer status (watching brief) with the High Court.[12] Subsequently, they filed *amicus curiae* briefs and mobilized their resources to bring public attention to the case.

The question of whether to "go public" posed a dilemma for the groups because they were uncertain if public attention would work to their advantage. According to Ravi Nekoo, "The initial view was that if the case became too big, it would become a political issue and the courts would then succumb to political pressure."[13] But after extensive deliberation, a decision was made to go public. Ravi explained that the decision was based upon the consensus view among rights activists that " ... prior to Shamala there were so many other cases that just went nowhere."[14]

Women's groups met with the Ministry of Women and Family Development on April 8, 2003, to discuss their concerns about women's rights when a husband

---

[12] Malik Imtiaz Sarwar also held a watching brief for the Malaysian Bar Council.

[13] Interview with Ravi Nekoo, February 18, 2012.

[14] Even though they eventually lost the case, Ravi held the view that going public was the right choice: "I still think the publicity was useful. Not in getting the desired result, but in raising public awareness ... when we go to court in small groups to argue, we get nowhere. Only when it became a little bigger – with many lawyers coming and representing their own groups with [press] coverage – it's only then that the courts take us more seriously. Otherwise, the case would have been thrown out of court a long, long time ago." Interview with Ravi Nekoo, February 18, 2012.

converts to Islam.[15] Thereafter, they initiated a public awareness campaign and advocated for amendments to the Marriage and Divorce Act to protect women's rights in such circumstances. The day after the court decision in *Shamala v. Jeyaganesh*, the Malaysia Hindu Sangam and the Malaysian Consultative Council of Buddhism, Christianity, Hinduism, Sikhism, and Taoism (MCCBCHST) also went public, issuing press statements condemning the court decision.[16] This was the first time that *any case* concerning the contested civil/shariah court jurisdiction was covered in the leading online news outlet, *Malaysiakini*. Over the next twelve years, 1,800 stories would be published in *Malaysiakini* alone. The total number of articles published across all news outlets in Malaysia (and abroad) very likely exceeded 10,000 stories.[17]

The year 2004 thus marked a watershed moment when Article 121 (1A) cases became politically salient. The solid line in Figure 5.1 illustrates the number of Article 121 (1A) decisions each year, through 2015. Beginning in 1991, there were anywhere from one to seven Article 121 (1A) High Court decisions reported each year. The stacked columns in Figure 5.1 illustrate the number of news stories and op-eds that focused on these cases in *Malaysiakini*. Beginning with the first *Malaysiakini* story on *Shamala v. Jeyaganesh* in 2004, the Article 121 (1A) cases were covered more intensively than any other issue. In 2014, 360 articles and op-eds ran in *Malaysiakini* alone, or nearly one story per day. Coverage was similar among the many other English-, Chinese-, Malay-, and Tamil-language newspapers, not to mention radio and television. In short, the news was saturated with coverage of the cases. This media attention dramatically broadened the audience for the 121 (1A) cases. This audience expansion is directly attributable to the efforts of liberal rights groups to bring the cases to the public's attention, and to the media's enthusiastic coverage.[18]

LIBERAL RIGHTS GROUPS MOBILIZE

As a direct result of the High Court decision in *Shamala v. Jeyaganesh*, thirteen liberal rights groups formed a working coalition. The coalition named itself "Article 11," after the provision of the Federal Constitution that guarantees the freedom of religion. The coalition included prominent organizations, including the All Women's Action Society (AWAM), the Malaysian Bar Council, the National

---

[15] "Reform Marriage Law, Say Women's Groups," *Malaysiakini* August 26, 2003. Sisters in Islam had a separate meeting on September 29 with the Attorney General's chambers and other stakeholders. There they presented concrete suggestions to amend the Law Reform (Marriage and Divorce) Act.

[16] "Religious Leaders Irked by Decision on Conversion Case," *Malaysiakini*, April 14, 2004.

[17] The figure for *Malaysiakini* was tabulated. The extrapolation of total news coverage surpassing 10,000 stories is based on a rough estimate of the frequency of coverage in Malaysia's many other news outlets.

[18] As we will see, liberal coverage was soon matched by countervailing efforts of conservative groups in the Malay press.

Human Rights Society (HAKAM), the Malaysian Civil Liberties Society, Suara Rakyat Malaysia (SUARAM), the Women's Aid Organization (WAO), and Sisters in Islam. The Article 11 coalition also included the Malaysian Consultative Council of Buddhism, Christianity, Hinduism, Sikhism, and Taoism (MCCBCHST), an umbrella organization that represents the concerns of non-Muslim communities. The objective of the Article 11 coalition was to focus public attention on the erosion of individual rights and to "ensure that Malaysia does not become a theocratic state" (Malaysian Bar Council 2006). Article 11 produced a website, short documentary videos providing firsthand interviews with non-Muslims who were adversely affected by Article 121 (1A), analysis and commentary from their attorneys, and recorded roundtables on the threat posed by Islamic law.[19] Women's groups continued to lobby the government. Illustrative of this multi-pronged approach is the September 29, 2004, meeting hosted by the Attorney General's chambers to discuss proposed amendments to the Law Reform (Marriage and Divorce) Act 1976.[20]

Liberal rights activists also worked to establish an "Interfaith Commission" composed of representatives of various faith communities in Malaysia. Among other roles, the proposed commission would work to "advance, promote and protect every individual's freedom of thought, conscience and religion" by examining complaints and making formal recommendations to the government.[21] This explicit focus on individual rights raised the ire of conservatives, who feared that such a commission would serve as a platform to challenge the shariah courts. These concerns were compounded by the fact that the principal organizer of the two-day organizing conference was the Malaysian Bar Council, an organization that was hardly viewed as impartial in disputes over shariah versus civil court jurisdictions. Moreover, as an *Utusan Malaysia* article highlighted for its Malay readers, the main financial sponsor for the conference was the Konrad Adenauer Foundation, a German research foundation associated with the Christian Democratic Union Party of Germany.[22] Conservative NGOs spoke out loudly against the notion of an interfaith commission. Nonetheless, the Bar Council went ahead to organize a "National Conference on the Initiative towards the Formation of the Interfaith Commission of Malaysia" on February 24–25, 2005. Conservative NGOs boycotted the conference, condemned it in the press, and called on the government to stop the proceedings.[23] Media coverage only grew

[19] http://www.article11.org/ [last accessed March 2, 2010]. The website has since closed.
[20] Representatives also attended the meeting from the Shariah Judicial Department, ABIM, the Ministry for Women and Family Development, JAIS, PERKIM, the Shariah Lawyers Association, and others.
[21] Draft Interfaith Commission of Malaysia Bill, Article 4 (1) (a). For the text of the Draft Bill and other primary source materials pertaining to the Interfaith Commission initiative, see S. Hadi Abdullah (2007).
[22] *Utusan Malaysia*, Feb 28, 2005. *"Jangan Cetuskan Isu Agama Elak Perbalahan Kaum"* [Do Not Spark Religious Issues; Avoid Racial Disputes]
[23] See, for example, *"Majlis Peguam Tidak Sensitif Kepada Kesucian Islam"* [The Bar Council is not Sensitive to the Sanctity of Islam] *Harakah*, January 16–31, 2005; *"Pelbagai Pihak Bantah Syor Tubuh*

more intense after the conference, with conservatives drawing attention to the prominent position of international law and individual rights in the conference platform, and the implications that this would have for Islamic law.[24] In response to the uproar, Prime Minister Abdullah Badawi called on the Bar Council to cease discussion of the Interfaith Commission proposal.

Soon thereafter, the Court of Appeal rejected Lina Joy's second petition. It did not go unnoticed that the 2–1 split decision mirrored the emerging divide in Malaysian society. Two Muslim justices, Abdul Aziz Mohamad and Arifin Zakaria, wrote the majority opinion while Gopal Sri Ram, a non-Muslim, wrote the dissenting opinion. Given that the Lina Joy case would soon become the most well-known apostasy case, it is striking that there had been virtually no media coverage until the Court of Appeal decision. *Malaysiakini* ran its first article on Lina Joy on September 19, 2005, but the case was subsequently discussed in over 400 articles and letters to the editor. The Article 121 (1A) cases had become *the* salient political issue of the decade.

Having failed with the initiative to forge an Interfaith Commission, the Malaysian Consultative Council of Buddhism, Christianity, Hinduism, Sikhism, and Taoism (MCCBCHST) made a bold move, but this time it was away from the media spotlight. The MCCBCHST submitted a detailed memorandum to the government "to highlight the real societal problems faced by a significant minority of persons professing religions other than Islam in Malaysia."[25] The style and substance of the memo suggest that it was written by the same attorneys who were litigating the cases. The detailed memo outlined some of the major Article 121 (1A) cases and illustrated how the heavy regulation of the religious sphere produced legal conundrums and miscarriages of justice. The MCCBCHST memo called for political intervention: "We urgently need legislative redress for these very severe social problems."[26]

As if to underline the legal problems detailed in the MCCBCHST memo, another "body snatching" case captured national attention in late 2005. This time, the public spectacle turned around the burial of Moorthy Maniam, a national hero who was the first Malaysian to have successfully climbed Mount Everest. Moorthy was injured in a training accident and later fell into a coma, dying six weeks later. Although Moorthy was known by his family and the public as a practicing Hindu, his wife was informed by the religious authorities that Moorthy had converted to Islam

---

Suruhanjaya Antara Agama" [Various Parties Oppose the Recommendation for the Establishment of an Inter-Religious Commission] *Utusan Malaysia*, February 24, 2005; "*Kerajaan Perlu Bertegas Tolak Penubuhan IRC*" [Government Needs to be Firm in Rejecting the Establishment of the IRC] *Harakah*, February 16–28, 2005.

[24] See, for example, "The IFC Bill: An Anti-Islam Wish List" Baharuddeen Abu Bakar, *Harakah Daily*, March 27, 2005.

[25] "Respect the Right to Profess and Practice One's Religion," submitted to the government on October 20, 2005.

[26] Two years and several major court decisions later, the MCCBCHT went public with the text of the 2005 memorandum, under the title "Unity Threatened by Continuing Infringements of Religious Freedom."

and that he must, therefore, be buried in accordance with Muslim rites by the religious authorities. If Moorthy had converted to Islam, it was news to everyone. Moorthy had carried out Hindu rituals on television just weeks before he fell into his coma.

Upon his death on December 20, 2005, Moorthy's widow, Kaliammal Sinnasamy, filed a lawsuit to prevent the Islamic Religious Affairs Council from taking her husband's body for burial. A hearing was scheduled for December 29, 2005, but in the meantime, the Islamic Religious Affairs Council raised a petition in the Kuala Lumpur Shariah High Court for the release of the body for a Muslim burial.[27] After examining the facts of the case and citing relevant civil court case law, the Shariah High Court declared that Moorthy was a Muslim at the time of his death. The shariah court decision ordered the hospital to surrender Moorthy's body to the Islamic Religious Affairs Council for burial in accordance with Muslim rites. The decision also directed the police to provide the necessary assistance to ensure proper execution of the court order. The order was served on the hospital, but the hospital director refused to release the body on the advice of the legal advisor for the Ministry of Health. Television, radio, and newspaper outlets all covered the unfolding drama.

The High Court of Kuala Lumpur heard Kaliammal's petition the following week, but the judge dismissed the case on the grounds that the federal civil courts did not have the competence or jurisdiction to decide on Moorthy's religious status as a result of Article 121 (1A).[28] For all practical purposes, Kaliammal was denied recourse to *any legal forum* since, as a non-Muslim, she did not have standing with the Shariah High Court. Moorthy's body was released to the religious authorities under a heavy security presence and buried on the same day, enraging the non-Muslim community.[29] The Malaysian Consultative Council for Buddhism, Christianity, Hinduism, Sikhism, and Taoism (MCCBCHST) held an emergency session on the same day. The MCCBCHST called on the government to amend the Constitution and to vest the federal courts with authority to determine the validity of conversions into and out of Islam. The MCCBCHST organized a candlelight vigil for the same evening in front of the Kuala Lumpur High Court to publicly mourn the High Court decision. More direct political action followed.

With the Lina Joy and Moorthy decisions generating extensive news coverage, civil society groups continued with their urgent calls for the repeal of Article 121 (1A). On January 5, 2006, the DAP organized a "Parliamentary Roundtable on

[27] *Dalam Perkara Permohonan Perisytiharan Status Agama Si Mati Mohammad Abdullah@Moorthy a/l Maniam* [2006] *Jurnal Hukum* v 21 (2) 210.

[28] *Kaliammal a/p Sinnasamy lwn Pengarah Jabatan Agama Islam Wilayah Persekutuan (JAWI) dan lain-lain* [2006] 1 MLJ 685. It should be noted that this was another case where the High Court judge issued a ruling in Bahasa Malaysia rather than English, a symbolic move that marks this as a "Malay" issue.

[29] Moorthy's widow appealed the case, only to have the Court of Appeal affirm the earlier High Court decision on August 20, 2010.

FIGURE 5.2: Kaliammal Sinnasamy, the wife of the late Moorthy Maniam, holds his picture as she leaves the courtroom with her daughter in Putrajaya. The Court of Appeal affirmed that the High Court had no jurisdiction to determine the religious status of her deceased husband.
REUTERS/Alamy/Bazuki Muhammad.

Article 121 (1A)" that included prominent opposition politicians and civil society activists. The roundtable passed a resolution calling for the repeal of Article 121 (1A) of the Federal Constitution. Two weeks later, nine of Prime Minister Badawi's non-Muslim cabinet ministers submitted a formal memorandum requesting the review and repeal of Article 121 (1A).[30] The move was unprecedented. It stirred immediate protest from Muslim NGOs and the Malay-language press. Prime Minister Badawi responded to the pressure by publicly rejecting the memorandum two days later. Badawi's refusal to consider the problems generated by Article 121 (1A) did nothing to resolve the underlying legal conundrum. Lina Joy was granted permission to approach the Federal Court, the highest appellate court in Malaysia, in April 2006. The following month, the *Subashini v. Saravanan* child conversion/custody case hit the headlines. And in July 2006, Siti Fatimah Tan Abdullah applied to convert out of Islam. It had become painfully clear that each case would create enormous controversy. The judicial system was hardwired to reproduce the same legal tensions. Worse still, the pressure from civil society groups began to make it more difficult for the courts to solve the legal conundrums. NGOs were now regularly submitting amicus curia briefs, requesting formal observer status in the cases, or requesting to

[30] *New Straits Times*, January 20, 2006.

intervene as formal participants in the lawsuits.[31] They were, in other words, mobilizing both inside and outside the courts.

The Article 11 coalition and the Malaysian Bar Council went on to organize a series of public forums across Malaysia. The first in Kuala Lumpur was titled "The Federal Constitution: Protection for All." The discussion addressed the cases of Lina Joy, Moorthy Maniam, and Shamala Sathiyaseelan among others. It drew over 600 participants, with speakers including prominent human rights lawyer Malik Imtiaz Sarwar, Ivy Josiah (president of the Women's Aid Organization), and prominent lawyer and soon-to-be Malaysia Bar Council President, Ambiga Sreenevasan. The Article 11 coalition continued with a nationwide road show, hitting Malacca in April, Penang in May, and Johor Bahru in July of 2006. The road show campaign was coupled with a petition to the Prime Minister, signed by 20,000 concerned Malaysians, calling on the government to affirm that "Malaysia shall not become a theocratic state" (Malaysian Bar Council 2006).

MUSLIM NGOs MOBILIZE

But others saw it differently. Politicians and conservative NGOs also framed the Article 121 (1A) cases as presenting challenges to rights, but not individual rights. Rather, the message from conservatives was that the rights of the Muslim community, and Islam itself, were under attack.[32] PAS president, Abdul Hadi Awang, used the Article 11 forums to his advantage at the PAS annual party convention in 2006. Opening the conference, he told 1,000 party delegates that "Never before in the history of this country has the position of Islam been as strongly challenged as it is today."[33] Abdul Hadi Awang urged the government, conservative NGOs, and all Muslims to defend Islam in the face of Article 11 challenges. Similarly, delegates at the 2006 UMNO General Assembly used the issue to burnish their religious credentials. An UMNO Penang delegate, Shabudin Yahaya, railed the crowd with his declaration that, "there are NGOs like Interfaith Commission, Article 11 Coalition, Sisters in Islam and Komas who are supported and funded by this foreign body called Konrad Adenauer Foundation."[34]

Although the Article 11 forums had been tremendously successful in generating media attention, coverage in the Malay language press was not favorable.

---

[31] For instance, in *Subashini v. Saravanan* the Women's Aid Organization, Women's Development Collective, Women's Center for Change, Sisters in Islam, and the Malaysian Bar Council all held watching briefs. As noted in Chapter 6, Islamic religious authorities similarly intervened in many Article 121 (1A) cases.

[32] Moreover, Islam and Malay ethnic identity were virtually one and the same. A perceived challenge to Islam was framed as a challenge to Malays. This view is summed up in the PAS press release of May 5, 2008, "Only Islam Can Defend Malay Honor – PAS President" [*Hanya Islam yang dapat angkat martabat Melayu – Presiden PAS*].

[33] "PAS to Muslims: Close Ranks, Defend Islam," *Malaysiakini*, June 7, 2006.

[34] "Muslims Face Threats from Within and Without," *Malaysiakini*, November 17, 2006.

FIGURE 5.3: Protesters hold signs that read "Bar Council, Don't Threaten Islam" and "Don't Challenge Islam" during a demonstration against a public forum on legal issues related to religious conversion held by the Malaysian Bar Council in Kuala Lumpur, August 9, 2008.
REUTERS/Alamy/Bazuki Muhammad.

The Malay-language (and state-owned) newspaper *Berita Harian* ran articles with headlines that included "Warning: Stop Questioning the Constitution." Its sister newspaper, *Utusan Malaysia*, published an op-ed from the Minister of Education himself under the banner "Never Question Article 121 (1A)."[35] As with the Interfaith Commission initiative before it, the Article 11 forums were depicted as a challenge to the shariah courts and Islam. The Article 11 forum in Penang was disrupted by several hundred protesters with posters reading, "Fight Liberal Islam," "Don't Seize our Rights," and "Don't Insult God's Laws."[36] Mohd Azmi Abdul Hamid, the leader of *Teras Pengupayaan Melayu* and organizer of the protest, explained that the real intent of liberal rights activists was to undermine the shariah courts. "Under the pretext of human rights, they condemned Islamic principles and the shariah courts. They have a hidden motive to place the shariah laws beneath the civil laws."[37] When another large protest gathered outside the next Article 11 forum in Johor Bahru, the forum was stopped half way through by police seeking to preserve "public order."

Liberal rights groups were not the only organizations to mobilize in a coordinated fashion. A more formidable counter-mobilization was already underway in the name of defending Islam. A group of lawyers calling themselves Lawyers Defending Islam (*Peguam Pembela Islam*) held a press conference to announce their formation at the Federal Territories Shariah Court building on July 13, 2006.

---

[35] *Berita Harian*, July 25, 2006; *Utusan Malaysia*, July 24, 2006.   [36] *Malaysiakini*, May 15, 2006.
[37] *Malaysiakini*, June 5, 2006.

Their explicit aim was to "take action to defend the position of Islam" in direct response to the activities of the Article 11 coalition. A few days later, a broad array of conservative NGOs united in a coalition calling itself Muslim Organizations for the Defense of Islam (*Pertubuhan-Pertubuhan Pembela Islam*), or Defender (*Pembela*) for short. *Pembela* brought together over fifty organizations including ABIM, *Jamaah Islah Malaysia* (JIM), the Shariah Lawyers' Association of Malaysia, and the Muslim Professionals Forum.[38] *Pembela's* founding statement explains that they were motivated to organize as a result of the Moorthy Maniam and Lina Joy cases, which challenge "the position of Islam in the Constitution and the legal system of this country."[39] Underlining their extensive grassroots base, *Pembela* gathered a maximum-capacity crowd of 10,000 supporters at the Federal Mosque in Kuala Lumpur and issued a "Federal Mosque Resolution" outlining the threat posed by liberal rights activists.[40] The following day, *Pembela* released an open letter to the Prime Minister and the press, reiterating the threat they believed the recent court cases posed to Islam and the shariah courts:

> Since Independence forty-nine years ago, Muslims have lived in religious harmony with other religions. Now certain groups and individuals have exploited the climate of tolerance and are interfering as to how we Muslims should practice our religion. They have used the Civil Courts to denigrate the status of Islam as guaranteed by the Constitution. There are concerted attempts to subject Islam to the Civil State with the single purpose of undermining the Shariah Courts. The interfaith groups and the current Article 11 groups are some of the unwarranted attempts to attack Islam in the name of universal human rights.[41]

The messages were unmistakable: The shariah courts and Islam are one in the same; universal human rights are inimical to Islam; the shariah courts and Islam are imperiled by the civil courts; and Muslims are being pushed around. In nearly all of this heated rhetoric, conservatives asserted that liberal rights pose a fundamental challenge to Islam and the shariah. Subsequent to *Pembela's* mobilization, Prime Minister Badawi issued an executive order that all Article 11 forums should be stopped immediately.

THE INTERNATIONAL DIMENSION OF THE RIGHTS-VERSUS-RITES BINARY

By 2006, *Lina Joy v. Majlis Agama Islam Wilayah Persekutuan* was receiving widespread coverage in the international press. Prominent news outlets such as the

---

[38] *Pembela* later grew to encompass the activities of more than seventy NGOs.

[39] Pembela Press Release, "*Pertubuhan-Pertubuhan Pembela Islam Desak Masalah Murtad Ditangani Secara Serius*" [Defenders of Islam Urge Seriousness in Handling the Apostasy Problem], July 17, 2006.

[40] Pembela, "Federal Mosque Resolution," July 23, 2006. The gathering was also widely covered in the press. See "Muslim Community Asked to Defend the Position of Religion in the Constitution." [*Umat Islam diminta pertahan kedudukan agama dalam perlembagaan*] *Bernama*, July 24, 2006.

[41] Pembela, "*Memorandum Mengenai Perkara Murtad Dan Memeluk Agama Islam*" [Memorandum on Apostasy and Conversion to Islam].

New York Times, the *Wall Street Journal*, the *Washington Post*, the *Guardian*, the BBC, the *International Herald Tribune*, *The Economist*, *Time* magazine, and dozens of others covered the case. Liberal rights activists were eager to share the story with the international press in the hope that outside pressure on the Malaysian government might spur legal change where domestic activism had failed. Hungry for such stories, the international media was happy to oblige. Thus, the rights-versus-rites binary was circulated internationally, affirming an enduring trope that liberal rights and Islam are fundamentally at odds with one another.

Liberal rights activists leveraged international pressure in other ways, too. In litigation, lawyers for Lina Joy made extensive reference to international law and the international human rights conventions signed by the Malaysian government. They also accepted legal assistance from the United States-based non-governmental organization, the Becket Fund for Religious Liberty. The Becket Fund not only submitted an amicus curiae brief to the Federal Court of Malaysia, but they also testified before the United States Congressional Human Rights Caucus about the threat to individual rights in Malaysia.[42] The United States Department of State also focused attention on Lina Joy and other cases in their International Religious Freedom Reports (2000–2010). Likewise, the United Nations Commission on Human Rights and the United Nations Human Rights Council made multiple inquiries at the request of Malaysian rights organizations. The UN Commission and Council repeatedly reminded the Malaysian government of their commitments under international law (2006, 2008, 2009).

This internationalization of *Lina Joy v. Majlis Agama Islam Wilayah Persekutuan* was not without a cost. And one could reasonably argue that it was a strategic misstep. Although liberal rights advocates viewed their strategies as entirely legitimate and compelling, they fit perfectly with the opposing narrative that Western powers seek to undermine Islam in Malaysia. What better proof of Western interference could be offered than the hundreds of Western newspaper articles that covered the plight of Lina Joy? And what better evidence of Western interference could be offered than regular criticisms in the annual United States Department of State Human Rights Reports and the United States Department of State International Religious Freedom Reports? Liberal rights activists were slow to accept the fact that all three strategies – litigation, consciousness-raising public events, and appeals to international law and outside pressure – provided conservatives with more ammunition to claim that Islam was under siege.

Conservative NGOs organized dozens of public forums and flooded the Malay-language press with hundreds more articles and opinion pieces on the need to defend Islam from liberalism, particularly from "liberal Muslims" who posed an insidious threat to the *ummah* from within. For example, *Harakah Daily* explained

---

[42]   Becket Fund for Religious Liberty, "Legal Opinion of the Becket Fund for Religious Liberty" [Amicus brief submitted in the case of *Lina Joy lwn Majlis Agama Islam Wilayah Persukutuan dan lain-lain*].

to its readers that "the challenge of apostasy ... is planned, encouraged, cultivated, and funded by the enemies of Islam here and abroad, and disguised as human rights."[43] The Becket Fund's involvement was noted and criticized.[44] Demonstrating their grassroots support, *Pembela* submitted a 700,000-signature petition to the Prime Minister on September 29, 2006, dwarfing the 20,000 signatures that the Article 11 coalition could muster. The petition demanded that "the government must take a stand in refusing Western efforts and non-governmental organizations that plot together using the local NGOs, academics, and individuals to influence the policies and laws related to Muslims." No doubt, the two-hour meeting that was arranged for conservative NGO leaders with the Prime Minister was a result of their ability to mobilize such broad-based support.

AFTER LINA JOY: DIMINISHED ROOM FOR INFORMAL ACCOMMODATION

Mobilization reached a fevered pitch in the weeks leading up to the final Federal Court decision in *Lina Joy v. Federal Territories Islamic Religious Affairs Council*. *Pembela* and PAS called on Muslims to assemble at the Palace of Justice in Putrajaya and for others to pray in mosques all across the country for a court decision that would "favor Islam."[45] The Federal Court issued its highly anticipated decision on May 30, 2007. In another split decision, the Court decided 2–1 to dismiss Joy's petition. Once again, the split decision mapped onto the religious divide. The two Muslim justices, Chief Justice Ahmad Fairuz and Justice Alauddin, authored the majority decision, while Richard Malanjum authored the dissenting opinion. Conservative NGOs were satisfied with the decision, but liberal rights groups and organizations representing non-Muslim communities were outraged.[46] Rather than resolving the rights-versus-rites binary, the Lina Joy decision confirmed the widespread view that Islam and liberal rights are fundamentally at odds with one another.

The political spectacle that came with *Lina Joy v. Majlis Agama Islam Wilayah Persekutuan* exacerbated difficulties for the attorneys and shariah court judges who

---

43 "Kes Lina Joy Usaha Terancang Hapuskan Islam" [Lina Joy's Case is a Planned Effort to Undermine Islam] *Harakahdaily*, July 15, 2006.
44 "Agensi Amerika didakwa beri sokongan sepenuhnya kepada Lina Joy" [American Agency Accused of Giving Full Support to Lina Joy] *Harakahdaily*, August 15, 2006.
45 *Harakah*, "Kes Lina Joy: Umat Islam Diminta Solat Hajat" [Lina Joy Case: Muslims Asked to Pray] May 29, 2007.
46 See Aliran media statement, "Lina Joy Verdict: No Freedom, No Compassion" (May 30, 2007); Women's Aid Organization, All Women's Action Society, and Sister's in Islam statement, "Constitutional Right to Freedom of Belief Made Illusory" (May 31, 2007); Malaysian Bar Council press statement, "Federal Constitution Must Remain Supreme" (May 31, 2007); SUARAM press statement (May 31, 2007); Malaysia Hindu Sangam press statement (May 30, 2007); Christian Federation of Malaysia press statement (May 30, 2007); Council of Churches of Malaysia press statement (May 30, 2007); Catholic Lawyer's Society Press statement (June 6, 2007); Malaysian Consultative Council of Buddhism, Christianity, Hinduism, Sikhism, and Taoism press release (June 19, 2007).

had, in the past, attempted to find ways to negotiate Malaysia's increasingly bureau-cratized religious sphere.[47] A striking example of this was a case concerning a woman named Siti Fatimah, who went by the name of Revathi Masoosai. Revathi was born to ethnic Indian converts to Islam, but she was raised by her Hindu grandmother. Thus, Revathi was raised a Hindu, while she was officially registered as a Muslim. Later in life, Revathi married a Hindu man in accordance with Hindu religious rites, but they did not register the marriage with the state, simply because there is no legal avenue to record a marriage between an officially registered Muslim and a non-Muslim in Malaysia. As a further result of this legal limbo, their child's birth was unregistered. Thus, Revathi did not enjoy the legal protections that would be afforded by way of marriage. What happened next illustrates the legal conundrums that are the product of Malaysia's hyper-regulated – and now intensely politicized – religious sphere. After giving birth, Revathi applied to have her official religious status changed. But at her hearing at a Malacca Shariah High Court, she was detained and sent to a "religious rehabilita-tion center" for six months against her will.[48] Her baby was taken from her husband (presumably because he is a non-Muslim) and put in the custody of Revathi's Muslim parents. The authorities released Revathi after six months of detention, but in the meantime, her ordeal had become the focus of national attention.[49]

Revathi's case is not offered simply as a shocking anecdote. Rather, I use her case to illustrate the legal conundrums that result from Malaysia's hyper-regulated religious sphere. The Malaysian federal and state governments establish rigid racial and religious categories that deny Muslims and non-Muslims the possibility of entering an official marriage. Yet situations like Revathi's are bound to emerge in a multi-religious and multiethnic society like that of Malaysia. Lawyers at the Legal Aid Center in Kuala Lumpur report that they see cases like this on a weekly basis.[50] In times past, individuals in Revathi's situation could secure state recognition of a different religious status by affirming a statutory declaration before a commissioner of oaths and registering a new name in the civil court registry through a deed poll. States only began restricting conversion and codifying penalties for apostasy in the 1980s. And, as noted in Chapter 4, the National Registration Department only began to require documentation from a shariah court starting in 2001. Even then, indivi-duals like Revathi were sometimes able to secure a statement affirming that they

---

[47] Interview with lawyers Latheefa Koya and Fadiah Nadwa Fikri, June 29, 2009.

[48] Malacca does not provide a formal legal avenue for conversion out of Islam. Instead, it criminalizes conversion with fines, jail terms, or mandatory counseling in a rehabilitation camp.

[49] Press reports indicate that Revathi was brought to the Malacca Shariah High Court on July 5, 2007. The court ordered that Revathi would remain "Muslim" and that she and her daughter must reside with Revathi's Muslim parents, away from her husband. Revathi's attorney launched a habeas corpus application in the Shah Alam High Court, but the case was dismissed because of Revathi's release. Mohamad Haniff Khatri Abdulla, the lawyer for the government, urged the court to dismiss the case, against the pleas of Karpal Singh, the attorney for Revathi's husband. See *Malaysiakini*, July 6, 2007, "Woman Released from Islamic Rehab Camp."

[50] Interview with lawyers Latheefa Koya and Fadiah Nadwa Fikri, Kuala Lumpur, June 29, 2009.

were not – and had never been – practicing Muslims.[51] After the Lina Joy decision, intense political pressure made it difficult even for sympathetic shariah court judges to facilitate a change of official religious status, and even in cases that are so thoroughly nonsensical, like that of Revathi's. Her case, and many others like hers, are easily narrated as miscarriages of religious freedom. But, in fact, they are much more complicated as they are rooted in deeper legal and institutional paradoxes of the Malaysian state, with antecedents that stretch back to colonial governance. These are not easily undone, particularly because they are locked in through competing, entrenched institutions.

THE RISE OF THE HINDU RIGHTS ACTION FORCE (HINDRAF)

The ethnic Indian community did not take these court decisions lying down. A new organization calling itself the Hindu Rights Action Force (more commonly known as Hindraf) launched in 2006. For our purposes, it is significant to note that Hindraf was initiated as a direct response to a 2005 Article 121 (1A) court decision that had denied Kaliammal Sinnasamy the right to bury her husband, Moorthy Maniam. But Hindraf also tapped into longstanding grievances in the ethnic Indian community. Although ethnic Indian Malaysians are not homogeneous regarding socioeconomic status, much of the community has long suffered from political, social, and economic marginalization. As the reader will recall from Chapter 3, most of Malaysia's ethnic Indians are Tamils who were brought to Malaysia as bonded laborers to work in rubber plantations.[52] With Malaysia's rapid economic development in the 1970s and 1980s, many estates were converted to other forms of economic activity, including industry, infrastructure, shopping centers and housing, and other development projects. In this great transformation, there was little, if any, effort to integrate estate workers into the rapidly changing economy, and the bulk of ethnic Indians were further marginalized. A variety of indicators from average income, to educational attainment, to life expectancy, to incarceration rates reflect the plight of the community and the growing gap between ethnic Indians and other Malaysians.

Hindraf's founders had initially established an organization called "Police Watch" to document police abuse of ethnic Indians.[53] But in the wake of the Moorthy Maniam court decision, they launched Hindraf with a decidedly religious

---

[51] Interview with lawyer Latheefa Koya, Kuala Lumpur, 2011. Another attorney with experience in these types of situations explained to me that clients are advised by their lawyers to demonstrate a complete lack of knowledge of Islam when requesting a declaration that they are not Muslim. This includes purposefully orchestrating visual cues that suggest they are not Muslim, such as entering the court with an awkwardly positioned hijab, in a fashion that might suggest that she had no prior experience with covering her hair.

[52] A smaller group of non-labor migrants were also recruited by the British from Ceylon and South India to work for the colonial administration. Finally, a group of lawyers, doctors, and merchants came from elsewhere.

[53] Interview with P. Uthayakumar, 2009

FIGURE 5.4: Some of the tens of thousands of Indian Malaysians who mobilized to claim their rights on November 25, 2007, under the banner of Hindraf (Hindu Rights Action Force). The placard reads "Peaceful Assembly – Article 10 of the Federal Constitution" (which guarantees peaceful assembly). Later that day, Hindraf supporters faced teargas and water cannon. Hindraf organized to challenge a long history of oppression, but the immediate catalyst was the court decision that had denied Kaliammal Sinnasamy the right to bury her husband, Moorthy Maniam.
Photo: Andrew Ong / Malaysiakini.com.

frame of reference and a more extensive array of grievances. That an ethnic Indian rights movement would mobilize because of long-term marginalization is no surprise. But Hindraf chose to organize along religious lines rather than ethnic lines. The religious frame was one further indication that Malaysian politics, long defined by its ethnic cleavages, was increasingly polarized along religious lines. The religious frame also served a more practical purpose: it facilitated political organization through a network of Hindu temples. This avenue of mobilization proved indispensable in the rural areas of the Klang Valley. As in other times and places, religious infrastructure facilitated collective action. Moreover, Hindu temples themselves became symbolic. As rural estates were plowed under to make way for development projects, Hindu temples were demolished in the process. Each temple demolition made the news headlines (especially in the Tamil-language newspapers), and each served as emotionally charged reminders of the marginalized status of ethnic Indians.

One of Hindraf's early initiatives was to file a lawsuit against the British government, suing for the "pain, suffering, humiliation, discrimination, and continuous colonization" that resulted from British exploitation of Indians as bonded laborers.

Hindraf called on the ethnic Indian community to come in person to deliver a petition to the office of the British High Commission in Kuala Lumpur. The authorities denied a request for a protest permit in anticipation of the thousands of protesters who were expected to gather. Roads were blocked leading to the city center, and police used water cannons and tear gas to disperse protesters. Nonetheless, an estimated 30,000 protesters flooded into downtown on November 25, 2007, exceeding all expectations. The protest organizers were charged with sedition and served two years in prison, but their initiative electrified the ethnic Indian community. The mobilization catalyzed widespread anger with the government. The percentage of ethnic Indians reporting dissatisfaction with "the way things are going in the country" slid substantially from 86 percent to 44 percent between in November 2006 and December 2007.[54] The government's declining legitimacy was also reflected in its poor performance in the 2008 elections.

FROM THE 2008 ELECTION TO "1MALAYSIA"

For the first time in fifty years, and indeed since national independence, the ruling *Barisan Nasional* (BN) lost its two-thirds parliamentary majority in the 2008 elections. The BN also lost control of state legislatures in Penang, Selangor, and Kedah. The vote tally was so close that were it not for extensive gerrymandering, the *Barisan Nasional* would have retained power only by a razor-sharp margin.[55] This blow was in large part due to the dwindling support from the ethnic Chinese and ethnic Indian (non-Muslim) communities, as reflected in the poor performance of the ethnic Chinese and ethnic Indian component parties in the *Barisan Nasional*. Compared with the 2004 parliamentary elections, the Malaysian Chinese Association (MCA) lost over half of its parliamentary seats. The Malaysian Indian Congress (MIC) lost a stunning two-thirds of its seats.[56] The election also delivered a significant shake-up within the MIC. Samy Vellu, the longest-serving president of the MIC, lost his seat after having held it for eleven consecutive terms that had stretched nearly three decades. Neither the MCA or the MIC recovered in subsequent elections, ultimately contributing to the stunning defeat of the BN coalition in the historic 2018 general elections.

---

[54]   Merdeka Center for Opinion Research (2007). During the same period, satisfaction among the ethnic Chinese community had slipped from 65 percent to 54 percent, while satisfaction held steadier in the ethnic Malay community, having dropped from 75 percent to 71 percent. In a subsequent poll, ethnic Indians identified "ethnic affairs and inequality" as "the most important problem in the country today." By way of comparison, 13 percent of ethnic Chinese and only 5 percent of ethnic Malays selected "ethnic affairs and inequality" as the leading problems. See Merdeka Center for Opinion Research (2008).

[55]   The popular vote was 50.27 percent for *Barisan Nasional* versus 46.75 percent for the opposition coalition, *Pakatan Rakyat*. The opposition secured 88 of 222 seats in the Parliament.

[56]   The MCA dropped from thirty-one seats in the 2004 election to fifteen in 2008. The MIC dropped from nine seats in the 2004 election to three seats in 2008. In terms of the popular vote, the MCA lost 33 percent, and the popular vote for the MIC fell 31 percent.

It is impossible to know the extent to which anger over the Article 121 (1A) cases influenced voters in the 2008 elections, but these controversies played a defining role for many Malaysians. In face-to-face interviews with "everyday Malaysians" of varying ethnicity in the summer of 2009, the overwhelming majority of non-Muslim respondents said that 121 (1A) cases influenced their vote in the 2008 elections, and many stated that government mishandling of the cases moved them to abandon the MCA and MIC. While these interviews are from a non-random sample, they are suggestive. More systematic opinion polling by the Merdeka Centre for Survey Opinion Research (2006) suggests similar conclusions. 58 percent of ethnic Chinese and 79 percent of ethnic Indian respondents indicated that non-Malay parties were ineffective in safeguarding non-Muslims vis-à-vis Islamization.[57] One might expect the UMNO leadership would take heed of these election results and adopt legal reforms to mitigate the tensions between the shariah and civil court jurisdictions, but the opposite outcome prevailed. The government is equally concerned with consolidating its Malay-Muslim base, and religion is one of the primary tools that the government uses to rally support. This results in an arguably duplicitous policy of relying on religious and ethnic cleavages to rally a Malay-Muslim base of support, while at the same time adopting more superficial policies that claim to advance ethnic and religious harmony.

Reeling from the blow in the 2008 parliamentary elections, Deputy Prime Minister Najib launched a new public relations initiative in September 2008, "1Malaysia." The campaign sought to mend rifts across racial and religious lines through a renewed emphasis on religious harmony and national unity.[58] When Prime Minister Najib Abdul Razak took office on April 3, 2009, he made the "1Malaysia" concept the motto of his new administration. The "1Malaysia" logo became ubiquitous – for years it was found everywhere on billboards, in government buildings, in newspapers, and on television. The initiative was criticized for being heavy on public relations, with no real substance. The real question was whether the prime minister would have the gumption and ability to push through institutional reforms to address the virtual conveyor belt of new legal controversies. To Najib's chagrin, another conversion/custody case hit the news wires on the same day that he became Prime Minister.[59] *Indira Gandhi v. Muhammad Ridzuan Abdullah* (detailed in Chapter 4) concerned the unilateral change of

---

[57]   The Merdeka Centre 2006 report is itself suggestive of the ways that Islam and government policy are conflated for many. When non-Muslims were asked whether they perceived Islamization as threatening, 58 percent of ethnic Chinese and 71 percent of ethnic Indians answered affirmatively. Yet, the Merdeka report summarizes the question as "Is *Islam* threatening?" [Emphasis added]. Although Islam and the project of state Islamization are two very different things, the survey conflates them.

[58]   Another prominent Malay rights group, Perkasa, was formed in the same month. Perkasa's founder, Ibrahim Ali, hammered on the importance of Article 121 (1A) and pledged that Perkasa would act as "the last bastion to defend the Malay-Islamic agenda." *Utusan Malaysia*, September 22, 2008, "Another Organization Established to Defend Malay Rights" [Lagi pertubuhan pertahan hak Melayu ditubuh].

[59]   "Anguished Mom Knocks on PM's Door," *Malaysiakini*, April 17, 2009.

religious status for Indira Gandhi's three children without her knowledge or consent. Gandhi's case illustrates how the status quo continued to enable individuals like Muhammad Ridzuan to claim child custody simply by changing the children's official religious status, thereby circumventing his legal obligations under a civil law marriage.[60]

CONSTRUCTING THE MEDIA FRAME

Indira Gandhi v. Muhammad Ridzuan Abdullah illustrates how Article 121 (1A) cases escalated to national political sensations overnight. Analysis of media coverage also provides insight into how media segmentation along ethnolinguistic lines exacerbates ethnic and religious polarization. The fact that Indira's predicament first reached the news by way of a press conference on April 3, 2009, speaks volumes. *Indira Gandhi v. Muhammad Ridzuan Abdullah* provided a brilliant opportunity for politicians to serve as champions for the rights of the ethnic Indian community. Knowing full well that media attention was the surest way to leverage pressure on the government, local DAP State Assemblyperson, A. Sivanesan, and Parliament Member from Ipoh, M. Kulasegaran, organized the press conference. And knowing the extent to which conversion/custody cases electrified the opposition, Democratic Action Party (DAP) leader Lim Kit Siang held another news conference with Indira Gandhi on April 21, 2009. We can recall that rights groups and attorneys had introduced the strategy of "going public" with considerable ambivalence in Shamala's fight for child custody back in 2004. Five years later, this media-savvy strategy was par for the course.

Indira's plight provided fodder for Tamil-language newspapers to run front-page articles for weeks on end. Two major newspapers serving the ethnic Indian community, *Makkal Osai* and *Malaysia Nanban*, provided extensive coverage with long exposés devoted to the latest twists and turns.[61] The story broke with front page banners reading, "Eleven-Month-Old Baby Converted to Islam" in *Makkal Osai* and "Conversion of Child: Mother's Worst Fears Come True" in *Malaysia Nanban*. Along the way, the papers gave a voice to critics of Najib's "1Malaysia" gloss, pointing to the more unpleasant realities on the ground. *Makkal Osai* carried a statement from the Malaysia Hindu Sangam President, that "at a time when Malaysians welcome the 1Malaysia concept, we still have instances where ulama have no qualms about converting an 11-month-old infant

---

60 Another unilateral child conversion was reported the following week in *Makkal Osai* and *Tamil Nesan*. In this case, the wife, K. Nalina Devi, converted two children without the consent of her husband, T. Tharmakannoo. Unlike Indira's case, the dispute did not generate long-term media coverage, perhaps because T. Tharmakannoo was reported as having an income of only RM650 per month, making legal action more difficult.

61 The other major Tamil paper, *Tamil Nesan*, generally represents the views of the Barisan Nasional's component party, the Malaysian Indian Congress. Perhaps because of this, *Tamil Nesan* carried relatively less coverage of Indira's plight.

FIGURE 5.5: Democratic Action Party (DAP) stalwart Lim Kit Siang and DAP Assemblyperson A. Sivanesan speak at a press conference at the Party Headquarters with Indira Gandhi and her two eldest children concerning litigation over custody rights. Article 121 (1A) cases were championed at the highest levels of government. Photo: The Nutgraph.

who is still being breastfed."[62] The unfolding drama was also covered extensively in English-language newspapers, which cater primarily to urban-educated Malaysians. By contrast, there was not a single mention of Indira's plight in the three most prominent Malay-language newspapers, *Utusan Malaysia*, *Berita Harian*, or *Harakah*, from April 3–22, 2009. The ethnic Indian community and urban-educated Malaysians were acutely aware of the unfolding drama. But this was not the case for the bulk of the ethnic Malay community, whose primary language for news and events is Bahasa Malaysia.[63] Media segmentation along ethnolinguistic lines made all the difference.

Faced with growing discontent in the ethnic Indian community and pressure from opposition parties and rights groups, Prime Minister Najib issued a surprise

---

[62] Malaysia Hindu Sangam President, Datuk A. Vaithilingam, quoted in "Rumblings in MIC" *The Nutgraph*, April 14, 2009.

[63] In 2009, Malaysian-language newspapers were read by 28 percent of the public, whereas Chinese-language newspapers were read by 18 percent, Tamil-language papers were read by 6 percent, and English-language newspapers were read by 9 percent of the public (Perception Media, 2009). A Merdeka Center for Opinion Research poll conducted in 2008 indicated that most Malaysians received most information concerning the 2008 elections from the newspapers. Peninsula Malaysia Voter Opinion Poll conducted March 14–21, 2008.

cabinet decision on April 23, 2009. The cabinet announced that in unilateral conversion situations like Indira's, the child's official religious status must not be changed without the consent of both parents. The Prime Minister wished to avoid the reoccurrence of politically explosive cases involving conversion and child custody, but whether the government would pass the appropriate legislative changes into law was an entirely different matter. The cabinet decision was met with rare praise from non-Muslim religious associations and rights groups, but conservative Muslim groups such as *Pembela, Jamaah Islah Malaysia* (JIM), ABIM, PAS, and the Malaysian Shariah Lawyers Association fiercely opposed the reform initiative.

Remarkably, Malay-language newspapers *Utusan Malaysia, Berita Harian,* and *Harakah* only began covering *Indira Gandhi v. Muhammad Ridzuan Abdullah* after the announcement of the cabinet decision. *Berita Harian*'s front-page article was neutral in tone, only detailing the cabinet decision and its rationale, with quotes from Minister in the Prime Minister's Office, Tan Seri Nazri Aziz.[64] The following day, the tone of Malay-language papers changed dramatically, as they reported on emerging opposition to the cabinet decision among conservative NGOs. *Utusan Malaysia* ran the headline "100 NGOs Protest Cabinet Decision." The article provided a platform to Malaysian Shariah Lawyers Association President Mohamad Isa Abd. Ralip and the Secretary General of the Lawyers for the Defense of Islam (*Peguam Pembela Islam*), Zainul Rijal Abu Bakar.[65] *Berita Harian* carried similar coverage with a bold title declaring that the "[Cabinet Reform] Clashes with Shariah."[66] *Harakah* ran similar articles, with titles including "Muftis Must Rise up to Object to Cabinet Decision," "Sacrificing Religion Does Not Create Unity," and "Pembela Defends Muslims from the Religious Conversion Conflict."[67] The Malay-language press showed little concern for the plight of non-converting spouses or the legal/institutional issues that exacerbated the legal conundrum, such as the fact that non-converting spouses had no legal recourse in the shariah courts. Rather, the dominant frame focused attention on how the proposed reforms would adversely affect the authority of the shariah courts, the rights of the converting Muslim spouse, and the position of Islam in the country. The contrast between Malay-language press and the Tamil- and English-language coverage could not have been starker. Media segmentation along ethnolinguistic lines facilitated the compartmentalization of strikingly different narratives.[68]

---

[64] "Child to Follow Parent's Original Religion," *Berita Harian*, April 24, 2009. *Utusan Malaysia* ran a similar article on the same day.

[65] *Utusan Malaysia*, April 25, 2009.   [66] *Berita Harian*, April 25, 2009.

[67] "Muftis Must Rise up to Object to Cabinet Decision," *Harakah* April 28, 2009; "Sacrificing Religion Does Not Create Unity," *Harakah* April 29, 2009; "Pembela Defends Muslims from the Religious Conversion Conflict," *Harakah* April 30, 2009.

[68] This is partly by design. The government encourages compartmentalization by restricting reform groups from publishing in the Malay language (Bahasa Malaysia). The clearest case of this was the Minister of Home Affairs refusal to license the reform group *Aliran* to publish in Bahasa Malaysia, even though they were already publishing in English. The case went all the way to the Supreme Court in *Persatuan Aliran Kesedaran Negara v. Minister of Home Affairs. Aliran* lost the case, preventing them from reaching a wider, Malay-language readership.

REFORM BLOCKED

Democratic Action Party Parliamentarian M. Kulasegaran pressed the government to make the necessary legislative changes that would give the cabinet decision the force of law, but concrete reforms did not follow. This lack of follow-through reveals much about the intractability of these legal conundrums. Criticism from conservative NGOs, the religious bureaucracy, and the Malay press suggests that legislative change can be delivered only at a political cost to the government. Moreover, it quickly became apparent that Malaysia's complicated federal structure would make legal reform all the more difficult. The bills were to be tabled in Parliament in late June 2009, but because the proposed amendments concerned issues related to Islam, the government referred the issue to the Conference of Rulers, which convened a special session on June 29, 2009.[69] In turn, the Conference of Rulers decided that the state religious authorities must first vet the proposed amendments due to state jurisdiction over religious matters as specified in the Federal Constitution.[70] Parliamentary debate on the legislative reforms was put on hold, pending approval from the state religious authorities. Months later, Mohamed Nazri from the Prime Minister's Office announced that the federal government was unable to produce results because they could not secure the cooperation of the state religious authorities.[71] Fending off criticism, Nazri challenged the state legislatures – particularly those that had fallen to opposition parties in the 2008 elections – to approach the state religious authorities, since religious matters fall within the mandate of state governments.

Nazri's argument was a cop-out because UMNO had the ability to push through reform of the Marriage and Divorce Act for the Federal Territories, which is under the jurisdiction of the federal government. Yet they did not. Moreover, a constitutional amendment to Article 12 (4) of the Federal Constitution could have put an end to unilateral conversions. As the reader will recall, Article 12 (4) was read literally by the civil courts as enabling a parent to convert a child, without the consent of her or his spouse, because Article 12 (4) mentions "parent or guardian" in the singular.[72] Regardless of whether reform was stymied due to Malaysia's complex federal structure or the simple lack of political will, the result is the same. At the time of writing, no legislative amendments have been made, leaving the legal conundrums unresolved.

---

[69] Amendments were proposed for the Law Reform (Marriage and Divorce) Act 1976, Administration of Islamic Law (Federal Territories) Act 1993, and Islamic Family Law (Federal Territories) Act 1984.

[70] "State Religious Authorities Sitting on Conversion Bills," *Malaysiakini*, July 14, 2010. Pushback was apparent in many venues. For example, see *Utusan Malaysia*, "Defending the Rights of the Islam is Compulsory" [*Wajib Pertahan Hak Islam*], July 28, 2009; *Utusan Malaysia*, "Don't Disturb the Syariah Courts" [*Jangan kacau Mahkamah Syariah*], December 8, 2009.

[71] "Muslim Conversion Law Reforms hit 'dead end'," *Malaysiakini* October 18, 2010.

[72] Article 12 (4) of the Constitution stipulates that " . . . the religion of a person under the age of eighteen years shall be decided by his parent or guardian."

FIGURE 5.6: Journalists are briefed by K. Shanmuga following a court hearing related to the child custody/conversion cases of Deepa Subramaniam and Indira Gandhi on July 24, 2014. Activist lawyers played crucial roles in litigating cases and explaining their significance to the public.
Photo by Yu Ren Chung.

Tan Cheow Hong v. Fatimah Fong Abdullah@Fong Mee Hui underlined the fact that unilateral child conversion/custody battles would continue without legal reform. In this case, an ethnic Chinese couple, Tan Cheow Hong and Fong Mee Hui, had been separated for three years when Fong converted to Islam in 2010. Fong obtained a custody order from a shariah court. The child, Tan Yi Min, had been living with her father, but Fong Mee Hui (now Fatimah Fong Abdullah) went to Yi Min's school to collect her with the assistance of Selangor Islamic Affairs Department (JAIS) officers and police. In a public confrontation that made news headlines, Fong Mee Hui presented the shariah court custody order to school officials and left with her child after a short altercation. The next day, Fatimah Fong Abdullah changed her daughter's official religious status to Islam. Her husband attempted to challenge the shariah court custody order and the change of official religious status of the children by way of the civil courts. However, as in prior cases, the civil courts declined to intervene because they had no jurisdiction in matters related to the shariah courts. Similarly, in *Viran a/l Nagapan v. Deepa a/p Subramaniam*, the husband converted in 2012 and changed the official religious status of the two children to Islam without the wife's consent.[73] The High Court granted

---

[73] *Viran a/l Nagapan v. Deepa a/p Subramaniam* [2014] MLJU 1391; *Viran a/l Nagapan v. Deepa a/p Subramaniam* [2015] 3 MLJ 209; *Viran a/l Nagapan v. Deepa a/p Subramaniam* [2016] MLJU 05; *Viran a/l Nagapan v. Deepa a/p Subramaniam* [2016] 1 MLJ 585.

FIGURE 5.7: Deepa Subramaniam speaking with reporters after a Federal Court hearing concerning the custody of her children. Her case, along with other custody/conversion battles, became a national spectacle.
The Sun/Sun Media Corporation, Sdn Bhd.

Deepa custody of the children in 2014. Deepa recovered the children, only to despair over the abduction of one of the children just two days later. Subsequently, the father initiated legal action to contest the custody order based on Article 121 (1A). The legal battles in *Viran a/l Nagapan v. Deepa a/p Subramaniam* continued non-stop for several years (as did the press coverage), with no end in sight at the time of writing. Cases concerning the conversion out of Islam similarly continued.[74]

SHAPING ISLAM THROUGH THE FRIDAY KHUTBAH

The religious establishment amplified the Islam-versus-liberalism trope in the Friday sermons prepared weekly by the Department of Islamic Development Malaysia (*Jabatan Kemajuan Islam Malaysia* – JAKIM) and by state-level Islamic religious departments, such as *Jabatan Agama Islam Negeri Selangor* (JAIS).[75] These sermons provide a direct window onto religious knowledge production and the particular

[74] *Mohd Syafiq Abdullah @ Tiong Choo Ting v. Director of Jabatan Agama Islam Sarawak & Ors* [2015] MLJU 1150; *Hj Raimi bin Abdullah v. Siti Hasnah Vangarama bt Abdullah and another appeal* [2014] 3 MLJ 757.

[75] Mosques can use the JAKIM-prepared *khutab*, or those prepared by the parallel state-level religious administration, such as *Jabatan Agama Islam Negeri Selangor* (JAIS). JAKIM *khutab* are archived at <http://www.islam.gov.my/e-khutbah> (last accessed August 1, 2016). Earlier, JAKIM archived *khutab*

inflection of Islam that federal and state religious administrations would like to impress upon Malaysian Muslims. Interestingly, the content of JAKIM sermons changed significantly over time, in parallel with the controversies around the Article 121 (1A) cases.

From 2003–2007, most JAKIM sermons addressed the sorts of moral and ethical issues that one would expect to find in any religious setting. They addressed the central place of charity, generosity, and compassion in Islam,[76] the imperative of a strong moral foundation for youth,[77] the importance of parenting,[78] the necessity for perseverance in difficult times,[79] the virtues of frugality and the perils of extravagant behavior,[80] warnings about the scourge of drugs and gambling,[81] and the problem of corruption.[82] Public service themes were also peppered into the sermons, including messages promoting awareness of HIV/Aids,[83] fire safety,[84] personal hygiene and diet,[85] and the need to protect the environment.[86] Some sermons carried political themes. For example, Palestinian rights were presented as a Muslim cause.[87] Nationalist tropes were invoked on the anniversaries of Malaysia's independence. And there were frequent appeals for loyalty to the monarchy and exhortations on the need to defend Malaysia from external threats.[88] However, beginning around 2008, the tone of many Friday sermons became more overtly political, and they focused far more on the appropriate place of Islam in the legal and political order and the threat that is posed by liberalism. Consider, for example, the *khutbah* that JAKIM prepared for delivery on Friday, December 26, 2008:

> Recently, there have been attempts, whether deliberate or not, to threaten the special position of Islam as the official religion of Malaysia, as stated in Article 3 of the Federal Constitution of Malaysia. These attempts to challenge Islam are made through all kinds of methods. Among them is the organization of forums and dialogues, and the spreading of articles that insult Islam through blogs and also through meddling with Islamic ceremonies.
>
> In Article 3 of the Federal Constitution, Islam is the religion of the Federation; but other religions may be practiced in peace and harmony in any part of the Federation. This provision recognizes that Islam's position is higher than any other religion, and the Yang di-Pertuan Agong is the head of the Federation, whereas the Malay kings are the heads of Islam in their respective states. Therefore, when Islam was made the religion of the Federation, it meant the people and the governing system must, in unity, place Islam as the main basis for the country's governance . . . .

---

going back to 2003 at <http://www.islam.gov.my/khutbah-online> (last accessed April 3, 2015). This link has since been removed.

[76] For examples, see February 3, 2006; February 10, 2006.

[77] April 7, 2006; May 19, 2006; December 1, 2006; July 6, 2007.   [78] November 23, 2007; June 9, 2006.

[79] May 5, 2006.   [80] April 21, 2006; May 26, 2006; July 28, 2006; June 13, 2008.

[81] February 17, 2006; June 29, 2007; June 27, 2008.   [82] May 2, 2008; October 10, 2008.

[83] December 22, 2006; May 25, 2007.   [84] May 4, 2007.

[85] March 10, 2006; December 12, 2008; February 13, 2009.   [86] September 15, 2006; August 17, 2007.

[87] August 11, 2006; December 8, 2006; January 2, 2009.   [88] June 1, 2007.

The JAKIM *khutbah* embraces a revisionist interpretation of Article 3 on par with the public statements made by *Pembela*. Islam is imagined as the basis of governance, superior to any other normative order. The mantra that Islam is the "ruling religion" of the country is a refrain that is regularly emphasized in JAKIM sermons.[89] Conventional views of Article 3 are not only pronounced unfaithful to the Federal Constitution; they are said to "challenge Islam" itself. The *khutbah* goes on to describe the intentions of anyone who does not subscribe to this vision of Article 3:

> There are groups in this country that use the law to challenge the sovereignty of Islam ... What is even more unfortunate is that there are Muslims who are not aware of this game because it hides behind the disguise of freedom and human rights. All kinds of international conventions are forced on Islamic nations, which then bind us. This is in line with the propaganda [being spread] by the international media. The most commonly used issue is women's rights and also gender equality. Besides that, certain groups try to raise suspicion and doubt towards the truth of Islam by mixing traditions or Western values as part of Islamic teaching.[90]

The *khutbah* frames Muslims who embrace liberal rights as either naive or knowingly complicit in a project to undermine Islam. The possibility of being a devout Muslim *and* a committed liberal is not entertained. The *khutbah* also implicates international law in this global conspiracy. Any "mixing" of "Western" values with "Islamic teachings" – especially in women's rights and gender equality – is to be condemned. JAKIM repeats similar tropes in other Friday sermons. Pluralism and liberalism were presented as threats to Islam and to the faith of Muslims.[91] Muslims are reminded that Malaysia faces an internal threat from those who stir up "sensitive issues" related to religion, and courts are singled out as the principal avenue through which Islam is challenged.[92]

JAKIM does not refer to the Article 121 (1A) cases by name, but the connection could not be clearer. For example, consider the JAKIM *khutbah* delivered in the immediate aftermath of the High Court decision in the Catholic Herald case.[93]

> The pulpit reminds the congregation and all Muslims that we need to understand what motivates the use of the word Allah, which is championed by certain groups. If we look closely, this issue has strong ties to the issue of pluralism, which is the concept that all religions are the same. In fact, some Muslims support this struggle and created Liberal Islam. The supporters of Liberal Islam worked hard to loosen the

---

[89]   For additional examples, see August 27, 2010; January 22, 2010; July 29, 2011; December 9, 2011; June 1, 2012; May 31, 2013.

[90]   December 26, 2008.

[91]   For example, see the sermons from March 9, 2012; October 11, 2013; June 7, 2014; October 24, 2014; March 20, 2015; February 5, 2016.

[92]   March 23, 2012

[93]   *Titular Roman Catholic Archbishop of Kuala Lumpur v. Menteri Dalam Negeri & Anor* [2010] 2 CLJ 208.

hold on special names or terms that have been the strength of Islam, so that the creed of the Muslim people becomes fragile and breaks apart. (JAKIM, January 8, 2010)

This rhetoric helped to fuel church burnings across Malaysia from January 8–15, 2010. Two weeks later, in the immediate aftermath of violence on houses of worship, a JAKIM *khutbah* proved even more inflammatory. Here, the JAKIM focused on the place of non-Muslims in Malaysia, referring to them as *"Kafir Dzimmi."*[94] The *khutbah*, titled "Kafir Dzimmi and Kafir Harbi," explains that Muslims are benevolent hosts to non-Muslims, but that Muslims should not be infinitely patient or passive. JAKIM explains that non-Muslims entered a social contract with Muslims in the form of the Federal Constitution and that the *"Kafir Dzimmi"* must respect this arrangement, which requires that non-Muslims bow to Islamic supremacy. The *khutbah* explains that "one of the important agreements in the Constitution is to acknowledge that Islam is the religion of the Federation, *which opens the path for Islam to become the ruling religion in this country"* [emphasis added]. In articulating this vision of Article 3, JAKIM provides a legal rationale for *Ketuanan Melayu* (literally "Malay Dominance" or "Malay Supremacy," the political concept that underpins Malay nationalism). Moreover, this reading of Article 3 attempts to endow the concept of *Ketuanan Melayu* with religious legitimation. JAKIM explains that those who hold a different view of Article 3 and refuse to bow to Islamic supremacy may, in fact, be *"Kafir Harbi"* agents – those non-Muslims who are at war with Muslims.[95] JAKIM recalls that the Prophet and Islamic law " ... teach us not to follow wild emotions." Yet, in the next sentence, the *khutbah* clarifies that, "the pulpit would like to remind the congregation that having good relations with non-Muslims does not mean we forget our responsibility to Islam. Islam provides for no tolerance when it comes to questions of faith and devotion." In other words, in such circumstances, the gloves must come off.

Muslims are also warned that some among them are also willing to sacrifice the interests of their religion, their race, and their nation in pursuit of selfish interests and ideologies.[96] The sermon, released in advance of Heroes' Day (*Hari Pahlawan*) in 2011, brings together core themes that are present in many of JAKIM's more political sermons and is, therefore, worthy of extended quotation. The *khutbah*, titled "National Heroes Are the Backbone for Islam's Protection in the Federal Constitution," begins with Article 3 as its focal point:

---

[94] *Dzimmi* (Arabic: *Dhimmi*) is the historical term that referred to non-Muslims in an Islamic polity. The word means "protected person." This status gave non-Muslims rights to carry on within their communities in exchange for payment of a special tax. The term assumes a relationship of dominance. Moreover, the qualifying term *"kafir"* carries a colloquial inflection that is roughly on par with English use of the term "infidel." See the *khutbah* of January 22, 2010, titled "Kafir Dzimmi and Kafir Harbi."

[95] The sermon goes on to discuss the Cabinet decisions of May 16, 1986 and January 3, 2008, in which non-Muslims were prohibited from using the word "Allah" in publication.

[96] For example, see the *khutbah* of April 13, 2012.

Article 3 (1) of the Federal Constitution provides that Islam is the religion of the Federation ... The big question is, who are the national heroes who will be the backbone for Islam's protection in the Federal Constitution? ...

Although history shows that Islam was accepted as the religion of the Federation and the Malay Kings are given the necessary acknowledgement, the position of Islam still invites all kinds of interpretations by the people of this country. The position of Islam has been questioned and debated by those who refuse or fail to understand the position of Islam. The dissenting voices of certain groups continue to echo in their false interpretation of the position of Islam in the Federal Constitution until it results in confusion among Muslims who believe that Islam is for ceremonial purposes only. The pulpit wishes to assert that if this misinterpretation is allowed to continue, Islam will be viewed as a religion that is equal in position with other religions and has no special rights.

Lately, we also hear of groups that make fun of Islam using all kinds of methods and tricks. They challenge the legitimacy of shariah law and the authority of Islamic institutions such as the Department of the Mufti and the shariah courts. Fatwas have been challenged with claims that they clash with the freedom of religion. Shariah law has been accused of being backwards because it clashes with international conventions that promote democracy and Western human rights. They also infuse liberal beliefs and pluralism ... aiming to threaten and erode the values of the Muslim people.

Even more unfortunate is that enemies of Islam seize this opportunity to lower the position of Islam. They demand an interfaith commission that goes against the Federal Constitution; they question the implementation of shariah sentences; they support apostasy cases; they demand that homosexuals, lesbians and transgender people be given freedom to practice their activities. They also question the position of the Malay Kings, the special rights of the Malay people, and the position of Islam as the official religion of the Federation ...

Why does this happen? ... First, Muslims themselves are divided into different groups. Second, they are willing to sacrifice their honor and the interests of the religion for their own interests and their group's interest. Third, there are Muslims who conspire with certain groups to question Islam as the official religion of this country, using the excuse of defending the rights of others. Therefore, the pulpit wishes to remind [you] that if Muslims continue to be divided, lose their integrity, and are used by others, sooner or later the protection of Islam in the Federal Constitution will be eroded and Muslims of this country will receive an unfortunate fate similar to countries where their people are hunted and expelled from their own land. (JAKIM, July 29, 2011)

The message is unequivocal: Islam and Islamic law are enshrined in the legal system, but they face powerful threats from non-Muslims; Islam and Islamic law are put at risk by wayward, confused, and self-serving Muslims; and, finally, Islam and Islamic law are besieged by liberalism, pluralism, and "Western" human rights. JAKIM's dire warnings suggest that these dangers constitute nothing short of an existential threat to the Muslim community. If Islam's position in the Federal Constitution is eroded, Muslims will be "hunted and expelled from their own land."

The rhetoric around the Article 121 (1A) cases also grew more intense outside of the state-monopolized religious establishment. *Ikatan Muslimin Malaysia* (Isma) president Abdullah Zaik Abd Rahman positioned liberalism as the diametric opposite of Islam and claimed that liberalism and pluralism were part of a global conspiracy to destroy Malay identity.[97] *Utusan Malaysia* headlines called on the government to "curb extremist liberalism,"[98] to "wipe out liberalism,"[99] and to "block liberalism, pluralism."[100] Liberalism, Malaysians were told, "poses a major threat to the nation, the religion of Islam, and the survival of the Malay people."[101] The messaging from the top of the Malaysian political establishment thus came to echo the polarized political discourse from the most hyperbolic ideologues. On more than one occasion, Prime Minister Najib called on Muslims to avoid liberalism and pluralism, going so far as to say that these values threatened national security.[102] High-ranking government ministers echoed these sentiments on many occasions, both to ward off conservative criticism of the government and to bolster Malay unity in the face of an increasingly fraught political order.[103]

These developments illustrate the radiating effects of courts on civil society activism. The decisions gave new energy and focus to variously situated civil society groups, both liberal and conservative. Court decisions catalyzed the formation of entirely new NGOs and coalitions of NGOs – most notably, the Article 11 Coalition and *Pembela*. The work of these NGOs, in turn, played a direct role in shaping a political context that increasingly constrained judges who might otherwise work to find pragmatic solutions. Without a doubt, the dynamic was one of polarization. A further impact of polarization is clearly illustrated by the fact that Sisters in Islam, a women's rights organization that works to advance women's rights (and liberal rights more generally) through the framework of Islamic law, proved unable to negotiate a "middle way." Instead, Sisters in Islam assumed a leadership position in the Article 11 Coalition. They were portrayed by conservative detractors as "Sisters against Islam." On the other side of the spectrum, conservative NGOs that had previously staked out a broad range of positions on various issues – from ABIM to the Muslim Professionals Forum – found themselves working in cooperation under *Pembela*.

It is notable that judicialization drew the involvement of actors with little or no expertise in matters of religion. Litigants, lawyers, judges, political activists, journalists, government officials, and many others fielded claims and counter-claims inside

---

97   *Malay Mail Online*, October 15, 2014.
98   "*Mengekang ekstremis liberalisme*," *Utusan Malaysia*, November 9, 2014.
99   "*Beratu banteras anaman liberalisme*," *Utusan Malaysia*, October 5, 2016.
100 "*Bendung Liberalism, Pluralisme*," *Utusan Malaysia*, May 20, 2014.
101 "*Beratu banteras anaman liberalisme*," *Utusan Malaysia*, October 5, 2016.
102 For example, see *Malaysiakini*, May 15, 2014.
103 "Shi'ism, Liberalism, among threats to Muslim Faith, says Minister," *Bernama*, October 3, 2013.

and outside the courts. Most of these actors have little, if any, specialized knowledge of Islamic law or the Islamic legal tradition. Yet these competing claims are none-theless consequential. Those with little or no training in Islamic law are the primary actors that drive the judicialization of religion, and they are central agents in the production of new religious knowledge. What is so striking in the polarized dis-course in Malaysia is that Islam is increasingly defined vis-à-vis liberalism. More to the point, Islam is increasingly defined *against* liberalism. Likewise, liberalism and secularism come to be defined vis-à-vis Islam, indeed *against* Islam. As the reader will recall, these dichotomies are facilitated, even encouraged, by the legal claims that are made in the court of law and the political claims fielded in the court of public opinion. All too easily, Islam is pitted *against* liberal rights; individual rights are pitted *against* collective rights; religion *against* secularism, and so on. These binaries elevate the "legal-supremacist" conceptualization of "Islam as law" (Ahmed 2016), and they further position Anglo-Muslim law as the full and exclusive embodi-ment of the Islamic legal tradition. Likewise, these binaries elevate "secularism" and "liberalism" as monolithic ideological formations of their own. Secularism and liberalism are positioned as inherently inimical to religion (and vice-versa) in political discourse. Self-positioned Islamists make countless claims that liberalism, secularism, and pluralism are a threat to Islam. Liberal rights activists ironically reinforce and validate the claims of their rivals by emphasizing the incompatibility of Islamic law with liberal rights and secularism. Each side finds agreement in the zero-sum nature of the conflict. Given the ease with which these binary tropes are advanced, it is crucial to remain mindful that they are, in fact, constructed binaries. That is, binary forms emerge as a function of the institutional environment in which Islam and liberalism are represented. Islam and liberal rights are not autonomous, pure, and coherent formations. And in contexts like that of contemporary Malaysia, they are increasingly co-constitutive.

6

The Rights-versus-Rites Binary in Popular Legal Consciousness

"If men define situations as real, they are real in their consequences."
– William Isaac Thomas

There is little question that binary polemics dominated elite-level contestation. But did these polemics shape the common-sense understandings of ordinary Malaysians? This chapter turns from the political spectacle to popular legal consciousness. I draw on open-ended interviews, focus group discussions, and original survey data to explore how everyday Malaysians understood the Article 121 (1A) controversies and what they meant for the future of their country. The data suggests that the cases were perceived in starkly different terms across Malaysia's ethnic and religious "legalscape." Despite divergent understandings of the cases, however, most Malaysians were united in the assumption that legal tensions were inevitable, and a concrete manifestation of a basic incompatibility between Islam and liberalism. The second part of the chapter turns to the efforts of Sisters in Islam, a Malaysian non-governmental organization that challenges these binary constructions and works to expand women's rights from within the framework of the Islamic legal tradition. I examine the unique strategies that Sisters in Islam undertakes to confront the rights-versus-rites binary, which is now deeply entrenched in the popular imagination.

RIGHTS-VERSUS-RITES IN POPULAR LEGAL CONSCIOUSNESS

To examine the hold of the rights-versus-rites binary in popular legal consciousness, I assembled a multiethnic research team to conduct one hundred semi-structured interviews with ordinary Malaysians.[1] These interviews were supplemented by

---

[1] Interviews were conducted in the summer and fall of 2009 by the author (in English only) and a team of research assistants at a variety of locales in greater Kuala Lumpur. Interviews were conducted in Bahasa Malaysia, Chinese, English, and Tamil (whichever language was appropriate to the respondent) in the neighborhoods of Kampung Baru, Kampung Kerinchi, Subang Jaya, Brickfields, Seri Kembangan, Shah Alam, and Bangsar. These areas were selected to represent the diverse ethnic and socioeconomic

a nationwide survey with a sampling frame that ensured a maximum error margin of ±3.03 percent at a 95 percent confidence level.[2] Finally, a series of focus groups were convened.[3] All three sets of data suggest that popular legal consciousness closely aligned with the rights-versus-rites binary advanced by political activists and further amplified by the media.

As we saw in Chapter 5, conservative organizations frequently claimed that the Article 121 (1A) cases represented deliberate attempts to undermine Islam and the shariah courts. These claims appear to have resonated with the public. Sixty-two percent of Muslims surveyed believed that the Article 121 (1A) cases were "examples of efforts by some individuals and groups to undermine Islam and the shariah courts in Malaysia." By way of comparison, only eight percent of non-Muslims viewed these cases as efforts to undermine the shariah courts. Muslim respondents almost all spoke of Islam being "the religion of the country" and most expressed the view that the Muslim community must be allowed to govern its own affairs without interference from the civil courts. The Article 121 (1A) cases and the controversies that surrounded them were not understood as the result of the tight regulation of religion. Instead, many understood the legal controversies as the result of too little regulation and bold attempts by non-Muslims to undermine the position of Islamic law in the country. One respondent explained that legal disputes come about

---

composition of metropolitan Kuala Lumpur. Given that selection of respondents was non-systematic and confined to neighborhoods in and around Kuala Lumpur, they should be taken as suggestive, and not necessarily representative of national trends. They were primarily used to gain a deeper contextual understanding of the results of the nationwide survey.

[2] The national telephone survey was nationwide in scope. It used appropriate sampling techniques to ensure that respondents represented the composition of the Muslim community in Malaysia across relevant demographic variables including region, sex, and urban–rural cleavages. Execution of the telephone survey, including the sampling of respondents, was conducted by the Merdeka Center for Opinion Research, the leading public survey research group in Malaysia. The sampling population was drawn from the national telephone directory, which comprises all households with fixed-line telephones. In stage one of the sampling, a random number generator was used to produce a sample of three million fixed-line phone numbers from the national directory. The resulting list was then checked to ensure that it was proportional to the number of Muslim residents in each state per 2006 Malaysian census figures. In stage two, a randomly generated respondent telephone list was prepared, comprising five times the desired sample size of one thousand respondents. In step three, interval sampling was applied to the respondent telephone list. One respondent was contacted in each household on December 9–13, 2009. Respondents were balanced to ensure an equal number of males and females. The random stratified sample of 1,043 Malaysian Muslims ensures a maximum error margin of ±3.03 percent at a 95 percent confidence level. Additional findings from the nationwide survey are detailed in Moustafa (2013a).

[3] Four focus group sessions were organized on July 14, 20, and 21, 2013 in Petaling Jaya. Each focus group lasted approximately 1.5 hours and drew participants from across metropolitan Kuala Lumpur. The first focus group was composed of Malay participants with a Malay facilitator; the second group was made up of ethnic Indian Malaysians with an ethnic Indian facilitator; the third group had ethnic Chinese Malaysians with an ethnic Chinese moderator; the final focus group was ethnically mixed, with both ethnic Malay and ethnic Chinese facilitators. The focus group questions were designed by the author and executed with the assistance of the Merdeka Center for Opinion Research, which provided organization and assistance.

"because we don't have full implementation of the shariah law here in Malaysia." He clarified that, "we claim that we are an Islamic country but our shariah law is still not that strong. If we don't strengthen shariah law, we will be weakened and they [non-Muslims] will be able to overrule us [Muslims] using the civil court."[4] This view, which was reflective of the mindset of many in the Malay community, pointed to an immediate threat, a diagnosis of the problem, and a solution. The immediate threat is that non-Muslims "will be able to overrule us." The diagnosis of the problem is that "shariah law is still not that strong." And the solution to the problem is "full implementation of shariah law."[5] This "Islam under siege" threat perception matched the frames of understanding provided by the most outspoken conservative activists and nongovernmental organizations virtually one-to-one.

Muslim respondents also had a strong tendency to understand the shariah courts as faithful expressions of Islam, unmediated by human agency. Concerning the Lina Joy case, for example, respondents explained that the government must stringently regulate apostasy because it is forbidden in Islam. Three-quarters of Muslim respondents believed that Joy should be barred from changing her official religious status without the permission of the shariah court. In the national survey, an even greater majority, 96.5 percent, stated that Muslims should not be permitted to change their religion. Rather than drawing popular attention to the variety of possible positions concerning apostasy in the Islamic legal tradition, the polarized framing around the case appears to have strengthened a view that the state is obliged to prevent apostasy. Similarly, most Muslim respondents understood the child custody cases of *Gandhi v. Pathamanathan* and *Shamala v. Jeyaganesh* in religious terms.[6] Although viewed as regrettable by many, Gandhi's loss of custody was considered the only acceptable outcome.

It is nonetheless important to note that Muslim respondents were not uniform in their understanding of the cases. When asked about *Gandhi v. Pathamanathan* in the open-ended interviews, nearly one-third of Muslim respondents held that Gandhi's husband should *not* have the legal right to convert the children without his wife's approval. One-third also shared the view that the civil court was the proper forum to address the dispute, not the shariah court. Similarly, one-fifth of Muslim respondents argued that Lina Joy had the right to change her religious status and that she should not be answerable to the shariah court. Muslim respondents who voiced these opinions tended to have a better understanding of the details of the cases, especially their legal ambiguities. Perhaps because of this, these respondents also

[4] Interview in Subang Jaya, July 20, 2009.
[5] The same respondent concluded his statement by insisting that "We cannot play around with issues of religion, especially Islam. Because we are Muslims, we must follow the shariah law to a tee. We only have two choices: either we follow the shariah law or we don't."
[6] We focused on *Gandhi v. Pathamanathan* because the case was in the news at the time that the interviews were conducted. The facts of *Gandhi v. Pathamanathan* resembled *Shamala v. Jeyaganesh* (and many other conversion/custody cases), so much so that respondents frequently confused the names of the protagonists and the cases.

tended not to view the cases as efforts by groups and individuals to challenge Islam and the shariah courts. This finding supports the hypothesis that the stylized narratives advanced in the Malay media tended to have less of an influence on respondents who understood the technical complexities that had triggered the Article 121 (1A) cases.

It is not surprising that non-Muslim respondents, on the other hand, viewed the cases through the prism of minority rights vis-à-vis the state and the Malay Muslim community. Every non-Muslim respondent believed that an injustice had befallen Gandhi when her husband sought child custody in the shariah courts. Like their Malay counterparts, non-Muslims did not attribute the outcomes to the ambiguities, contradictions, complexities of the Malaysian legal system, or the rigid regulation of religion. Rather, they associated the outcomes with a broader pattern of legal discrimination against non-Malays and non-Muslims. In discussions of *Gandhi v. Pathamanathan*, for example, respondents frequently commented on the economic advantages that Malay Muslims enjoyed at the expense of non-Muslim Indian and Chinese Malaysians. Respondents frequently vented their frustration that Malays enjoyed access to lucrative government contracts, discounts on housing, government scholarships for study at home and abroad, reserved spaces at universities, and many other benefits. In other words, the Article 121 (1A) cases were understood in relation to a whole array of longstanding political and economic grievances of the ethnic Indian and ethnic Chinese communities.

An elderly, ethnic Indian man whom I interviewed articulated the grievances that are common to many non-Muslims, while voicing nostalgia for an era when religious cleavages were less pronounced and state resources were distributed more equitably. After a lengthy discussion of several prominent Article 121 (1A) court cases, he explained that:

> Thirty-five years back, we didn't have these issues. Everyone was happy. I went to school with the Chinese and Bumis. We really mingled around. There was no problem. But now come a lot of issues. They are segregating the people. It is government policy that they're segregating [us]. We didn't have problems with our Muslim friends and our Chinese friends. No, we went to school, and we didn't have problems. The Muslims can buy any property for thirty percent less. It's another discrimination. Indians get good marks in school, but the Malays get the scholarships. It's the government policy that is disuniting the people. These are the sort of things that people get fed up with.

At this point in the interview, I asked the respondent, "So are these [economic] issues more important than the court cases that we discussed earlier?" To which he replied, "Both are the same to me. Both are important." The fact that the discussion of the court decisions naturally flowed into a discussion of economic, social, and political grievances illustrates the dynamic of "issue expansion" at work. Before the extensive media coverage of the Article 121 (1A) cases, ordinary Malaysians had little awareness of the legal tensions that were brewing in the courts. But after 2004, the extraordinary political spectacle around Lina Joy, Shamala Sathiyaseelan, and Moorthy Maniam made each of the cases household names. The cases became powerful metonyms for wider ethnic and religious grievances.

The cases were clearly at the front of people's minds. Respondents were not only familiar with the cases, but some launched into a conversation about them *before we had the opportunity to initiate discussion*. For example, the first substantive interview question was "how do you see the state of religious and race relations in the country today?" Before we could proceed to the next question, many respondents offered detailed descriptions of the injustices suffered by Indira Gandhi and others, as examples to support their assessment of poor race and religious relations in Malaysia. Similarly, when asked about specific court cases, respondents frequently referenced other Article 121 (1A) cases that had also been covered heavily in the press, including *Kaliammal v. Islamic Religious Affairs Council, Subashini v. Saravanan,* and *Shamala v. Jeyaganesh.* The frequency of this cross-referencing suggests that these cases were salient in popular legal consciousness among "everyday Malaysians."

Not surprisingly, non-Muslim Indian and Chinese respondents universally viewed the civil courts as the appropriate judicial forum to resolve legal controversies, even if they were skeptical that justice would be delivered. Whereas Malays viewed litigation as an attack on Islam and a threat to the autonomy of the shariah courts, non-Muslims experienced the cases as just another example of Malay Muslim dominance over religious and ethnic minorities. And just as most Muslim respondents understood the Article 121 (1A) cases as a threat to the Muslim community, non-Muslims viewed them as fundamental(ist) threats to their communities. The radiating effects of these court decisions varied starkly across ethnic and religious communities.

Beyond these differing threat perceptions, there were shared assumptions across ethnic and religious lines. The first shared assumption was that the cases were deeply consequential for the future of Malaysia, beyond the individuals involved and beyond the specific issues at hand, such as religious freedom. Eighty-five percent of Muslim respondents and eighty percent of non-Muslim respondents reported that they had strong views about the outcome of the cases. This is a striking confirmation of the broadening audience and the tremendous "expansion" of issues and concerns that were (made to be) associated with the cases. Media outlets and political activists had framed the cases to resonate with longstanding sensitivities and grievances, stirring passions across ethnic and religious lines. The cases effectively became metonyms for the most pressing social and political issues of the day, including fundamental questions of state identity and the contested foundations of the political order. The audience extended to the entire nation, with most everyone invested in the outcome.

A second shared assumption was that the cases were the result of a fundamental incompatibility between Islam and liberal rights. In one of the

TABLE 6.1 *Islamic law and shariah courts in popular legal consciousness*

Statement	Agree	Disagree	Do Not Know
Each of the laws and procedures applied in the shariah courts is clearly stated in the Qur'an.	0.785	0.153	0.059
Islamic law changes over time to address new circumstances in society.	0.505	0.479	0.015
Islam provides a complete set of laws for human conduct and each of these laws has stayed the same, without being changed by people, since the time of the Prophet (s.a.w.).	0.785	0.153	0.059

most striking findings of the national survey, respondents were asked to agree or disagree with the statement: "Each of the laws and procedures applied in the shariah courts is clearly stated in the Qur'an." 78.5 percent of respondents agreed, while only 15.3 percent disagreed (Table 6.1). As examined in Chapter 2, few of the substantive provisions and none of the procedures applied in the shariah courts are found in the Qur'an. The Islamic Family Law Act and parallel state-level enactments merely provide a codified and select representation of a diverse body of *fiqh*. An important consequence of codification is that, for many, Islam is equated with the law, and a legalistic understanding of Islam is elevated above all others. Islamic law is also understood as fixed. Respondents were almost equally divided by the statement "Islamic law changes over time to address new circumstances in society," with only slightly more respondents agreeing (50.5 percent) than disagreeing (48 percent). As previously explained, the idea that Islamic law evolves with new understandings and in new contexts is a core concept in Islamic legal theory. Yet those surveyed were divided in evaluating the statement. The next statement approached the issue in a more direct and strongly worded fashion: "Islam provides a complete set of laws for human conduct, and each of these laws has stayed the same, without being changed by people, since the time of the Prophet (s.a.w.)." An overwhelming 82 percent of respondents agreed with the statement, a remarkable result given that human agency is acknowledged as being central to the development of Islamic law among Muslim jurists.

For both Muslims and non-Muslims, the shariah courts were understood as embodying "shariah law." Malaysians were therefore primed to assume that jurisdictional scuffles are part of a zero-sum struggle for or against the "implementation" of Islamic law. In these circumstances, Islam is pitted against liberal rights, individual rights are pitted against collective rights, and religion against secularism. These binaries elevate the "legal-supremacist" conceptualization of "Islam as law" and they further position Anglo-Muslim law as the full and exclusive embodiment of the

Islamic legal tradition (Ahmed 2016). Indeed, most political discourse is premised upon this stark binary.

Another question on the nationwide survey probed the salience of these binary formations. Respondents were asked to consider the question, "Are the Federal Constitution and the shariah compatible or incompatible with one another?" 45.5 percent responded that they are incompatible, 44.9 percent responded that they are compatible, and 9 percent said they "do not know."[7] Those respondents who viewed the Constitution and the shariah as incompatible were asked the follow-up question, "Should one of these be a final authority above the other?" Here, a remarkable 80.2 percent responded that the "shariah" should be the final authority.[8] These findings hint at the effect of the binary tropes that have circulated in the media for years in Malaysia. These popular understandings pose significant challenges to the perceived legitimacy of the Malaysian legal order. Moreover, because Islam is used as an instrument of public policy, these beliefs carry important implications for a host of substantive issues. Women's rights provide an important example. When the public believes that the shariah courts apply God's law, unmediated by human agency, people who question or debate those laws are easily framed as working to undermine Islam. Indeed, it is the presumed divine nature of the laws applied in the shariah courts that provides the rationale for criminalizing the expression of alternative views in the Shariah Criminal Offenses Act. As a further result, laws concerning marriage, divorce, child custody, and other issues critical to women's well-being are difficult to approach as matters of public policy.

The salience of the rights-versus-rites binary was also evident in many of the open-ended interviews. In the discussion of the Lina Joy case, for example, one respondent explained, "she says that she is exercising her human rights, but here in Malaysia our official religion is Islam." When asked to elaborate, the respondent suggested that Islam and liberalism were incompatible and that the appropriate resolution to the tension would be "to just use shariah law in Malaysia [and get rid of civil law]."[9] Another respondent explained that:

> The shariah court is submissive to the civil court. When anything is deferred to the civil court, the civil court wins, and the shariah court loses. [This shows that] we don't put Islam first; we put the constitution first. If you ask me what the solution is, I have to say it's the shariah court and shariah law because these things [Islamic fundamentals] you can't change. You can amend a constitution. It's passed on your whim and fancy. But the Qur'an you cannot change. If it's "A" today, it's going to be

[7] That an equal proportion found the constitution and the shariah incompatible is in tension with the claim of Islamist lawyers that Malaysia is an Islamic state by virtue of Article 3 of the Federal Constitution itself. Yet, at the same time, rhetoric around the incompatibility between liberal rights and Islamic law is a prominent trope that is emphasized in political posturing and political discourse among Islamists and secularists alike.

[8] 16.5 percent indicated that the Malaysian Constitution should be the final authority, while 3.2 percent answered: "do not know."

[9] Subang Jaya, July 20, 2009.

"A" until the end of the day. But for the constitution, if you have "A" today, and you have two-thirds majority, it can be "B".[10]

Echoing the same binaries that are played out in the media, many of the respondents explained that Islam and liberal rights are locked in opposition. When it comes to the Article 121 (1A) cases, self-identified secularists and Islamists understand themselves as pitted against one another. They are united by the perception that they are locked in a zero-sum struggle between the "implementation" of Islamic law vs. civil law.[11]

Another set of survey questions probed whether Malaysian Muslims conceive of Islamic law as uniform in character, with a single "correct" answer to any given issue or, alternatively, whether the Islamic legal tradition provides a framework through which Muslims can arrive at equally valid yet differing understandings of God's will. One way of approaching this issue was to assess popular understandings of the *fatwa*. As detailed previously, a *fatwa* is a non-binding opinion by a religious jurist. It is widely accepted among Sunni legal scholars that for any given question, jurists are likely to arrive at a variety of views, all of which should be considered equally valid if they follow the accepted methods of one of the four schools of jurisprudence. But do lay Muslims understand *fatwas* in the same way?

To explore this issue further, respondents were asked, "If two religious scholars issue conflicting *fatwas* on the same issue, must one of them be wrong?" The majority (54.2 percent) answered yes, while 39.5 percent answered no. In one sense, this majority response is in harmony with Islamic legal theory; most scholars believe that there is a correct answer to any given question, but that humans can never know God's will with certainty in this lifetime. However, in another survey question, the same respondents were asked: "Is it appropriate in Islam for the '*ulama* to issue differing *fatwas* on the same issue?" On this question, 40.5 percent answered yes while the majority, 54.2 percent, answered no. Taken together, the responses suggest that most respondents believe that there is a single "correct" answer for any given issue *and* that religious scholars can and should arrive at the same answer in the here and now. In other words, most lay Muslims tend to understand Islamic law as constituting a single, unified code rather than a body of equally plausible juristic opinions (See Table 6.2).

The finding that most lay Muslims understand Islamic law as a legal code yielding only one correct answer to any given question is a testament to how the modern state,

---

[10]   Subang Jaya, July 22, 2009.

[11]   A more recent survey commissioned by the Institute for Democracy and Economic Affairs (IDEAS) and executed by the Merdeka Centre for Survey Research sought to measure popular understandings of liberalism. The 2016 survey found that nearly one-third (29 percent) of Muslims believed that liberalism was bad for Malaysia, compared to only 13 percent of non-Muslims (13 percent). IDEAS presented the data as an encouraging indication that two-thirds of Muslims have not bought into the polarized rhetoric around Islam and liberalism. Yet the pronounced difference across Muslim and non-Muslim communities is nonetheless significant. *Malaysiakini*, March 24, 2017.

TABLE 6.2 *Uniformity or plurality of Islamic law in popular legal consciousness*

Question	Yes	No	Do Not Know
If two religious scholars issue conflicting *fatwas* on the same issue, must one of them be wrong?	0.542	0.395	0.062
Is it appropriate in Islam for the *'ulama* to issue differing fatwas on the same issue?	0.405	0.542	0.050

with its codified and uniform body of laws and procedures, has left its imprint on popular legal consciousness. Only about 40 percent of respondents conceive of the possibility that two or more religious opinions can be simultaneously legitimate, a remarkable divergence from core axioms in Islamic legal theory. Whereas Islamic jurisprudence is diverse and fluid, it is understood by most Malaysians as singular and fixed. Implementation of a codified version of Islamic law through the shariah courts is assumed to be a religious duty of the state. And, indeed, it appears that most Malaysians believe that the shariah courts apply God's law directly, unmediated by human agency.

When public policy is legitimized through the framework of Islamic law, this vision of Islamic law as code narrows the scope for debate and deliberation. It is no wonder that women's rights activists have encountered such difficulty in mobilizing broad-based public support for their effort to reform Muslim family law codes. It is also not surprising that they often find themselves on the losing end of debates with conservatives. Women's rights activists, even those operating within the framework of Islamic law, are easily depicted by their opponents as challenging core requirements of Islamic law, or even Islam itself. Conversely, the discursive position of conservative actors is strengthened. Religious officials, political parties, and other groups wishing to preserve the status quo can easily position themselves as defenders of the faith.

This can be seen in other areas as well. Islamic law is used as the pretext for outlawing "deviant" sects, policing public morality (Liow 2009: 128–31), and curtailing freedom of expression (SUARAM 2008, 69–71).[12] In each of these areas, Islamic law is not only cast in a conservative vein; it is also deployed in a manner that shuts down public debate and deliberation. This vision of Islamic law is encouraged by the government, the growing religious bureaucracy, the Islamic Party of Malaysia (*Parti Islam se-Malaysia*, or PAS), and Islamist organizations such as ABIM (Liow 2009; Mohamad 2010). Such rhetorical positioning is regularly deployed in public policy debates because speaking in God's name proves to be the most effective and expedient avenue for a variety of state and non-state actors to undercut their opponents.

---

[12] By 2008, the Malaysian government had outlawed fifty-six "deviant" sects, including the Shia.

OVERCOMING BINARIES: THE WORK OF SISTERS IN ISLAM

The data presented in this chapter confirms what women's rights activists have long known: the state's selective codification of Islamic law is understood by many as the faithful implementation of divine law. Because of this conflation, rights activists cannot easily question or debate family law provisions without being accused of working to undermine Islam. The Malaysian women's rights organization Sisters in Islam identifies this rights-versus-rites binary as a formidable obstacle. Sisters in Islam co-founder Zainah Anwar explains, "Very often Muslim women who demand justice and want to change discriminatory law and practices are told 'this is God's law' and therefore not open to negotiation and change" (2008b, 1). These informal obstacles underline the critical importance of "legal consciousness."

Sisters in Islam has a unique approach to overcoming the rights-versus-rites binary in popular legal consciousness.[13] Instead of pursuing a strictly secular mode of political activism, it engages with liberal rights constructs *and* the Islamic legal tradition simultaneously with apologies to no one. Sisters in Islam insists that there is no contradiction whatsoever in being a committed Muslim and a committed liberal because core values of justice and equality are inherent to Islam. It takes aim at the laws governing marriage, divorce, and other aspects of Muslim family law that have been codified in a manner that provides women with fewer rights than men. Along with a rising number of Muslim feminists, it insists that the Islamic legal tradition is *not* inherently incompatible with contemporary notions of liberal rights. It explains that existing inequities are reflective of the biases and shortcomings of human agency, not core values of Islam. Instead of working to abolish religion in the public sphere, Sisters in Islam works to recover the core spirit of justice and equality in Islam. It explains that the Islamic legal tradition is not a uniform legal code but is instead a diverse and open-ended body of jurisprudence that affords multiple guidelines for human relations, some of which are better suited to contemporary circumstances.

This is a new mode of political engagement. While women's rights initiatives were advanced through secular frameworks through most of the twentieth century, efforts to effect change in family law from within the framework of Islamic law have gained increasing traction in recent years. To varying degrees, women have pushed for family law reform within the framework of the Islamic legal tradition in Egypt (Singerman 2005; Zulficar 2008), Iran (Mir-Hosseini 2008), Malaysia (Azza Basarudin 2016; Nik Noriani Nik Badlishah 2003, 2008; Norani Othman 2005), Morocco (Salime 2011), and many other Muslim-majority countries. This opens a new terrain for debate and dialogue. In some cases, this strategy yields concrete, progressive legal reforms. Among all the women's groups operating in this mode of

---

[13]   More recently, Sisters in Islam has been joined by like-minded NGOs, such as the Islamic Renaissance Front.

engagement, Sisters in Islam has been a pioneer in these endeavors since its establishment in 1987.

As a central part of its message, Sisters in Islam invokes the core conceptual distinction between the *shariah* (God's way) and *fiqh* (human understanding). As examined in Chapter 2, Islamic legal theory regards the *shariah* as immutable, whereas *fiqh* is the diverse body of legal opinions that are the product of human reasoning and engagement with the foundational sources of authority in Islam, the Qur'an, and the Sunnah. In this dichotomy, God is infallible, while humankind's attempt to understand God's way is imperfect and fallible. Islamic legal theory holds that humans should strive to understand God's way, but that human faculties can never deliver certain answers; people can only reach reasoned deductions about what God's will might be. To be sure, jurists in the classical era did not use the specific terms "*shariah*" and "*fiqh*," but they recognized these conceptual distinctions nonetheless.

The conceptual distinction between God's perfection and human fallibility is of critical importance because it serves as the basis for a normative commitment within Islamic legal theory toward respect for diversity of opinion as well as temporal flexibility in jurisprudence. Since the vast corpus of Islamic jurisprudence is the product of human agency, scholars of Islamic law recognize Islamic jurisprudence as open to debate and reason and subject to change as new understandings win out over old. By invoking the *shariah/fiqh* distinction and the open-ended jurisprudential tradition within Islam, Sisters in Islam engages conservatives on their own discursive terrain. The common rebuke that women's rights activism challenges "God's law" is met with the powerful rejoinder that Islam simply does not have a single position on most issues.

To overcome the rights-versus-rites binary in popular legal consciousness, Sisters in Islam conducts a variety of public education programs with the central purpose of highlighting the distinction between *shariah* and *fiqh*. This entails a number of interrelated strategies, all of which are meant to disrupt and critique the state monopoly on religious knowledge production, spur new knowledge production, and provide alternatives that empower women while nonetheless remaining faithful to the Islamic legal tradition. These strategies include the commissioning of detailed studies of various issues pertaining to women's rights in the Islamic legal tradition (e.g., polygamy, domestic violence, marriage, and divorce); producing and distributing question and answer booklets concerning various aspects of gender in Islam; documenting the "lived realities" of Muslim family law on Malaysian women; drawing attention to more progressive formulations of Muslim family law in other Muslim-majority countries; penning regular columns and op-eds in major newspapers; organizing reading groups and study sessions; running a telephone hotline for women in need of legal assistance; and, increasingly, engaging with the issues of the day in real time via digital and social media. Sisters in Islam also organizes intensive, multi-day training sessions for journalists, lawyers, human rights activists, women's groups, and even government officials and members of parliament. Each of these workshops provides a crash course on the fundamentals of *usul al-fiqh*, on Muslim family law and shariah court administration in Malaysia, and the possibilities for progressive legal change within the framework of Islamic law. By training journalists, lawyers, human rights activists, and government officials, Sisters in Islam is able to "scale up" its message through key actors, some of whom might otherwise reinforce the rights-versus-rites binary in their work.

Sisters in Islam runs an impressive operation with modest resources, yet it faces formidable obstacles. As examined in Chapter 2, the Malaysian state has significant legal and administrative infrastructure that is designed to monopolize religious knowledge production. The Administration of Islamic Law Act and parallel state-level enactments establish a monopoly on the administration of mosques, including the licensing, appointment, and disciplining of imams. Federal and state agencies also dictate the content of Friday *khutbah*. The reach of the state extends to other areas as well, including religious content in public education (Azmil Tayeb 2018), state television and radio, quasi-independent institutions such as IKIM (Institute for Islamic Understanding), the *shariah* court administration, and state and federal fatwa councils. Between these various institutions, the government controls formidable resources for shaping popular understandings of Islam as fixed, singular, state-centric, and unmediated by human agency.

Sisters in Islam must also contend with legal challenges. The group might have been banned long ago were it not for its tenacity and the elite-level connections of a few of its members.[14] Most of the activities of Sisters in Islam are illegal by a straightforward reading of the Shariah Criminal Offenses Act and parallel state-level enactments. There have been periodic calls from conservative NGOs for the government to close Sisters in Islam. A lawsuit was initiated to bar it from using "Islam" in its title.[15] More concretely, one of its books was banned for several years until Sisters in Islam prevailed in litigation to lift the ban.[16] A still-unfolding case involves a *fatwa* issued by the Selangor Fatwa Committee that condemns Sisters in Islam for subscribing to "religious liberalism and pluralism." The *fatwa* calls on the Malaysian Communications and Multimedia Commissions to ban and seize any

---

[14] Among other elite connections, Marina Mahathir (the daughter of the former Prime Minister, Mahathir Mohamad) is a core member of Sisters in Islam.

[15] For example, the youth wing of PAS (Federal Territories and Selangor) called for the banning of SIS in 2005. Interestingly, the PAS women's wing issued public statements opposing the call. See *Malaysiakini*, "Haramkan Sisters in Islam, kata Pemuda PAS WP," April 15, 2005; *Malaysiakini*, "PAS Women against Youth Call to Ban SIS," April 20, 2005. *Dewan Pemuda Masjid Malaysia's* (Masjid Youth of Malaysia) filed suit on March 22, 2010, to prevent SIS from using the name "Sisters in Islam." See *Dewan Pemuda Masjid Malaysia v. SIS Forum.* [2011] MLJU 518.

[16] The ban on Norani Othman's book, *Muslim Women and the Challenge of Islamic Extremism*, was overturned in court. I had the honor of attending these hearings. Ironically, although the book had been banned for several years, I managed to find a copy of it in the library of the conservative think tank IKIM. For the court decision, see *SIS Forum v. Dato' Seri Syed Hamid Bin Syed Jaafar Albar (Menteri Dalam Negeri)*.

publication that might be considered "liberal and plural" because of the threat it poses to Islam. Sisters in Islam contested the *fatwa* in High Court, but Justice Datuk Hanipah Farikullah dismissed the claim under the premise that the shariah courts have exclusive jurisdiction over the matter, as per Article 121 (1A). Sisters in Islam appealed the decision with a positive result. The Court of Appeal ordered another High Court judge to consider the merits of the case. To date, the issue has not reached a conclusion.

Sisters in Islam was not the only organization that was exploring new ways to engage ordinary Malaysians. Many of the activists who were at the forefront of litigation efforts readily acknowledged the limitations of depending exclusively on the courts to secure liberal rights. One of the most prominent attorneys litigating religious freedom cases over the last fifteen years, K. Shanmuga reflected on the frustrations that an exclusive reliance on litigation entailed.

> The group of us who started the Centre are all primarily litigation lawyers, who slowly became disenchanted with the litigation process as a means of achieving real social change. This was a result of the bitter experiences in the majority of our public interest cases. Government lawyers came with technical and petty objections on procedure, which were upheld by judges reluctant to deal with the real subject matter of the controversy. International human rights protections were not respected and extensive arguments on them were summarily dismissed as being irrelevant and not binding in Malaysia. It was clear to us, then, that taking matters to court would never really solve real problems. (Kanesalingam 2013)

Haris Ibrahim, another prominent lawyer who had litigated many of the religious freedom cases, abandoned the law altogether and founded *Saya Anak Bangsa Malaysia* (SABM) in 2009.[17] Frustrated with the lack of headway in the courts, Haris sought to build a grassroots movement for social and political change. SABM was initiated with considerable fanfare, which included a nationwide "roadshow" (reminiscent of the Article 11 roadshow before it) with stops in Perak, Sabah, Sarawak, Terengganu, Kelantan, Pahang, Malacca, Kedah, and Penang.

Likewise, the Malaysian Bar Council launched a "MyConstitution Campaign" ("Kempen PerlembagaanKu") in the same year as SABM. The campaign was billed as an effort to "educate and empower the *rakyat* and to create greater awareness about the Federal Constitution."[18] The Bar Council developed a series of pocket-sized guides in easy-to-read language (with cartoon graphics and all) explaining the fundamental rights of citizenship guaranteed by the Constitution. The campaign focused on direct engagement with youth (particularly at schools and universities) and it heavily engaged with social media. Edmond Bon, one of the driving forces behind the MyConstitution Campaign, also founded the Malaysian Centre for

---

[17]   *Saya Anak Bangsa Malaysia* roughly translates to "My race is Malaysian" or "I am Malaysian." More
       on https://harismibrahim.wordpress.com/
[18]   Malaysian Bar Council, Circular 292/2009.

Constitutionalism and Human Rights (MCCHR) with Long Seh Lih in 2012. Like the MyConstitution Campaign, the MCCHR focused its energy on the next generation of legal activists. It opened a resource center and organized workshops, conferences, and training sessions on strategic litigation in the service of liberal rights advocacy.

A related initiative, the LoyarBurok blog, was founded by six young lawyers, including Edmond Bon, Long Seh Lih, and two lawyers who worked extensively on freedom of religion cases, K. Shanmuga and Fahri Azzat.[19] "LoyarBurok" literally means "bad lawyer" and is slang in Malaysia for a person who is full of hot air. The humor in the title captures the irreverent tone that characterizes the outlet. Yet the purpose is anything but frivolous. LoyarBurok is meant to generate informed debate at the intersection of law and politics. More fundamentally, LoyarBurok aims to inspire legal mobilization in the service of social and political change. The blog serves as a repository of court decisions, case notes from key legal battles, analysis of select judgments, and perspectives on the latest round of public interest litigation.

All of these organizations, in their own way, are working to elevate and galvanize popular legal consciousness. If there is any hopeful note to be found, it is the fact that a variety of organizations, working through both secular and religious discourses, have joined together for progressive change. This is particularly manifest in the work of the Joint Action Group for Gender Equality (JAG), a coalition of seven women's rights groups, including Sisters in Islam, that has worked together since 1985.

---

[19] LoyarBurok served as the progenitor of the MCCHR. The alternate name of the MCCHR is, in fact, *Pusat Rakyat LoyarBurok* (the LoyarBurok People's Centre). For more on the genesis of LoyarBurok, see Kanesalingam (2013).

7

"Islam is the Religion of the Federation"

Over half of all Muslim-majority countries have constitutional clauses that proclaim Islam the religion of state. For Malaysia, it is Article 3. Clause 1 of Article 3 declares, "Islam is the religion of the Federation ... "[1] For decades, the clause received little attention. The federal judiciary understood the clause to carry ceremonial and symbolic meaning only. However, recent years have seen increasing litigation around the meaning and intent of the clause. Recent federal court decisions introduce a far more robust meaning, which practically elevates Islamic law as the new *grundnorm* in the Malaysian legal system. Jurisprudence on the matter is still unfolding, but what is clear – and what has been clear for quite some time – is that two legal camps hold radically divergent visions of the appropriate place for Islamic law and liberal rights in the legal and political order. This chapter builds on the legal and political context of the preceding chapters to make sense of the increasing contestation over Article 3, as well as the federal judiciary's shifting jurisprudence on the matter. I argue that the Article 121 (1A) cases provided a unique opportunity for Islamist lawyers to push for sweeping new interpretations of Article 3, which have gained surprising traction in the civil courts.

LITIGATING ARTICLE 3 IN CHE OMAR BIN CHE SOH

Che Omar bin Che Soh v. Public Prosecutor was the first case in which the Supreme Court (as it was called at the time) considered the meaning of Article 3.[2] The occasion for the landmark 1988 decision was a constitutional challenge to the mandatory death penalty for the trafficking of drugs. The appellant claimed that the provision did not conform to Islamic jurisprudence and was therefore unconstitutional by virtue of Article 3 (1) of the Federal Constitution.[3] The Supreme Court

---

[1] The full clause reads, "Islam is the religion of the Federation; but other religions may be practised in peace and harmony in any part of the Federation."
[2] *Che Omar bin Che Soh v. Public Prosecutor* [1988] 2 MLJ 55.
[3] The specific arguments turned around whether the Fire Arms (Increased Penalties) Act conformed to Islamic jurisprudence on matters *qisas* and *huddud* punishments. Ironically, the attorneys for the

decision in *Che Omar bin Che Soh v. Public Prosecutor* denied the appeal, affirmed the "secular" nature of the Malaysian state, and restricted the meaning of Article 3 (1) to matters of ritual and ceremony. However, the decision simultaneously validated a narrative that is increasingly championed by Islamist attorneys and judges. Given the importance of *Che Omar bin Che Soh v. Public Prosecutor*, it is worth examining the text and the reasoning of the decision in some detail.

In considering the meaning of Article 3 (1), the Lord President of the Supreme Court, Salleh Abas, articulated the significance of the constitutional challenge as follows:

> If the religion of Islam ... means only such acts as relate to rituals and ceremonies, the argument has no basis whatsoever. On the other hand, if the religion of Islam or Islam itself is an all-embracing concept, as is normally understood, which consists not only the ritualistic aspect but also a comprehensive system of life, including its jurisprudence and moral standard, then the submission has a great implication in that every law has to be tested according to this yard-stick.[4]

With this framing of the case, the stakes were monumental. Either Article 3 would be considered purely symbolic, with no legal effect, or it would carry the implication that *every* law on the books should be similarly "tested" against Islam and Islamic law. Before indicating which of these two positions had legal merit, Salleh Abas avowed the all-embracing reach of Islam and the importance of Islamic law, regardless of what state law might say on the matter. Here, the Lord President references the writings of the Islamist thinker *par excellence*, Syed Abul A'la Maududi:

> There can be no doubt that Islam is not just a mere collection of dogmas and rituals but it is a complete way of life covering all fields of human activities, may they be private or public, legal, political, economic, social, cultural, moral or judicial. This way of ordering the life with all the precepts and the last of such guidance is the Quran and the last messenger is Mohammad S.A.W. whose conduct and utterances are revered. (See S. Abdul A'la Maududi, *The Islamic Law and Constitution*, 7th Ed., March 1980.)[5]

With Islam defined as "a complete way of life, covering all fields of human activities," the Lord President Salleh Abas turned to the question of what the framers of the Federal Constitution meant by Article 3:

> Was this the meaning intended by the framers of the Constitution? For this purpose, it is necessary to trace the history of Islam in this country after the British intervention in the affairs of the Malay States at the close of the last century.

---

appellant were not Muslim, but they were very much interested in Islamic law insofar as it might save their client's skin.

[4] *Che Omar bin Che Soh v. Public Prosecutor* [1988] 2 MLJ at 55–56

[5] *Che Omar bin Che Soh v. Public Prosecutor* [1988] 2 MLJ at 56.

Before the British came to Malaya, which was then known as Tanah Melayu, the sultans in each of their respective states were the heads not only of the religion of Islam but also as the political leaders in their states, which were Islamic in the true sense of the word, because, not only were they themselves Muslims, their subjects were also Muslims and the law applicable in the states was Muslim law . . . .When the British came, however, through a series of treaties with the sultans beginning with the Treaty of Pangkor and through the so-called British advice, the religion of Islam became separated into two separate aspects, *viz.* the public aspect and the private aspect. The development of the public aspect of Islam had left the religion as a mere adjunct to the ruler's power and sovereignty. The ruler ceased to be regarded as God's vicegerent on earth but regarded as a sovereign within his territory. The concept of sovereignty ascribed to humans is alien to Islamic religion because in Islam, sovereignty belongs to God alone. By ascribing sovereignty to the ruler, *i.e.* to a human, the divine source of legal validity is severed and thus the British turned the system into a secular institution. . . . Thus, it can be seen that during the British colonial period, through their system of indirect rule and establishment of secular institutions, Islamic law was rendered isolated in a narrow confinement of the law of marriage, divorce, and inheritance only . . .[6]

Whether the Lord President was aware or not, this stylized narrative legitimized the Islamist claim that the pre-colonial Malay Peninsula was "Islamic in the true sense of the word." The Court decision not only advanced the Islamist talking point that sovereignty belonged "to God alone" in the pre-colonial era, but also the implication that this historical schism can be corrected. The decision does not elaborate on how God's sovereignty was actualized in the pre-colonial era, nor does the decision provide clues as to how God's sovereignty might be restored so that Malaysia can once again be "Islamic in the true sense of the word." After affirming this narrative, the Lord President only explains that, as a strictly legal matter, Article 3 must be read narrowly:

In our view, it is in this sense of dichotomy that the framers of the Constitution understood the meaning of the word "Islam" in the context of Article 3. If it had been otherwise, there would have been another provision in the Constitution which would have the effect that any law contrary to the injunction of Islam will be void . . . .

As the reader will recall from Chapter 3, important context is missing from this historical account, particularly concerning the intent of the framers of the Constitution. Missing is the irony that the most determined resistance to Article 3 came from those who were meant to be the guardians of Islam – the Sultans. Also missing is the story of how Justice Abdul Hamid came to play a pivotal role on the Reid Commission at the eleventh hour (Stilt 2015). Perhaps most crucial is the fact that the Alliance had agreed to the text of Article 3 only on the condition that, "the

---

[6] *Che Omar bin Che Soh v. Public Prosecutor* [1988] 2 MLJ at 56.

observance of this principle ... shall not imply that the State is not a secular State" (Fernando 2006: 253).[7] Nonetheless, the Supreme Court decision constructed an account in which Malaysia was subject to a legal straitjacket imposed by the British and that Malaysian judges, even if they wished to correct this historical injustice, were duty-bound to apply secular law. In the closing text of the decision, Salleh Abas explains that:

> We have to set aside our personal feelings because the law in this country is still what it is today, secular law, where morality not accepted by the law is not enjoying the status of law. Perhaps that argument should be addressed at other forums or at seminars and, perhaps, to politicians and Parliament. Until the law and the system is changed, we have no choice but to proceed as we are doing today.[8]

The seminars and other activities that Salleh Abas suggested in *Che Omar bin Che Soh* were, in fact, organized through the 1980s and 1990s. A series of workshops and conferences focused primarily on the administration of Muslim law and the formalization of the shariah judiciary. Within these forums and elsewhere, a few Islamist thinkers explored the possibilities for expanding the meaning and ambit of Article 3 beyond the constraints articulated by Lord President Salleh Abas in his 1988 landmark decision. One of the most influential thought-pieces, already cited in this book, is a law review article by Mohammad Imam (1994) that provides extensive argumentation for why Article 3 (1) must be understood to carry the broad meaning denied in *Che Omar bin Che Soh*.

ARTICLE 121 (1A) AS A SPRINGBOARD TO ARTICLE 3 LITIGATION

A few lawyers began to make these arguments in court. There, they found a receptive audience among a few civil court judges. One of the earliest such decisions was the 2001 High Court ruling in *Lina Joy v. Majlis Agama Islam* (Chapter 4). In that case, Haji Sulaiman Abdullah represented the Islamic Religious Council of the Federal Territories. In oral arguments, he submitted to the court that "There is nothing which is outside the scope of Islamic law and adat because Islam ... is a complete way of life and ... controls all aspects of our life" (Dawson and Thinu 2007: 154). Justice Faiza Tamby Chik concurred, connecting these broad claims to Article 3 and the implications that this meaning holds for all facets of social and political life. Specifically citing the scholarship of Mohammad Imam and others, Justice Faiza advanced a "purposive interpretation" to Article 3 (1).[9] He averred that " ... the position of Islam in art 3(1) is that Islam is the main and dominant religion in the Federation. Being the main and dominant religion, the Federation has a duty to

---

7 As explained in Chapter 3, this was the text of the Alliance joint memorandum to the Reid Commission requesting that "The religion of Malaysia shall be Islam."

8 *Che Omar bin Che Soh v. Public Prosecutor* [1988] 2 MLJ 56-57.

9 *Lina Joy v. Majlis Agama Islam Wilayah Persekutuan & Anor* [2004] 2 MLJ at 128.

protect, defend and promote the religion of Islam."[10] Justice Faiza took another page out of Mohammad Imam's playbook with his focus on Article 11 (3) of the Federal Constitution, which states that "Every religious group has the right . . . to manage its own religious affairs . . . ."[11] Justice Faiza argued that Article 11 (3) supports the view that Article 121 (1A) provides for the absolute supremacy of the shariah courts in any matter related to Islam, even in cases when individual rights are curtailed as a result. For Justice Faiza, the right of religious communities (as provided in Article 11 (3)), must supercede an individual's rights (as provided in Article 11 (1)) anytime it comes to Islam. Indeed, what emerges in Justice Faiza's decision is a series of interlocking interpretations of select articles that collectively elevate the supremacy of Islam in the Federal Constitution.

Justice Faiza's 2001 decision in *Lina Joy* was an outlier at the time, but similar interpretations of Article 3 would find their way to the apex Federal Court as the decade progressed. The Federal Court's Article 3 jurisprudence is largely the fruit of the concerted efforts of a small number of Islamist lawyers enabled by Article 121 (1A) and the spectacle that surrounded those cases. Article 121 (1A) provided a unique opportunity for Islamists to advance an expansive interpretation of Article 3 and a new vision for the role of Islam in the legal and political order. Once Article 121 (1A) litigation reached the court of public opinion, the polarized political environment that followed (Chapter 5) made it increasingly uncomfortable for judges who did not share the revisionist view of Article 3 (1). Given the centrality of Article 121 (1A) to Article 3 jurisprudence, a refresher on Article 121 (1A) may be useful.

As the reader will recall from Chapter 3, the Mahathir administration introduced Article 121 (1A) as a constitutional amendment in 1988. On its face, the amendment sought to clarify matters of jurisdiction between the civil courts and the shariah courts. The clause states that the High Courts "shall have no jurisdiction in respect of any matter within the jurisdiction of the Syariah courts." However, rather than clarify matters of jurisdiction, Article 121 (1A) exacerbated legal ambiguities and produced new legal tensions. Cases concerning the religious status of the dead, religious freedom for the living, and battles over child custody/conversion marked a fault line down the middle of the Malaysian judiciary. As I argued in Chapter 4, these legal dilemmas were a product of tightening state regulations on religion, the formalization of the shariah judicial system, and the introduction of Article 121 (1A). As the legal system was made increasingly rigid, boundary maintenance between the federal civil courts and the state shariah courts was judicialized. The fact that one jurisdiction was meant to implement "Islamic law" and the other "secular law" made this jurisdictional fault line ripe for ideological polarization.

To be sure, there were a variety of motives among those who raised Article 121 (1A) objections to civil court jurisdiction. For some litigants, Article 121 (1A) provided a means to achieve strategic advantage in domestic squabbles, as in custody/

---

[10] Ibid, 130.   [11] Ibid, 126.

conversion cases where conversion to Islam (or the threat thereof) provided leverage in divorce settlements.[12] In other circumstances, such as the freedom of religion and "body-snatching" cases, it is the religious bureaucracy and state lawyers that invoke Article 121 (1A) to affirm their role as gatekeepers for the religious community. For others, Article 121 (1A) provides an instrument to expand the ambit of the shariah courts and the position of Islam in the constitutional order. It is this last set of actors – those with an ideological agenda – to which we now turn.

For a handful of activist lawyers, Article 121 (1A) is part of a long-term strategy motivated by specific ideological commitments to build an "Islamic" legal order. These lawyers seized upon ambiguities in the law to advance a program of "Islamization" through the courts.[13] They invoked Article 121 (1A) at every opportunity to challenge civil court jurisdiction and to expand the ambit of the shariah courts.[14] A lead attorney in many of the Article 121 (1A) cases, Haniff Khatri Abdulla, was frank about this strategy as a means to expand the purview of the shariah courts and the place of Islam in the legal system more generally.[15] The "body snatching" cases, the religious conversion cases, and the child custody/conversion provided the most openings for strategic litigation.[16] Equally important, once the cases were politically salient, they provided opportunities for activists outside of the court to shape popular legal consciousness. As previously noted, 2004 was the watershed year

---

[12] In all the reported cases, the husbands contended that their conversions were sincere. However, anecdotal evidence suggests that wives are sometimes threatened by their husbands that if they do not agree to a divorce, or certain terms of divorce, they will lose control of their children by way of their unilateral conversion.

[13] Liberals contend that Islamist lawyers and some civil court judges *produced* ambiguities around the plain meaning of Article 121 (1A).

[14] Islamist lawyers explain that were it not for Schedule 9 of the Federal Constitution (which provides the states with authority to administer Anglo-Muslim law) Article 121 (1A) would be *the* main vehicle for "Islamizing" civil law. This is because, in their vision, Islamic law provides the basis for every aspect of state law, with the only exception being family law for non-Muslims.

[15] For a detailed presentation of this legal agenda, see Khatri et al. (2009). Haniff Khatri has been frank in private and public settings. He presented similar views publicly at the "Strategic Litigation Conference," October 3, 2015, organized by the MCCHR and the Malaysian Bar Council. I also had the opportunity to discuss these with Haniff Khatri and Abdul Rahim Sinwan in 2009, 2010, and 2014.

[16] There were a few other types of Article 121 (1A) cases. For instance, *Latifah bte Mat Zin* brought Article 121 (1A) into play in the context of dividing an estate following the death of an individual. A year later, the Federal Court decided *Abdul Kahar bin Ahmad v. Kerajaan Negeri Selangor*. In that case, Abdul Kahar was charged in the Syariah High Court of Selangor with expounding a doctrine contrary to Islamic law under the Shariah Criminal Offenses Enactment of Selangor. He was also charged for claiming himself to be a prophet, defiling the religion of Islam, defying the lawful orders of the Mufti, and disseminating opinions contrary to Islamic law. Abdul Kahar skipped out on the shariah court hearing and instead challenged the constitutionality of the state enactments in the civil courts. An Article 121 (1A) objection was raised to challenge civil court jurisdiction, and Islamist lawyers argued further that the shariah court should have some role in determining whether shariah court provisions are in harmony with the Federal Constitution. The Federal Court refused this logic but did not strike down the legislation in question. Abdul Kahar was sentenced to ten years in jail, RM 16,500 in fines, and six strokes of the rotan. He was released after seven years in prison after repenting.

when the Article 121 (1A) cases became politically salient. Beginning with the first *Malaysiakini* story on *Shamala v. Jeyaganesh*, Article 121 (1A) cases were covered more intensively than any other issue. This coverage broadened the audience for the 121 (1A) cases. This audience expansion is directly attributable to the efforts of liberal rights groups to bring the cases to the public's attention, and to the media's persistent scrutiny. Thirteen liberal rights groups formed a working coalition in the wake of the *Shamala v. Jeyaganesh* decision. This was subsequently surpassed by a coalition of over fifty conservative organizations mobilizing in the opposite direction. Together, this spectacle turned up the political heat for civil court judges.

Polarization also provided an opportunity for Islamist activists to introduce and amplify what I call the "harmonization trope." Although the term harmonization connotes an amicable reckoning, the clear objective in operational terms has been the "Islamization" of the Malaysian legal system beyond the ambit of the shariah court judiciary. Beginning in 2003, the Ahmad Ibrahim School of Law at the International Islamic University of Malaysia (IIUM) began to organize biennial conferences on the "Harmonization of Civil Law and Shariah." By 2005, the conference gained further endorsement when Justice Abdul Hamid Mohamad (soon to be Chief Justice of the Federal Court) officiated the function. The 2007 conference was organized jointly by the IIUM and the Attorney General's Chambers, with the further participation of the Department of Syariah Judiciary, Malaysia (JKSM). So close was the "harmonization" project to the corridors of power, the Headquarters of the Attorney General's Chambers provided the physical venue for the 2007 event. The 2007 conference ended with several resolutions, all of which articulated the need to amend "laws that are not Shari'ah compliant."[17] The fact that the Attorney General's Chambers posted the document on its official website spoke volumes as to the inroads that Islamist lawyers had made into the central functions of the federal government. Indeed, one need only examine the reports of the Advisory Division of the Attorney General's Chambers to see that the Shariah Section of the Attorney General's Chambers has an active agenda in sponsoring research on harmonization, which includes ongoing consultative meetings with prominent Islamist civil society organizations.[18] Such access to state authority is over and above the concerted efforts of the Attorney General's Chambers to litigate Article 121 (1A) cases in the same manner as freelance Islamist lawyers. This documentary evidence matched my observations in meetings with Nasir Bin Disa, then the head of the Shariah Section of the Advisory Division of the Attorney Generals Chambers, as well as other highly placed judges such as former Chief Justice Abdul Hamid Mohamad. Given these ideological strains within the Malaysian legal community and the

---

[17]   The resolutions are detailed in the document *"Projek Harmonisasi Antara Undang-Undang Syariah Dan Undang-Undang Sivil"* (On file with the author).

[18]   See the 2005–2006 report of the Advisory Division of the Attorney General's Chambers (on file with author).

polarized discourse more broadly, it is not surprising that revisionist readings of Article 3 appear to be gaining traction.

More recently, the civil courts have ceded jurisdiction in areas outside the domain of personal status law. A good example of this concerns the authority of the Shariah Advisory Council of the Central Bank of Malaysia vis-à-vis the civil courts. The Shariah Advisory Council was established in 2009 to issue binding rulings concerning "Islamic" finance. Commercial law had always been under the jurisdiction of the civil court administration, as per Schedule Nine of the Federal Constitution. However, with the rapid growth of Islamic finance, Islamist activists targeted this lucrative field of economic activity as "their own." *Mohd Alias Ibrahim v. RHB Bank Bhd & Anor* affirmed that decisions of the new Shariah Advisory Council are binding on the civil courts.[19] Islamist lawyers have also pushed an expansionist reading of Article 3 (1) to shift the *Grundnorm* of civil court jurisprudence. An important case in this regard concerns the seizure of books from an international book retailer.

The Borders Bookstore Case

On May 23, 2012, religious authorities raided and seized books from a Borders bookstore in Kuala Lumpur. ZI Publications had translated the book *Allah, Liberty and Love* by Canadian author Irshad Manji. Enforcement officers from the Federal Territories Islamic Religious Affairs Department (JAWI) raided the store with reporters in tow, seized copies of the book, and eventually charged the bookstore manager, a Muslim, under Article 13 of the Shariah Criminal Offenses Act. One week later, the Enforcement Division of the Selangor Department of Islamic Affairs raided the office of ZI Publications and seized additional copies of the book. Later, the owner of the publishing company, Ezra Zaid (son of Zaid Ibrahim), was charged under Article 16 of the Shariah Criminal Offences Enactment (Selangor), which states:

> Any person who —
>   (a) prints, publishes, produces, records or disseminates in any manner any book or document or any other form of record containing anything which is contrary to Islamic law; or
>   (b) has in his possession any such book, document or other form of record for sale or for the purpose of otherwise disseminating it, shall be guilty of an offence and shall be liable on conviction to a fine not exceeding three thousand ringgit or to imprisonment for a term not exceeding two years or to both.
>   (2) The Court may order any book, document or other form of record referred to in subsection (1) to be forfeited and destroyed notwithstanding that no person may have been convicted of an offence in connection with such book, document or other form of record.

[19] *Mohd Alias Ibrahim v. RHB Bank Bhd & Anor* [2011] 4 CLJ 654.

The first set of charges against Borders bookstore and the bookstore manager were contested in the Kuala Lumpur High Court. The High Court decided to exercise jurisdiction despite the Article 121 (1A) objections raised by JAWI.[20] In considering the case, the Court found that Borders could not be punished because it is a corporate entity (and hence "non-Muslim") and that it would be unjust to punish the Muslim bookstore manager because she worked under the direction of a non-Muslim supervisor. JAWI appealed the decision, but the Court of Appeal affirmed the High Court's reasoning in stronger wording yet.[21]

Meanwhile, Ezra Zaid sought a declaration that Article 16 of the Shariah Criminal Offences Enactment was invalid in ZI *Publications Sdn Bhd & Anor v. Kerajaan Negeri Selangor*.[22] Ezra's attorneys argued that the Selangor State Legislative Assembly did not have the power to legislate restrictions on freedom of expression. The Federal Court dismissed the request and explained that:

> . . . a Muslim in Malaysia is not only subjected [sic] to the general laws enacted by Parliament but also to the state laws of religious nature enacted by [the] Legislature of a state to legislate and enact offenses against the precepts of Islam. Taking the Federal Constitution as a whole, it is clear that it was the intention of the framers of our Constitution to allow Muslims in this country to be also governed by Islamic personal law. Thus, a Muslim in this country is therefore subjected to both the general laws enacted by Parliament and also the state laws enacted by the Legislature of a state. For the above reasons, we hold that the impugned section as enacted by the SSLA is valid and not ultra vires the Federal Constitution.[23]

The Federal Court decision underlined the reality that, despite the many financial advantages of being an ethnic Malay, Muslims enjoy fewer rights and freedoms compared with their non-Muslim counterparts. The decision also underscored an important class dimension to the enforcement of most shariah criminal offenses. Most of the punitive measures meted out by the shariah courts disproportionately affect those of more modest economic means. Moreover, they do so with far greater frequency.[24] The ZI Publications case was exceptional in that it drew the attention of the Malaysian elite to the chilling effect of shariah criminal offenses on freedom of expression.

The court's reasoning carried significant implications for the future of case law. Most important, the judges drew upon Article 3 to support the curtailment of fundamental rights. The Federal Court decision states, " . . . we are of the view that art 10 of the Federal Constitution must be read in particular with Arts 3 (1), 11, 74 (2) and 121. Article 3(1) declares Islam as the religion of the Federation

[20]   *Berjaya Books Sdn Bhd & Ors v. Jabatan Agama Islam Wilayah Persekutuan & Ors* [2013] MLJU 758.
[21]   *Jabatan Agama Islam Wilayah Persekutuan & Ors v. Berjaya Books Sdn Bhd & Ors* [2015] 3 MLJ 65.
[22]   *ZI Publications Sdn Bhd & Anor v. Kerajaan Negeri Selangor* [2016] 1 MLJ 153.
[23]   *ZI Publications Sdn Bhd & Anor v. Kerajaan Negeri Selangor* [2016] 1 MLJ at 164.
[24]   One of many examples that can be offered here are the periodic and highly publicized raids on lower-end hotels to combat *khalwat* ("close proximity") infractions.

. . . ."[25] The Federal Court goes on to explain that it is not only the shariah courts that are charged with administering Islamic law in Malaysia. The civil courts also have a role to play because the Federal Constitution must be read "harmoniously." With this reasoning, Article 3 takes a different legal meaning, one that is no longer tied to "rituals and ceremonies," which had been established by the Supreme Court in *Che Omar bin Che Soh v. Public Prosecutor*. Rather, Article 3 assumes an expansive meaning that provides a rationale for curtailing fundamental rights. In this upside-down world, fundamental rights provisions must bend to accommodate a new, expansive meaning for Article 3. Moreover, Islam is assumed to be in fundamental tension with liberal rights, although the Court provides no clear explanation as to why this must be the case.

The Catholic Herald *("Allah") Case*

The ZI Publications case is not the only decision where the meaning of Article 3 shifted. This change is also apparent in litigation over use of the word "Allah" in the Malaysian Catholic newspaper, the *Herald*. In this case, the publisher of the *Herald*, the Titular Roman Catholic Archbishop of Kuala Lumpur, received a letter from the Minister of Home Affairs forbidding them from using the word "Allah" in the Bahasa Malaysia version of its publication. The Minister of Home Affairs claimed that the use of the word violated the prohibition on proselytization to Muslims and, therefore, it posed a threat to public order. The Titular Roman Catholic Archbishop decided to fight in the High Court, drawing attention to the passage in Article 3 (1) that states " . . . religions other than Islam may be practiced in peace and harmony in any part of the Federation." Attorneys for the Church insisted that Catholics had long used the word "Allah." Moreover, attorneys argued that word is from Arabic and it is used by Christians and Muslims alike to refer to God. Finally, attorneys submitted that use of the word had nothing to do with proselytization. The High Court agreed with the Archbishop and issued a decision in favor of the *Herald*.[26] However, the Ministry of Home Affairs appealed the decision and managed to secure a more expansive interpretation for Article 3 from the Court of Appeal.[27]

The Court of Appeal decision hammered on what it claimed was the inescapable implication of the *first part* of Article 3 (1), which states that "Islam is the religion of the Federation." The main line of reasoning in the Court of Appeal decision is that Article 3 (1) is meant to secure the position of Islam in the country. This interpretation of Article 3 (1), coupled with the prohibition on proselytization in Article 11 (4),

---

[25] ZI Publications Sdn Bhd & Anor v. Kerajaan Negeri Selangor [2016] 1 MLJ at 160.

[26] *Titular Roman Catholic Archbishop of Kuala Lumpur v. Menteri Dalam Negeri & Anor* [2010] 2 CLJ 208. The Court also reasoned that the Church had the right to use the word "Allah" in accordance with Articles 10, 11, and 12 of the Federal Constitution.

[27] *Menteri Dalam Negeri & Ors v. Titular Roman Catholic Archbishop of Kuala Lumpur* [2013] 6 MLJ 468. For a more extensive treatment of the Court of Appeal judgment, with emphasis on the ethnocratic inflection of the legal reasoning, see Neo (2014).

provided the rationale for the Court to declare that the Ministry of Home Affairs had acted within its appropriate powers to ban the use of the word "Allah." The decision explains that:

> ... the fundamental liberties of the respondent in this case, has to be read with Art 3 (1) of the Federal Constitution ... The article places the religion of Islam at par with the other basic structures of the Constitution, as it is the third in the order of precedence of the articles that were within the confines of Part I of the Constitution. It is pertinent to note that the fundamental liberties articles were grouped together subsequently under Part II of the Constitution.[28]

The reasoning that the sequencing of constitutional provisions reflects their relative importance in the Malaysian constitutional order was dubious, to say the least. More significantly, this reading contradicted the clear text of Article 3 (4) of the Federal Constitution, which specifies that "nothing in this Article derogates from any other provision in the Constitution." The Court of Appeal decision contained even stronger and more direct language about the character of Article 3 and its meaning for the Malaysian legal order. In a passage penned by Justice Abdul Aziz Ab Rahim, the decision explains:

> [t]he position of Islam as the religion of the Federation, to my mind imposes certain obligation on the power[s] that be to promote and defend Islam as well to protect its sanctity. In one article written by Muhammad Imam, entitled *Freedom of Religion under Federal Constitution of Malaysia — A Reappraisal* ... it was said that: "Article 3 is not a mere declaration. But it imposes positive obligation on the Federation to protect, defend, promote Islam and to give effect by appropriate state action, to the injunction of Islam and able to facilitate and encourage people to hold their life according to the Islamic injunction spiritual and daily life."[29]

Justice Abdul Aziz Ab Rahim acknowledges the learned counsel for citing and supplying Muhammad Imam's scholarship. The learned counsel in the case was none other than Haniff Khatri, the lawyer behind many of the strategic litigation efforts to expand the meaning of Article 3. Khatri had already relied on Muhammad Imam's article in his manifesto titled "Moving Forward to Strengthen the Position of Islam UNDER the Federal Constitution" (Khatri et al. 2009). Moreover, Muhammad Imam's scholarship had already made an earlier appearance in none other than *Lina Joy v. Majlis Agama Islam Wilayah Persekutuan*. In that decision, Justice Faiza Tamby Chik relied on Imam's scholarship to support broad and sweeping claims about the meaning of Article 3 in the Malaysian legal order. Justice Faiza's High Court decision had shaped one of the most important Federal Court decisions on religious conversion. Another decision of Justice Faiza started

---

[28] *Menteri Dalam Negeri & Ors v. Titular Roman Catholic Archbishop of Kuala Lumpur* [2013] 6 MLJ 489-490.

[29] *Menteri Dalam Negeri & Ors v. Titular Roman Catholic Archbishop of Kuala Lumpur* [2013] 6 MLJ at 511.

FIGURE 7.1: Demonstrators chant slogans outside Malaysia's Court of Appeal in
Putrajaya, March 5, 2014.
REUTERS/Alamy/Samsul Said.

FIGURE 7.2: Activists gather with a sign reading "Save the word Allah" while they wait
outside of the Court of Appeal for a decision in the *Catholic Herald* case.
Choo Choy May/Malay Mail Online.

the Islamist ball rolling in the High Court judgment of *Shamala v. Jeyaganesh*.[30] The confluence of Islamist legal scholarship, Islamist strategic litigation, and the welcome reception by like-minded judges, such as Justice Faiza, demonstrates that "public interest litigation" and "cause lawyering" are not inevitably liberal in orientation (Sarat and Scheingold 2006; Teles 2012; Bennett 2017). My interviews with Islamist-oriented lawyers, highly placed attorneys in the Attorney General's Chambers, and even former Federal Court judges affirmed what is apparent in the court records themselves: strategic litigation occurs on both sides of the rights-versus-rites binary.

A striking dynamic in the *Catholic Herald* case is that it drew in the religious bureaucracy from across Malaysia. Religious councils from Terengganu, Melaka, Kedah, Selangor, Johor, and the Federal Territories intervened as formal parties to the dispute. Moreover, well-known Islamist lawyers, including Zainul Rijal, Mohamed Haniff Khatri Abdullah, and Abdul Rahim Sinwan, represented these religious councils. On the other side were prominent liberal rights attorneys Cyrus Das, Philip Koh, Benjamin Dawson, and Leonard Teoh among others. In total, 14 NGOs gained official (watching brief) status.

The Transgender Rights Case

Another high-profile case concerned transgender (*Mak Nyah*) rights in Negeri Sembilan. Section 66 of the Shariah Criminal Enactment of Negeri Sembilan forbids Muslim men from wearing women's attire or posing as a woman in public. The offense is subject to a fine of up to RM 1,000 and a prison term of up to six months. By 2010, activists in the *Mak Nyah* community had become vocal about periodic abuse at the hands of the religious authorities in the state of Negeri Sembilan. In 2012, four individuals from the *Mak Nyah* community initiated a case challenging Section 66 of the Shariah Criminal Enactment.[31] Each had repeatedly been detained, arrested, and prosecuted by the authorities. They sought protection from the civil courts from further punishment and harassment.[32] They filed a case in the High Court of Seremban, requesting a declaration that Section 66 of the Shariah Criminal Enactment is inconsistent with the Federal Constitution's provisions for the right to live with dignity (guaranteed by Article 5), the right to equal protection under the law (guaranteed by Article 8), the right to freedom of movement (guaranteed by Article 9), and the right to freedom of expression (guaranteed by Article 10). The lead attorney in the case was Aston Paiva, who was later

---

[30] *Shamala Sathiyaseelan v. Jeyaganesh Mogarajah & Anor* [2004] 2 MLJ 648.
[31] For more on the background to the case, activism around the case, and related issues of concern to the *Mak Nyah* community of Malaysia, see the website Justice for Sisters, at: https://justiceforsisters .wordpress.com [website last visited May 4, 2017].
[32] *Muhamad Juzaili Mohd Khamis & Ors v. State Government of Negeri Sembilan & Ors* [2015] 1 CLJ 954.

accompanied by Fahri Azzat. Both attorneys were cause lawyers embedded in liberal rights activist circles. Aston Paiva worked in the offices of Shanmuga Kanesalingam, and Fahri Azzat was one of the founding members of the Malaysian Centre for Constitutionalism and Human Rights. They won their bid for constitutional review in the High Court, but lost this first constitutional challenge. They subsequently secured leave to approach the Court of Appeal. At this point, the case was attracting national attention. Watching briefs were held by the Women's Aid Organization, Sisters in Islam, the All Women's Action Society, the Malaysian Centre for Constitutionalism and Human Rights, and others. *Amicus curiae* briefs came from Human Rights Watch and the Malaysian Bar Council. In a landmark ruling, the Court of Appeal, led by Justice Hishamudin Mohd Yunus, agreed to all the constitutional challenges put before them.

Victory for *Mak Nyah* rights in the Court of Appeal only set the stage for a more dramatic face off in the Federal Court.[33] The State Government of Negeri Sembilan, including the Islamic Affairs Department, the Chief Religious Enforcement Officer, the Chief Shariah Prosecutor, and the Religious Council of Negeri Sembilan, focused their energies on overturning the Court of Appeal decision. Intervenors from other state governments soon joined, including representatives from the Islamic Religious Councils of Perak, Penang, Johor, and the Federal Territories. A slew of *amicus curiae* briefs came from the United Malay National Organization (UMNO), the Women's Aid Organization, Sisters in Islam, the All Women's Action Society, the Attorney General's Chambers, the Shariah Lawyer's Association of Malaysia, the International Commission of Jurists, and a relatively new Islamist lawyer's group calling themselves Concerned Lawyers for Justice (*Persatuan Penguam Muslim Malaysia*), and others. Leading Islamist lawyers either litigated or submitted *amicus curiae* briefs, including Haniff Khatri, Zainul Rijal bin Abu Bakar, Abdul Rahim Sinwan, and others. In an anti-climactic decision, the Federal Court voided the Court of Appeal decision on a technicality. The Federal Court claimed that the specific procedures for approaching the High Court and the Court of Appeal were not followed, which therefore invalidated the Court of Appeal decision. The Federal Court did not address the constitutional issues at stake whatsoever.[34]

---

[33] *State Government of Negeri Sembilan & Ors v. Muhammad Juzaili Bin Mohd Khamis & Ors* [2015] MLJU 597.

[34] More recently, there was a successful challenge to the National Registration Department (NRD) refusal to change the official sex designation from woman to man. In a High Court of Kuala Lumpur decision on July 18, 2016, a man successfully won the right to reclassify his official sexual designation after having completed gender reassignment surgery in Thailand. Justice Nantha Balan decided that "The Plaintiff has a precious constitutional right to life under Article 5 (1) of the Federal Constitution and the concept of 'life' under Article 5 must necessarily encompass the Plaintiff's right to live with dignity as a male and be legally accorded judicial recognition as a male." Case 24NCVC-1306-08/2015. There are several interesting parallels here to litigation over the right to convert one's official religious status. Just as official conversion has important implications for an individual's rights and obligations, so too does a change in one's official sex designation, at least as far as Muslims are concerned. This is because Muslims have different rights and obligations depending on whether they are officially classified as men or women.

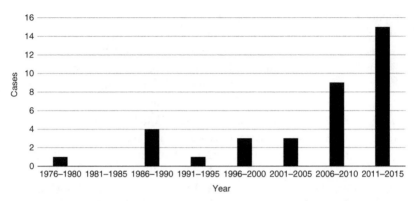

FIGURE 7.3: Reported Civil Court Decisions Concerning Article 3 (1), by Year
Source: Data compiled from the *Malayan Law Journal* and the *Current Law Journal*.

LIBERAL RIGHTS LITIGATION AS AN ENABLER OF ISLAMIST LEGAL MOBILIZATION?

The three cases reviewed above – the Borders bookstore case, the *Catholic Herald* case, and the *Mak Nyah* transgender rights case – all represented efforts to challenge the overreach of the religious authorities and defend liberal rights. Ironically, however, liberal litigation may have had the unintended effect of facilitating the efforts of Islamist legal activists to field a more expansive interpretation of Article 3. Figure 7.3 illustrates the fact that there was little attention given to Article 3 in civil court decisions through the mid-2000s. This relative neglect of Article 3 changed significantly through 2015.

The uptick in Article 3-related cases reflects increased contestation over the place of religion in the legal and political order, as well as the legal conundrums that were a product of the increasing regulation of religion and the formalization of shariah courts functions. Nonetheless, all three cases illustrate the way that liberal litigation provided Islamist lawyers with opportunities to field new, expansive interpretations of Article 3. They also provided opportunities for like-minded judges to build new case law. These new precedents shaped the trajectory of the law and narrowed the range of legal claims that could be fielded by liberal activists. Figure 7.4 illustrates the increasing number of reported civil court decisions that engage the key phrase "religion of the Federation" in Article 3 of the Federal Constitution.

The observation that liberal litigation may paradoxically facilitate the construction of Islamist-oriented case law is not to blame liberal activists for their own plight. Rather, it is to acknowledge the predicament that they face. Litigation can produce legal precedents that are exactly the opposite of the liberal protections that liberal rights advocates aim to secure. To describe their quandary in the new religious

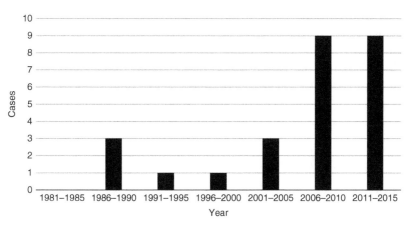

FIGURE 7.4: Reported Civil Court Decisions with the Term "Religion of the Federation"
Source: Data compiled from the *Malayan Law Journal* and the *Current Law Journal*.

FIGURE 7.5: Thousands gather in Padang Merbok, Kuala Lumpur, on February 18, 2017, to show support for amendments that would strengthen the Syariah Courts Act 335
Shafiq Hashim/NEWZULU/Alamy Live News.

idiom of Article 3 jurisprudence, "they're damned if they do and they're damned if they don't."

Litigation shifted case law over time. But perhaps more important than the new legal precedents is the way that judicialization fueled profound shifts in the broader political climate. Each successive case became a new focal point in debates over the place of Islam in the legal and political order. They inspired the formation of entirely new NGOs as well as coalitions of civil society groups on opposite sides of a polarizing rights-versus-rites binary.

Conclusion

In assessing the theoretical contribution of this book, one might ask whether the constitutive power of law and courts is as profound as the author claims. Stated as a counterfactual, one could query: Had Article 3 of the Malaysian constitution *not* specified that "Islam is the religion of the Federation ... "; had there *not* been a bifurcated judicial structure and separate family law provisions for Muslims and non-Muslims, and had there *not* been robust judicial institutions with broad public access, would Malaysia have witnessed a judicialization of religion nonetheless? After all, courts are made to contend with questions around religion even in countries that do not have these specific legal and institutional features (Sullivan 2005; Berger 2015).

A related counterfactual is the following: Absent judicialization, would the same questions and debates simply shift to a different forum? After all, the Islamic Party of Malaysia (*Parti Islam se-Malaysia*, or PAS) has roots that stretch back to independence, and religion has always figured prominently in electoral campaigns. It stands to reason that debates around religion would have played out in other arenas, even if they were absent from the legal field. What, then, are the uniquely constitutive functions of law and courts?

To be sure, any country with robust judicial institutions is bound to produce an expansive body of case law on religion. However, the Malaysian case suggests that some legal and judicial configurations exacerbate judicialization more than others. As I have sought to show throughout this book, the intensity, trajectory, and dynamics of these struggles can be traced to identifiable legal configurations that hardwired legal tensions. Not only did judicialization affect state policy, but the cases electrified the national imagination. Each successive case became a new focal point for debate over the place of Islam in the legal and political order. High-profile cases catalyzed the formation of new NGOs on opposite sides of a rights-versus-rites binary. Claims and counter-claims were fielded by litigants, lawyers, judges, political activists, journalists, and government officials. Most of these actors had little or no specialized training in Islamic jurisprudence or Islamic legal reasoning. Yet their competing claims were consequential nonetheless. In fact, judicialization positioned these players as central agents in the production of new religious knowledge. These actors overwhelmingly defined Islam vis-à-vis liberalism. More to the point, they defined Islam *against* liberalism (and vice-versa). The two sides found agreement only in the proposition that Malaysia faced a stark choice between secularism and Islam, between rights and rites. A zero-sum, winner-take-all struggle was constituted with courts taking center stage. For years, the press covered these cases daily, elevating the spectacle and keeping it fresh in people's minds. More than any other political forum, it was the courts that polarized public opinion and shaped a rights-versus-rites binary in legal and religious consciousness.

This is not to say that judicialization will provoke the same pattern of ideological polarization everywhere. In fact, the radiating effects of courts will vary according to different legal configurations and the broader sociopolitical ecosystems in which they are embedded. If we take Egypt as a comparative case, there are striking similarities as well as notable departures. Article 2 of the Egyptian Constitution affirms that "Islam is the religion of the state … and the principles of Islamic jurisprudence are the chief source of legislation." This is a much stronger formulation than Malaysia's Article 3 (1). However, most legal challenges that invoked Article 2 were, in fact, *liberal* in orientation (Moustafa 2007, 2010). That is, Article 2 was invoked to bolster liberal rights claims more often than an Islamist agenda.

It is telling that these liberal inflections of Article 2 received no mention in the Egyptian press, or in scholarly treatments of judicial politics in Egypt (except Moustafa 2007, 2010).[1] Why? Because these cases did not invoke a secular/religious binary. As a result, they did not generate a political spectacle. The Article 2 cases in the Egyptian Supreme Constitutional Court (SCC) that drew attention were invariably those cases with legal claims that positioned Islam and liberal rights as binary opposites (Moustafa 2007). Even here, however, Egyptian Constitutional Court judges worked to square the dual constitutional commitments to Islam and liberal rights through liberal interpretations of the *Qur'an* and *fiqh* (Lombardi and Brown 2005). No doubt, this approach had much to do with the ideological orientation of justices on the SCC. Egypt's unified court structure also facilitated bridging. Whereas paralysis gripped Malaysian courts as the result of contested shariah versus civil court jurisdictions, the Egyptian Constitutional Court experienced no similar intra-judicial dynamics, and the SCC developed an Article 2 jurisprudence that was relatively liberal.

These dynamics notwithstanding, there were clear attempts by Islamist activists to push a political agenda through the courts in Egypt, but their legal victories were few and far between. As in Malaysia, Islamists made far better use of the courts as a megaphone from which to challenge the status quo, attract public attention, and assert broad claims about Islam and the role of the state in advancing (a specific

---

[1] A few other studies, such as Lombardi and Brown (2005), examine the liberal bent of SCC judgments, but to my knowledge, no other studies systematically examine the liberal inflection of Article 2 litigation in the SCC.

vision of) Islam. In any case, the Egypt/Malaysia comparison underlines the fact that legal institutions matter to broader political debates, and that specific institutional structures produce different patterns of ideological polarization.

The Egypt/Malaysia comparison also affirms that the radiating effects of law and courts cannot be fully appreciated without considering the broader socio-political environment. A secularist/Islamist cleavage was judicialized in both countries. However, the multiethnic composition of Malaysia, coupled with media segmentation along ethno-linguistic lines, meant that media coverage of high-profile cases exacerbated the compartmentalization of starkly different narratives of what was at stake for the country. For many Malays, the cases triggered historically rooted anxieties about national identity (anxieties that were encouraged by most of the Malay political elite). For non-Muslims, on the other hand, the cases were tied up with a host of economic and political grievances around the increasingly ethnocratic character of the Malaysian state.

The Malaysian case illustrates how the radiating effects of courts can trigger more expansive political reverberations. Consider, for example, the fundamental realignment that appears to be well underway in the Malaysian political order. Since national independence, "race" provided the organizing logic of political life, from the founding Alliance Party coalition to the present-day *Barisan Nasional*. However, the ascendant political cleavage is articulated in terms of religion more than race, with the Muslim/non-Muslim cleavage dominating political discourse.

Looking back over the past three decades, one can see the central role of law and courts in nurturing the rights-versus-rites binary that now dominates political discourse in Malaysia. Although race and religion have long been intertwined, it is religion that is more deeply entrenched in the Federal Constitution, and in the logic of the legal system more broadly. The latent tensions between parallel tracks of state law are increasingly activated through litigation. The Article 121 (1A) cases, in particular, shifted the tone and emphasis of political discourse outside of the courts from race to religion. Religious cleavages have arguably eclipsed race, class, and other bases of political solidarity. In a broader political sense, Islam has been instrumentalized in the service of the Malay "race."

The very concept of race, and the legal category of "Malay," date back to the colonial era and they remain inextricably linked together by way of state law. What changed in recent years to produce a more intense judicialization of religion is the increasing rigidity of these official designations. Malaysians are regulated according to ascribed legal identities, never mind personal religious belief. This imposition creates difficult situations: lovers are unable to marry as the result of official religious status, individuals are unable to have conversions recognized; children are born out of wedlock and registered as such (with knock-on effects); and parents have lost custody of their children as a result of struggles over court jurisdiction. The thin volume of cases representing these sorts of issues may give the impression that very few individuals are affected. After all, the full universe of reported Article 121 (1A) cases does not total more than a few dozen. However, one must keep in mind that those who litigate represent only a tiny fraction of those Malaysians who face such legal conundrums. Gaining access to the High Courts is exceedingly difficult when the law is considered settled by way of a Federal Court decision. Even if a claimant has the financial and emotional fortitude to engage the legal system, they require legal standing to have their case heard. Reported cases therefore represent only the rare instances when a question of law has not been settled, opening the door for individuals to have their day in court. It is impossible to know the number of individuals who are negatively impacted by their official religious status. But surely the number is in the tens of thousands, if not hundreds of thousands.

Shachar (2001) is right to note that there is no inevitable conflict between multicultural accommodation and liberal rights. Creative institutional solutions can be found to protect individual rights while accommodating religious communities. But this can-do optimism may underestimate the path dependency of problematic institutional arrangements once they are forged. Working against the logic of Malaysia's pluri-legal system is something like attempting to break free from the children's toy, the "Chinese finger trap." The moment a person attempts to remove her fingers from the trap, the bamboo spiral contracts around her fingers, and grows tighter still the more she tries to break free.

Malaysia has been constructing such a finger trap for well over a century, from the initial formulation of Anglo-Muhammadan law in the colonial period, to the tightly regulated pluri-legal system of today. At each juncture – from British Malaya to contemporary Malaysia – the basic structure and logic of this pluri-legal system has remained remarkably stable, in part because entrenched interests have worked to preserve their mandate. And yet the increasing rigidity of official religious designations has, in recent years, catalyzed tensions within the legal system. The tensions between rights and rites are not inevitable. But one should not underestimate the capacity of institutions and individuals alike to construct them as binary opposites. Indeed, a supreme tragedy is that once this process starts, it tends to feed upon itself, reinforcing a false choice between Islam and liberal rights.

Religion of the State, Source Law, and Repugnancy Clause Provisions among Muslim-Majority Countries

Country	Year of Constitution (Most recent Amendment)	Religion of State Provision	Source Law or Repugnancy Provision
Afghanistan	2004	Article 2: "The sacred religion of Islam is the religion of the Islamic Republic of Afghanistan …"	Article 130: "In cases under consideration, the courts shall apply provisions of this Constitution as well as other laws. If there is no provision in the Constitution or other laws about a case, the courts shall, in pursuance of Hanafi jurisprudence, and, within the limits set by this Constitution, rule in a way that attains justice in the best manner"
Algeria	1989 (2008)	Article 2: "Islam shall be the religion of the State."	Article 9: "The institutions shall not indulge in: […] practices contrary to Islamic morals and the values of the November Revolution"
Bahrain	2002 (2012)	Article 2: "The religion of the State is Islam …"	Article 2: "… The Islamic Shari'a is a principal source for legislation …"
Bangladesh	1972 (2014)	Article 2A: "The state religion of the Republic is Islam …"	None
Brunei Darussalam	1956 (2006)	Part II (3.1): "The official religion of Brunei Darussalam shall be the Islamic Religion …"	None
Comoros	2001 (2009)	Preamble: "The Comorian people solemnly affirm their will to draw from Islam, the religion of the state, the permanent inspiration of the principles and rules that govern the Union"	Preamble: "The Comorian people solemnly affirm their will to draw from Islam, the religion of the state, the permanent inspiration of the principles and rules that govern the Union"
Djibouti	1992 (2010)	Article 1: "Islam is the Religion of the State …"	None
Egypt	2014	Article 2: "Islam is the religion of the State …"	Article 2: "… Islamic jurisprudence is the principal source of legislation"

Iran	1979 (1989)	Article 12: "The official religion of Iran is Islam and the Twelver Ja'fari school . . . and this principle will remain eternally immutable . . ."	Preamble: " . . . Legislation setting forth regulations for the administration of society will revolve around the Qur'an and the Sunnah. . . ."
Iraq	2005	Article 2: "Islam is the official religion of the State . . ."	Article 2: "Islam is the official religion of the State and is a foundation source of legislation: A. No law may be enacted that contradicts the established provisions of Islam B. No law may be enacted that contradicts the principles of democracy. C. No law may be enacted that contradicts the rights and basic freedoms stipulated in this Constitution"
Jordan	1952 (2016)	Article 2 "Islam is the religion of the State and Arabic is its official language"	Article 105: "The Sharia Courts alone shall have the jurisdiction – in accordance with their own laws – in . . . Matters of personal status of Moslems . . ."; Article 106: "Sharia Courts shall in their jurisdiction apply the provisions of the Sharia"
Kuwait	1962 (1992)	Article 2: "The religion of the State is Islam and Islamic Law shall be a main source of legislation"	None
Libya	2011 (2012)	Article 1: "Islam shall be its religion . . ."	Article 1: "Islamic Shari'a shall be the main source of legislation . . ."
Malaysia	1957 (2007)	Article 3 (1): "Islam is the religion of the Federation . . ."	None; but Schedule 9, List 2 of the Malaysian Constitution details specific areas of law that fall under the purview of state-level religious councils and shariah courts.

(Continued)

Country	Year of Constitution (Most recent Amendment)	Religion of State Provision	Source Law or Repugnancy Provision
Maldives	2008	Article 10 (a): "The religion of the State of the Maldives is Islam …"	Article 10 (a): " … Islam shall be the one of the [sic] basis of all the laws of the Maldives"; Article 10 (b): "No law contrary to any tenet of Islam shall be enacted in the Maldives" Also see Article 70 (b) and Article 142
Mauritania	1991 (2012)	Article 5: "Islam is the religion of the people and of the State"	None
Morocco	2011	Article 3: "Islam is the religion of the State …"	None
Oman	1996 (2011)	Article 2: "The religion of the State is Islam …"	Article 2: " … Islamic Sharia is the basis for legislation"
Pakistan	1973 (2015)	Article 2: "Islam shall be the State religion of Pakistan"	Article 227 (1): "All existing laws shall be brought in conformity with the Injunctions of Islam as laid down in the Holy Quran and Sunnah, in this part referred to as the Injunctions of Islam, and no law shall be enacted which is repugnant to such Injunctions" Also see Articles 203D, 203DD, and 230
Qatar	2003	Article 1: "Qatar is an Arab State, sovereign and independent. Its religion is Islam …"	Article 1: " … Islamic Law is the main source of its legislations …"
Saudi Arabia	1992 (2013)	General Principles: Article 1: "The Kingdom of Saudi Arabia is a sovereign Arab Islamic State. Religion: Islam …"	Article 1: "Constitution: The Holy Qur'an and the Prophet's Sunnah (traditions)"; Article 7: "The regime derives its power from the Holy Qur'an and the Prophet's Sunnah which rule over this and all other State Laws"; Also see Articles 8, 23, 26, 48

Somalia	2012	Article 2.1: "Islam is the religion of the State"	Article 2.3: "No law which is not compliant with the general principles of Shari'ah can be enacted"; Article 3.1: "The Constitution of the Federal Republic of Somalia is based on the foundations of the Holy Quran and the Sunna of our prophet Mohamed (PBUH) and protects the higher objectives of Shari'ah and social justice"; Article 4.1: "After the Shari'ah, the Constitution of the Federal Republic of Somalia is the supreme law of the country. It binds the government and guides policy initiatives and decisions in all departments of government"
Sudan	2005	None	Article 5.1: " … the Northern states of the Sudan shall have as its sources of legislation Islamic Sharia and the consensus of the people"
Syria	2012	None	Article 3: " … Islamic jurisprudence shall be a major source of legislation … "
Tunisia	2014	Article 1: "Tunisia is a free, independent, sovereign state; its religion is Islam, its language Arabic, and its system is republican"	None
United Arab Emirates	1971 (2009)	Article 7: "Islam is the official religion of the UAE … "	Article 7: " … . The Islamic Shari'a is a main source of legislation in the UAE … "
Yemen	2001 (2015 draft)	Article (2): "Islam is the religion of the state … "	Article (4): "Islamic Shari'ah is the source of legislation … "

Data Source: The Comparative Constitutions Project www.constituteproject.org/last accessed September 28, 2017.

Bibliography

Note: Malay names are alphabetized by the first name

NEWSPAPERS

Aliran
Berita Harian
Harakah
Makkal Osai
Malay Mail
Malaysiakini
Malaysia Nanban
New Straits Times
Nutgraph
Sin Chew
Utusan Malaysia

BOOKS AND ARTICLES

Abdul Hamid Mohamad. 2008. "Harmonization of Common Law and Shari'ah Law in Malaysia: A Practical Approach." Lecture delivered on November 6, 2008, at Harvard University Law School.

Abou El Fadl, Khaled. 2001. *Speaking in God's Name: Islamic Law, Authority and Women*. Oxford: Oneworld Publications.

Abou El Fadl, Khaled. 2004. *Islam and the Challenge of Democracy*. Princeton, NJ: Princeton University Press.

Agrama, Hussein Ali. 2012. *Questioning Secularism: Islam, Sovereignty, and the Rule of Law in Modern Egypt*. Chicago, IL: University of Chicago Press.

Ahmed, Farrah. 2015. *Religious Freedom Under the Personal Law System*. New Delhi: Oxford University Press.

Ahmed, Rumee. 2012. *Narratives of Islamic Legal Theory*. Oxford: Oxford University Press.

Ahmed, Shahab. 2016. *What is Islam? The Importance of Being Islamic*. Princeton, NJ: Princeton University Press.

Aks, Judith. 2004. *Women's Rights in Native North America: Legal Mobilization in the U.S. and Canada*. New York: LFB Scholarly Publications LLC.

Alba, R. 2005. "Bright vs. Blurred Boundaries: Second-Generation Assimilation and Exclusion in France, Germany, and the United States." *Ethnic and Racial Studies*, 28 (1): 20–49.

Ali, Shaheen Sardar. 2000. *Gender and Human Rights in Islam and International Law: Equal before Allah, Unequal before Man?* The Hague: Kluwer Law International.

Ali, Souad T. 2009. *A Religion not a State: Ali 'Abd al'Raziq's Islamic Justification of Political Secularism.* Salt Lake City: The University of Utah Press.

An-Na'im, Abdullahi Ahmed. 2002. *Islamic Family Law in a Changing World: A Global Resource Book.* Vol. 2. Zed Books.

An-Na'im, Abdullahi Ahmed. 2008. *Islam and the Secular State: Negotiating the Future of Shari'a.* Cambridge, MA: Harvard University Press.

Andaya, Barbara and Leonard Andaya. 2001. *A History of Malaysia.* Honolulu: University of Hawai'i Press.

Arjomand, Saïd Amir. 2007. "Islamic Constitutionalism." *Annual Review of Law Social Science* 3: 115–140.

Asad, Talal. 1986. "The Idea of an Anthropology of Islam." Center for Contemporary Arab Studies, Georgetown University.

Asad, Talal. 2001. "Reading a Modern Classic: W.C. Smith's 'The Meaning and End of Religion'." *History of Religions* 40(3): 205–222.

Asad, Talal. 2003. *Formations of the Secular: Christianity, Islam, Modernity.* Stanford, CA: Stanford University Press.

Asad, Talal. 2009. *Genealogies of Religion: Discipline and Reasons of Power in Christianity and Islam.* Johns Hopkins Press.

Azmil Tayeb. 2018. *Islamic Education in Indonesia and Malaysia: Shaping Minds, Saving Souls.* New York: Routledge

Azza Basarudin. 2016. *Humanizing the Sacred: Sisters in Islam and the Struggle for Gender Justice in Malaysia.* Seattle: University of Washington Press.

Baderin, Mashood. 2003. *International Human Rights and Islamic Law.* Oxford: Oxford University Press.

Baldwin, James. 2017. *Islamic Law and Empire in Ottoman Cairo.* Edinburgh University Press.

Bâli, Aslı Ü. and Hanna Lerner, eds. 2017. *Constitution Writing, Religion and Democracy.* New York: Cambridge University Press.

Barkey, Karen. 2008. *Empire of Difference: The Ottomans in Comparative Perspective.* Cambridge University Press.

Barr, Michael D. and Anantha Govindasamy. 2010. "The Islamisation of Malaysia: Religious Nationalism in the Service of Ethnonationalism." *Australian Journal of International Affairs* 64 (3): 293–311.

Bashi, Vilna. 1998. "Racial Categories Matter because Racial Hierarchies Matter: A Commentary." *Ethnic and Racial Studies* 21.5 (1998): 959–968.

Bayat, Asef. 2007. *Making Islam Democratic: Social Movements and the Post-Islamist Turn.* Stanford, CA: Stanford University Press.

Becket Fund for Religious Liberty. 2005. "Legal Opinion of the Becket Fund for Religious Liberty" [Amicus brief submitted in the case of *Lina Joy v. Majlis Agama Islam Wilayah Persekutuan dan lain-lain.*]

Benford, Robert and David Snow. 2000. "Framing Processes and Social Movements: An Overview and Assessment." *Annual Review of Sociology* 26: 611–39.

Bennett, Andrew, and Jeffrey T. Checkel, eds. 2014. *Process Tracing.* New York: Cambridge University Press.

Bennett, Daniel. 2017. *Defending Faith: The Politics of the Christian Conservative Legal Movement.* University Press of Kansas.

Berger, Benjamin. 2015. *Law's Religion: Religious Difference and the Claims of Constitutionalism*. Toronto: University of Toronto Press.

Berger, Peter and Thomas Luckmann. 1991. *The Social Construction of Reality: A Treatise in the Sociology of Knowledge*. Penguin UK.

Bottoni, Rossella, Rinaldo Cristofori, and Silvio Ferrari. 2016. "Religious Rules, State Law, and Normative Pluralism – A Comparative Overview."

Bowen, John R. 2003. *Islam, Law and Equality in Indonesia: An Anthropology of Pubic Reasoning*. Cambridge University Press.

Brown, Nathan J. 2012. *When Victory is not an Option: Islamist Movements in Arab Politics*. Cornell University Press.

Burak, Guy. 2015. *The Second Formation of Islamic Law: The Hanafi School in the Early Modern Ottoman Empire*. Cambridge, MA: Cambridge University Press.

Cady, Linell E. and Elizabeth Shakman Hurd, eds. 2010. *Comparative Secularisms in a Global Age*. Palgrave Macmillan.

Calhoun, Craig, Mark Juergensmeyer, and Jonathan VanAntwerpen. 2011. *Rethinking Secularism*. Oxford University Press.

Camroux, David. 1996. "State Response to Islamic Resurgence in Malaysia: Accommodation, Co-option, and Confrontation." *Asian Survey* 36 (9): 852–68.

Cardinal, Monique C. 2005. "Islamic Legal Theory Curriculum: Are the Classics Taught Today?" *Islamic Law and Society* 12: 224.

Cavanaugh, William T. 2009. *The Myth of Religious Violence: Secular Ideology and the Roots of Modern Conflict*. Oxford University Press.

Chandra, Kanchan, ed. 2012. *Constructivist Theories of Ethnic Politics*. Oxford University Press.

Charrad, Mounira. 2001. *States and Women's Rights: The Making of Postcolonial Tunisia, Algeria, and Morocco*. University of California Press.

Chaudhry, Ayesha. 2013. *Domestic Violence and the Islamic Tradition*. Oxford: Oxford University Press.

Comaroff, J. L. 2009. "Reflections on the Rise of Legal Theology: Law and Religion in the Twenty-First Century." *Social Analysis*, 53 (1), 193–216.

Cover, Robert M. 1983. "Foreword: Nomos and Narrative." *Harvard Law Review* 97: 4–68.

Dawson, Benjamin and Steven Thinu. 2007. "The Lina Joy Case and the Future of Religious Freedom in Malaysia." *Lawasia Journal 2017*: 151–164.

Dalacoura, Katerina. 2007. *Islam, Liberalism and Human Rights*. New York: IB Tauris.

Dirks, Nicholas B. 2001. *Castes of Mind: Colonialism and the Making of Modern India*. Princeton, NJ: Princeton University Press.

Dirks, Nicholas B. 1992. *Colonialism and Culture*. University of Michigan Press.

Djupe, Paul A. et al. 2014. "Rights Talk: The Opinion Dynamics of Rights Framing." *Social Science Quarterly* 95 (3): 652–668.

Dressler, Markus and Arvind Mandair. 2011. *Secularism and Religion-Making*. Oxford University Press, 2011.

Dudas, Jeffrey R. 2008. *The Cultivation of Resentment: Treaty Rights and the New Right*. Stanford, CA: Stanford University Press.

Dupret, Baudouin. 2007. "What is Islamic Law? A Praxicological Answer and an Egyptian Case Study." *Theory, Culture and Society* 24: 79–100.

Dzulkifli Ahmad. 2007. *Blind Spot: The Islamic State Debate, NEP, and other Issues*. Kuala Lumpur: Harakah.

Edelman, Murray. 1988. *Constructing the Political Spectacle*. Chicago, IL: University of Chicago Press.

Eisenstadt, S.N. 2000. "Multiple Modernities." *Daedalus* 129: 1–29.

Engel, David and Jaruwan Engel. 2010. *Tort, Custom, and Karma: Globalization and Legal Consciousness in Thailand*. Stanford University Press.

Euben, Roxanne. 1999. *Enemy in the Mirror: Islamic Fundamentalism and the Limits of Modern Rationalism*. Princeton, NJ: Princeton University Press.

Ewick, Patricia and Susan Silbey. 1998. *The Common Place of Law: Stories from Everyday Life*. Chicago, IL: University of Chicago Press.

Fadel, Mohammad. 2011. "A Tragedy of Politics or an Apolitical Tragedy?" *Journal of the American Oriental Society*, 131, (1).

Farish Noor. 2004. *Islam Embedded: The Historical Development of the Pan-Malaysian Islamic Party PAS, 1951–2003*. Kuala Lumpur: Malaysian Sociological Research Institute.

Fernando, Joseph. 2002. *The Making of the Malayan Constitution*. The Malaysian Branch of the Royal Asiatic Society (MBRAS).

Fernando, Joseph. 2006. "The Position of Islam in the Constitution of Malaysia." *Journal of Southeast Asian Studies* 37: 249–266.

Fitzpatrick, Peter. 1992. *The Mythology of Modern Law*. London: Routledge.

Fokas, Effie. "Directions in Religious Pluralism in Europe: Mobilizations in the Shadow of European Court of Human Rights Religious Freedom Jurisprudence." *Oxford Journal of Law and Religion* 4.1 (2015): 54–74.

Fox, Jonathan. 2008. *A World Survey of Religion and State*. New York: Cambridge University Press.

Galanter, Marc. 1983. "The Radiating Effects of Courts." In *Empirical Theories about Courts*, Keith Boyum and Lynn Mather, eds.

Gamson, William A. 1992. *Talking Politics*. Cambridge University Press.

Gamson, William A. and Andre Modigliani. "Media Discourse and Public Opinion on Nuclear Power: A Constructionist Approach." *American Journal of Sociology* 95.1 (1989): 1–37.

Ginsburg, Tom and Tamir Moustafa. 2008. *Rule by Law: The Politics of Courts in Authoritarian Regimes*. New York: Cambridge University Press.

Glendon, Mary Ann. 1991. *Rights Talk: The Impoverishment of Political Discourse*. The Free Press.

Glicksberg, Joseph. 2003. "The Islamist Movement and the Subversion of Secularism in Modern Egypt." Ph.D. Dissertation. Philadelphia, PA: University of Pennsylvania.

Goffman, Erving. 1986. *Frame Analysis: An Essay on the Organization of Experience*. Harvard University Press.

Goidel, Kirby, Brian Smentkowski, Craig Freeman. 2016. "Perceptions of Threat to Religious Liberty." *PS: Political Science and Politics*.

Gomez, Laura. 2010. "Understanding Law and Race as Mutually Constitutive." *Annual Review of Law and Social Science* 6: 487–505.

Government of Malaysia, Attorney General's Chambers. 2006. "Report 2005/2006."

Gramsci, Antonio. 1971. *Selections from the Prison Notebooks of Antonio Gramsci*. New York, NY: International Publishers.

Hallaq, Wael B. 2001. *Authority, Continuity, and Change in Islamic Law*. New York: Cambridge University Press.

Hallaq, Wael. 2009. *Sharī'a: Theory, Practice, Transformations*. New York: Cambridge University Press.

Hallaq, Wael. 2014. *The Impossible State: Islam, Politics, and Modernity's Moral Predicament*. New York: Columbia University Press.

Haltom, William and Michael McCann. 2004. *Distorting the Law: Politics, Media, and the Litigation Crisis*. Chicago, IL: University of Chicago Press.

Hamayotsu, Kikue. 2005. "Demobilizing Islam: Institutionalized Religion and the Politics of Co-optation in Malaysia." Ph.D. Dissertation: The Australian National University.

Harding, Andrew. 2012. *The Constitution of Malaysia: A Contextual Analysis*. Bloomsbury Publishing.

Harding, Andrew James and Amanda Whiting. 2011. "Custodian of Civil Liberties and Justice in Malaysia: The Malaysian Bar and the Moderate State." In *Fates of Political Liberalism in the British Post-Colony*. New York: Cambridge University Press.

Harrison, Peter. 1990. *"Religion" and the Religions in the English Enlightenment*. Cambridge University Press.

Hirschman, Charles. 1986. "The Making of Race in Colonial Malaya: Political Economy and Racial Ideology." *Sociological Forum* 1 (2): 330–361.

Hirschman, Charles. 1987. "The Meaning and Measurement of Ethnicity in Malaysia: An Analysis of Census Classification." *The Journal of Asian Studies*, 46 (3) 555–582.

Hirschl, Ran. 2011. *Constitutional Theocracy*. Cambridge, MA: Harvard University Press.

Hobsbawm, Eric. 1983. "Introduction: Inventing Traditions." In *The Invention of Tradition*. Eric Hobsbawm and Terence Ranger. New York: Cambridge University Press.

Hooker, M.B. 1975. *Legal Pluralism: An Introduction to Colonial and Neo-colonial Laws*. Oxford University Press.

Hooker, Michael Barry. 1984. *Islamic Law in South-east Asia*. Singapore: Oxford University Press.

Hooker, M.B. 2002. "Introduction: Islamic Law in South-East Asia." *Asian Law*, 4(3): 213–31.

Horowitz, Donald L. 1994. "The Qur'an and the Common Law: Islamic Law Reform and the Theory of Legal Change." *Am. J. Comp. L.* 42: 233.

Huang-Thio, S.M. 1964. "Constitutional Discrimination under the Malaysian Constitution." *Malaya Law Review* 6: 1.

Hurd, Elizabeth Shakman. 2008. *The Politics of Secularism in International Relations*. Princeton, NJ: Princeton University Press.

Hurd, Elizabeth Shakman. 2015. *Beyond Religious Freedom: The New Global Politics of Religion*. Princeton, NJ: Princeton University Press.

Hussin, Iza. 2007. "The Pursuit of the Perak Regalia: Islam, Law, and the Politics of Authority in the Colonial State." *Law & Social Inquiry* 32(3): 759–788.

Hussin, Iza. 2016. *The Politics of Islamic Law: Local Elites, Colonial Authority, and the Making of the Muslim State*. Chicago University Press.

Ibrahim, Ahmed Fekry. 2015. *Pragmatism in Islamic Law: A Social and Intellectual History*. Syracuse, NY: Syracuse University Press.

Ibrahim, Ahmad Mohamed. 2000. *The Administration of Islamic Law in Malaysia*. Kuala Lumpur: Institute of Islamic Understanding Malaysia (IKIM).

Imam, Muhammad. 1994. "Freedom of Religion under Federal Constitution of Malaysia – A Reappraisal." *Current Law Journal* lvii (June).

Jackson, Sherman. 1996. *Islamic Law and the State: The Jurisprudence of Shihab al-Din al-Qarafi*. Leiden: Brill Academic Publishers.

Jacobsohn, Gary. 2010. *Constitutional Identity*. Cambridge: Harvard University Press.

Jelen, T. G. 2005. "Political Esperanto: Rhetorical Resources and Limitations of the Christian Right in the United States." *Sociology of Religion*, 66 (3): 303–321.

Johansen, Baber. 1999. *Contingency in a Sacred Law: Legal and Ethical Norms in the Muslim Fiqh*. Leiden: Brill Academic Publishers.

Kagan, Robert A. 2001. *Adversarial Legalism: The American Way of Life*. Cambridge, MA: Harvard University Press.

Kanesalingam, Shanmuga. 2013. "Monkey in a Wig: Loyarburok, Undimsia, Public Interest Litigation and beyond." *Wisconsin International Law Journal* 31: 586.

Kamali, Mohammad Hashim. 2008. *Shari'ah Law: An Introduction*. Oxford: Oneworld Publications.

Kelsen, Hans. 1967. *Pure Theory of Law*. University of California Press.

Kendhammer, Brandon. 2016. *Muslims Talking Politics: Framing Islam, Democracy, and Law in Northern Nigeria*. University of Chicago Press.

Khatri Abdulla, Mohamed Hanniff, Abdul Rahim Sinwan, and Azril Mohd Amin. 2009. "Moving Forward to Strengthen the Position of Islam UNDER the Federal Constitution" https://membelaislam.wordpress.com/2009/06/10/moving-forward-to-strengthen-the-position-of-islam-under-the-federal-constitution/ (last accessed October 15, 2015).

Lau, Martin. 2005. *The Role of Islam in the Legal System of Pakistan*. Brill Publishers.

Lempert, Richard. 1978. "More Tales of Two Courts: Exploring Changes in the 'Dispute Settlement Function' of Trial Courts." *Law & Society Review* 13: 91–138.

Lerner, Hanna. 2011. *Making Constitutions in Deeply Divided Societies*. New York: Cambridge University Press.

Lindsey, Tim and Kerstin Steiner. *Islam, Law and the State in Southeast Asia*. (Volume III: Malaysia and Brunei). London: I.B. Tauris.

Liow, Joseph. 2009. *Piety and Politics: Islamism in Contemporary Malaysia*. New York: Oxford University Press.

Lombardi, Clark B. and Nathan J. Brown. 2005. "Do Constitutions Requiring Adherence to Shari'a Threaten Human Rights? How Egypt's Constitutional Court Reconciles Islamic Law with the Liberal Rule of Law." *Am. U. Int'l L. Rev.* 21: 379.

Lombardi, Clark B. 2006. *State Law as Islamic law in Modern Egypt: The Incorporation of the Sharia into Egyptian Constitutional Law*. Leiden: Brill Academic Publishers.

Maclean, Mavis, and John Eekelaar, eds. *Managing Family Justice in Diverse Societies*. Oxford: Hart Publishing.

Mahmood, Saba. 2016. *Religious Difference in a Secular Age: A Minority Report*. Princeton, NJ: Princeton University Press.

Malaysian Bar Council. 2006. "Petition: Reaffirming the Supremacy of the Federal Constitution" http://www.malaysianbar.org.my/letters_others/petition_reaffirming_the_su premacy_of_the_federal_constitution_.html?date=2016–06-01 [last accessed October 13, 2016].

Malaysian Bar Council. 2008. "Report of the Panel of Eminent Persons to Review the 1988 Judicial Crisis in Malaysia, Commissioned by Malaysian Bar Council, LAWASIA, International Bar Association's Human Rights Institute, Transparency International – Malaysia."

Mamdani, Mahmood. 1996. *Citizen and Subject: Contemporary Africa and the Legacy of Late Colonialism*. Princeton, NJ: Princeton University Press.

Mamdani, Mahmood. 2012. *Define and Rule: Native as Political Identity*. Cambridge, MA: Harvard University Press.

March, Andrew. 2009. *Islam and Liberal Citizenship: The Search for an Overlapping Consensus*. New York: Oxford University Press.

March, Andrew. 2015. "What Can the Islamic Past Teach Us About Secular Modernity?" *Political Theory* 43: 838–849.

Masoud, Tarek. 2014. *Counting Islam: Religion, Class, and Elections in Egypt*. Cambridge University Press.

Massad, Joseph A. 2015. *Islam in Liberalism*. Chicago, IL: University of Chicago Press.

Massoud, Mark Fathi. 2013. *Law's Fragile State: Colonial, Authoritarian, and Humanitarian Legacies in Sudan*. New York: Cambridge University Press.

Masuzawa, Tomoko. 2005. *The Invention of World Religions: Or, How European Universalism was Preserved in the Language of Pluralism*. Chicago, IL: University of Chicago Press.

Masud, Muhammad K., Brinkley Messick, and David Powers, eds. 1996. *Islamic Legal Interpretation: Muftis and their Fatwas*. Cambridge, MA: Harvard University Press.

Mather, Lynn and Barbara Yngvesson. 1980. "Language, Audience, and the Transformation of Disputes." *Law and Society Review* 15 (3): 775–821.

Maududi, Syed Abdul Aala. 1955. *Islamic Law and Constitution*.

Mawani, Renisa. 2009. *Colonial Proximities: Crossracial Encounters and Juridical Truths in British Columbia, 1871–1921*.

Maxwell, William George and William Sumner Gibson. 1924. *Treaties and Engagements Affecting the Malay States and Borneo*. London: J. Truscott & Son, Ltd.

Maznah Mohamad. 2010. "Bureaucratic Islam and the Secularization of the Sharia in Malaysia." *Pacific Affairs* 83 (3): 505–524.

MCCBCHS. n.d. "The First Ten Years." Unpublished document (on file with author).

MCCBCHST. 2007. "Respect the Rights to Profess and Practice One's Religion." Private memorandum to the Prime Minister. Unpublished document (on file with author).

MCCBCHST. 2007. "Unity Threatened by Continuing Infringements of Religious Freedom: Note of Protest by the Malaysian Consultative Council of Buddhism, Christianity, Hinduism, Sikhism & Taoism." (MCCBCHST).

McCann, Michael W. 1994. *Rights at Work: Pay Equity Reform and the Politics of Legal Mobilization*. Chicago, IL: University of Chicago Press.

Means, Gordon. 1972. "'Special Rights' as a Strategy for Development." *Comparative Politics* 5 (1): 29–61.

Mecham, Quinn and Julie Chernov Hwang, eds. 2014. *Islamist Parties and Political Normalization in the Muslim World*. Pittsburgh, PA: University of Pennsylvania Press.

Mehrez, Samia. 2008. *Egypt's Culture Wars: Politics and Practice*. Routledge.

Menchik, Jeremy. 2017. "The Constructivist Approach to Religion and World Politics." *Comparative Politics* 49.4: 561–581.

Menchik, Jeremy. 2016. *Islam and Democracy in Indonesia: Tolerance without Liberalism*. Cambridge University Press.

Merdeka Center for Opinion Research. 2006. "Public Opinion Voter Opinion Survey, Peninsular Malaysia, October 2006."

Merdeka Center for Opinion Research. 2007. "Peninsular Malaysia Voter Opinion Poll 4th Quarter 2007."

Merdeka Center for Opinion Research. 2008. "FNS Peninsula Malaysia Post-Election Poll."

Merry, Sally Engle. 1990. *Getting Justice and Getting Even: Legal Consciousness Among Working-Class Americans*. Chicago, IL: University of Chicago Press.

Merry, Sally Engle. 2000. *Colonizing Hawai'i*. Princeton, NJ: Princeton University Press.

Merry, Sally Engle. 2006. *Human Rights and Gender Violence: Translating International Law into Local Justice*. Chicago, IL: University of Chicago Press.

Migdal, Joel. 1988. *Strong Societies and Weak States: State–Society Relations and State Capabilities in the Third World*. Princeton, NJ: Princeton University Press.

Migdal, Joel S. 2001. *State in Society: Studying How States and Societies Transform and Constitute One Another*. Cambridge University Press.

Migdal, Joel, Atul Kohli, and Vivienne Shue. 1994. *State Power and Social Forces: Domination and Transformation in the Third World*. Cambridge University Press.

Milner, Anthony. 1998. "Ideological Work in Constructing the Malay Majority." In *Making Majorities*, Dru Gladney (ed.). Stanford, CA: Stanford University Press.

Mir-Hosseini, Ziba. 2000. *Marriage on Trial: A Study of Islamic Family Law*. London: I.B. Tauris.

Mir-Hosseini, Ziba. 2008. "A Woman's Right to Terminate the Marriage Contract: The Case of Iran." In *The Islamic Marriage Contract*, ed. Asifa Quraishi and Frank Vogel. Cambridge, MA: Islamic Legal Studies Program, Harvard Law School.

Mohamed Azam Mohamed Adil. 2007a. "Law of Apostasy and Freedom of Religion in Malaysia." *Asian Journal of Comparative Law* 2(1):1–36.

Mohamed Azam Mohamed Adil. 2007b. "Restrictions in Freedom of Religion in Malaysia: A Conceptual Analysis with Special Reference to the Law of Apostasy." *Muslim World Journal of Human Rights*, 4.

Mohd Al Adib Samuri and Peter Hopkins. 2017. "Voices of Islamic Authorities: Friday Khutba in Malaysian Mosques." *Islam and Christian–Muslim Relations*, 28.1: 47–67.

Moustafa, Tamir. 2000. "Conflict and Cooperation between the State and Religious Institutions in Contemporary Egypt." *International Journal of Middle East Studies*, 32: 3–22.

Moustafa, Tamir. 2007. *The Struggle for Constitutional Power: Law, Politics, and Economic Development in Egypt*. New York: Cambridge University Press.

Moustafa, Tamir. 2010. "The Islamist Trend in Egyptian Law." *Politics and Religion*, 3: 610–630.

Moustafa, Tamir. 2013a. "Islamic Law, Women's Rights, and Popular Legal Consciousness in Malaysia," *Law & Social Inquiry*, 38: 168–188.

Moustafa, Tamir. 2013b. "Liberal Rights versus Islamic Law? The Construction of a Binary in Malaysian Politics." *Law & Society Review*, 47: 771–802.

Moustafa, Tamir. 2014a. "Judging in God's Name: State Power, Secularism, and the Politics of Islamic Law in Malaysia." *Oxford Journal of Law and Religion*, 3: 152–167.

Moustafa, Tamir. 2014b. "Law and Courts in Authoritarian Regimes." *Annual Review of Law and Social Science*, 10: 281–299.

Muhammad Haniff Bin Hassan. 2007. "Explaining Islam's Special Position and the Politic [sic] of Islam in Malaysia." *The Muslim World* 97 (2): 287–316.

Nasr, Seyyed Vali Reza. 2001. *Islamic Leviathan: Islam and the Making of State Power*. Oxford University Press.

Nasr, Seyyed Vali Reza. 2005. "The Rise of Muslim Democracy." *Journal of Democracy*, 16.2: 13–27.

Neo, Jaclyn Ling-Chien. 2006. "Malay Nationalism, Islamic Supremacy and the Constitutional Bargain in the Multi-ethnic Composition of Malaysia." *International Journal of Minority and Group Rights*, 13: 95–118.

Neo, Jaclyn 2014. "What's in a Name? Malaysia's 'Allah' Controversy and the Judicial Intertwining of Islam with Ethnic Identity." *International Journal of Constitutional Law*, 12 (3) 751–768.

Nik Noriani Nik Badlishah. 2000. *Marriage and Divorce: Law Reform within Islamic Framework*. Kuala Lumpur: International Law Book Services.

Nik Noriani Nik Badlishah. 2003. *Islamic Family Law and Justice for Muslim Women*. Kuala Lumpur: Sisters in Islam.

Nik Noriani Nik Badlishah. 2008. "Legislative Provisions and Judicial Mechanisms for the Enforcement and Termination of the Islamic Marriage Contract in Malaysia." In *The Islamic Marriage Contract: Case Studies in Islamic Family Law*, ed. Asifa Quraishi and Frank Vogel, 183–98. Cambridge, MA: Harvard University Press.

Nongbri, Brent. 2013. *Before Religion: A History of a Modern Concept*. New Haven: Yale University Press.

Norani Othman. 2005. *Muslim Women and the Challenge of Islamic Extremism*. Kuala Lumpur: Sisters in Islam.

Osanloo, Arzoo. 2009. *The Politics of Women's Rights in Iran*. Princeton, N.J: Princeton University Press.

Otto, Jan Michiel. 2010. *Sharia Incorporated. A Comparative Overview of the Legal Systems of Twelve Muslim Countries in Past and Present*. Leiden University Press.

Peletz, Michael G. 2002. *Islamic Modern: Religious Courts and Cultural Politics in Malaysia*. Princeton, NJ: Princeton University Press.

Peletz, Michael G. 2015. "A Tale of Two Courts: Judicial Transformation and the Rise of Corporate Islamic Governmentality in Malaysia." *American Ethnologist*, 42: 144–160.

Pembela. 2006a. *"Pertubuhan-Pertubuhan Pembela Islam Desak Masalah Murtad Ditangani Secara Serius"* [Defenders of Islam Urges more Seriousness in Handling the Apostasy Problem].

Pembela. 2006b. "Federal Mosque Resolution."

Pembela. 2006c. *"Memorandum Mengenai Perkara Murtad Dan Memeluk Agama Islam."* [Memorandum on Apostasy and Conversion to Islam].

Perception Media. 2009. *Malaysia Press & PR Guide*. Kuala Lumpur: Perception Media.

Peters, Rudolph. 2005. *Crime and Punishment in Islamic Law: Theory and Practice from the Sixteenth to the Twenty-First Century*. New York: Cambridge University Press.

Pew Research Center. 2017. "Global Restrictions on Religion Rise Modestly in 2015, Reversing Downward Trend."

Powers, David S. 1992. "On Judicial Review in Islamic Law." *Law & Society Review*, 26: 315–342.

Puthucheary, Mavis. 1978. *The Politics of Administration: The Malaysian Experience*. Oxford University Press.

Quraishi, Asifa. 2006. "Interpreting the Qur'an and the Constitution: Similarities in the Use of Text, Tradition, and Reason in Islamic and American Jurisprudence." *Cardozo Law Review*, 28:67–121.

Quraishi, Asifa and Frank Vogel, eds. 2008. *The Islamic Marriage Contract: Case Studies in Islamic Family Law*. Cambridge, MA: Islamic Legal Studies Program, Harvard Law School.

Rabb, Intisar A. 2008. "We the Jurists: Islamic Constitutionalism in Iraq." *U. Pa. J. Const. L.*, 10: 527.

Rabb, Intisar. 2013. "The Least Religious Branch? Judicial Review and the New Islamic Constitutionalism." *UCLA Journal of International Law and Foreign Affairs*, 17: 75.

Raziq, Ali Abd al-. 1925. "al-Islam wa 'Usul al-Hukm."

Reporters without Borders. 2002. "2002 Press Freedom Index."

Redding, Jeffrey A. 2003. "Constitutionalizing Islam: Theory and Pakistan." *Va. J. Int'l L.*, 44: 759.

Roff, William R. 1967. *The Origins of Malay Nationalism*. New Haven, CT: Yale University Press.

Royal Commission of Inquiry on Immigrants in Sabah. 2014. http://www.sapp.org.my/rci/RCI-Eng.pdf. Last accessed June 9, 2017.

S. Hadi Abdullah. 2007. *The Initiative for the Formation of a Malaysian Interfaith Commission: A Documentation*. Kuala Lumpur, Malaysia: Konrad Adenauer Stiftung.

Sachedina, Abdulaziz. 2009. *Islam and the Challenge of Human Rights*. New York: Oxford University Press.

Saeed, Abdullah, and Hassan Saeed. 2004. *Freedom of Religion, Apostasy and Islam*. Ashgate Pub Limited.

Sajó, András. 2008. "Preliminaries to a Concept of Constitutional Secularism." *International Journal of Constitutional Law*, 6.3–4:605–629.

Salime, Zakia. 2011. *Between Feminism and Islam: Human Rights and Sharia Law in Morocco*. University of Minnesota Press.

Sarat, Austin and Stuart Scheingold. 2006. *Cause Lawyers and Social Movements*. Stanford University Press.

Scheingold, Stuart. 1974. *The Politics of Rights: Lawyers, Public Policy, and Political Change*. University of Michigan Press.

Scheppele, Kim Lane. 2004. "Constitutional Ethnography: An Introduction." *Law & Society Review*, 38.3: 389–406.

Schiappa, Edward. 2003. *Defining Reality: Definitions and the Politics of Meaning*. Carbondale, IL: Southern Illinois University Press.

Schonthal, Benjamin. 2016. *Buddhism, Politics and the Limits of the Law: The Pyrrhic Constitutionalism of Sri Lanka*. New York: Cambridge University Press.

Schonthal, Benjamin, Tamir Moustafa, Matthew Nelson, and Shylashri Shankar. 2016. "Is the Rule of Law an Antidote for Religious Tension? The Promise and Peril of Judicializing Religious Freedom." *American Behavioral Scientist*, 60 (2016) 966–986.

Schwedler, Jillian. 2006. *Faith in Moderation: Islamist Parties in Jordan and Yemen*. New York: Cambridge University Press.

Scott, James C. 1998. *Seeing like a State: How Certain Schemes to Improve the Human Condition Have Failed*. Yale University Press.

Sen, Amartya. 2006. *Identity and Violence*. New York: W.W. Norton & Co.

Sezgin, Yuksel. 2015. *Human Rights under State-Enforced Religious Family Laws in Israel, Egypt, and India*. New York: Cambridge University Press.

Sezgin, Yuksel and Mirjam Künkler. 2014. "Regulation of 'Religion' and the 'Religious': The Politics of Judicialization and Bureaucratization in India and Indonesia." *Comparative Studies in Society and History*, 56.2: 448–478.

Shachar, Ayelet. 2001. *Multicultural Jurisdictions: Cultural Differences and Women's Rights*. Cambridge University Press.

Shamsul A. B. 2001. "A History of an Identity, an Identity of a History: The Idea and Practice of 'Malayness' in Malaysia Reconsidered." *Journal of Southeast Asian Studies*, 32 (03), 355–366.

Shapiro, Martin. 1980. "Appeal." *Law & Society Review*, 14: 629–661.

Shapiro, Martin. 1981. *Courts: A Comparative and Political Analysis*. University of Chicago Press.

Singerman, Diane. 2005. "Rewriting Divorce in Egypt: Reclaiming Islam, Legal Activism, and Coalition Politics." *Remaking Muslim Politics: Pluralism, Contestation, Democratization*: 161–88.

Siraj, Mehrun. 1994. "Women and the Law: Significant Developments in Malaysia." *Law & Society Review*, 28 (3): 561–572.

Slater, Dan. 2010. *Ordering Power: Contentious Politics and Authoritarian Leviathans in Southeast Asia*. Cambridge University Press.

Sloane-White, Patricia. 2017. *Corporate Islam: Sharia and the Modern Workplace*. Cambridge University Press.

Smith, Wilfred Cantwell. 1963. *The Meaning and End of Religion*. Minneapolis, MN: Fortress Press.

Solanki, Gopika. 2011. *Adjudication in Religious Family Laws: Cultural Accommodation, Legal Pluralism, and Gender Equality in India*. New York: Cambridge University Press.

Sonbol, Amira El-Azhary. 2008. "A History of Marriage Contracts in Egypt." In *The Islamic Marriage Contract: Case Studies in Islamic Family Law*, ed. Asifa Quraishi and Frank Vogel.

Souaiaia, Ahmed E. 2009. *Contesting Justice: Women, Islam, Law, and Society*. Albany, NY: State University of New York Press.

Stahnke, Tad and Robert C. Blitt. 2005. "The Religion–State Relationship and the Right to Freedom of Religion or Belief: A Comparative Textual Analysis of the Constitutions of Predominantly Muslim Countries." *Georgetown Journal of International Law*, 36: 947.

Stevenson, Charles L. 1944. *Ethics and Language*. New Haven, CT: Yale University Press.

Stilt, Kristen. 2011. *Islamic Law in Action: Authority, Discretion, and Everyday Experiences in Mamluk Egypt*. Oxford University Press.

Stilt, Kristen. 2004. "Islamic Law and the Making and Remaking of the Iraqi Legal System." *George Washington International Law Review*, 36: 695.

Stilt, Kristen. 2015. "Contextualizing Constitutional Islam: The Malayan Experience." *International Journal of Constitutional Law*, 13: 407–433.

Suara Rakyat Malaysia (SUARAM). 2008. *Malaysia Human Rights Report 2008: Civil and Political Rights*. Petaling Jaya, Malaysia: SUARAM Kommunikasi.

Sullivan, Winnifred Fallers. 2005. *The Impossibility of Religious Freedom*. Princeton, NJ: Princeton University Press.

Sullivan, Winnifred Fallers, Elizabeth Shakman Hurd, Saba Mahmood, and Peter G. Danchin, eds. 2015. *Politics of Religious Freedom*. University of Chicago Press.

Tan, Nathaniel and John Ming Keong Lee, eds. 2008. *Religion Under Siege? Lina Joy, the Islamic State and Freedom of Faith*. Kinibooks.

Tarrow, Sidney. 1998. *Power in Movement: Social Movements and Contentious Politics*. Cambridge: Cambridge University Press.

Tate, C. Neal. 1995. "Why the Expansion of Judicial Power?" In *The Global Expansion of Judicial Power*, edited by C. Neal Tate and Torbjorn Vallinder. New York: New York University Press.

Teles, Steven M. 2012. *The Rise of the Conservative Legal Movement: The Battle for Control of the Law*. Princeton, NJ: Princeton University Press.

Tilly, Charles. 2006. *Why?* Princeton, NJ: Princeton University Press.

Tucker, Judith E. 2008. *Women, Family, and Gender in Islamic Law*. New York: Cambridge University Press.

United Nations Commission on Human Rights. 2006. "Civil and Political Rights, Including the Question of Religious Intolerance, Summary of Cases Transmitted to Governments and Replies Received."

United Nations Commission on Human Rights. 2008. "Report of the Special Rapporteur on Freedom of Religion or Belief, Summary of Cases Transmitted to Governments and Replies Received."

United Nations Human Rights Council. 2009. "Report of the Special Rapporteur on Freedom of Religion or Belief, Summary of Cases Transmitted to Governments and Replies Received"

United States Department of State. 2000–2010. International Religious Freedom Report.

Vogel, Frank E. 2000. *Islamic Law and Legal System: Studies of Saudi Arabia*. Leiden, Netherlands: Brill Academic Publishers.

Voules, A. B. 1921. *The Laws of the Federated Malay States 1877–1920*. (vol.2). Hazell, Watson & Viney.

Wadud, Amina. 1999. *Qur'an and Woman: Rereading the Sacred Text from a Woman's Perspective*. New York: Oxford University Press.

Walsh, Katherine Cramer. 2004. *Talking about Politics: Informal Groups and Social Identity in American Life*. University of Chicago Press.

Walton, Douglas. 2001. "Persuasive Definitions and Public Policy Arguments." *Argumentation and Advocacy*, 37(3).

Weiss, Bernard G. 1992. *The Search for God's Law: Islamic Jurisprudence in the Writings of Sayf Al-Din Al-Amidi*. Salt Lake City, UT: University of Utah Press.

Weiss, Meredith. 2006. *Protest and Possibilities: Civil Society and Coalitions for Political Change in Malaysia*. Stanford, CA: Stanford University Press.

Whiting, Amanda. 2012. "The Training, Appointment, and Supervision of Islamic Lawyers in the Federal Territories of Malaysia." *Pacific Rim Law and Policy Journal*, 21: 133.

Wickham, Carrie Rosefsky. "The Path to Moderation: Strategy and Learning in the Formation of Egypt's Wasat Party." *Comparative Politics* (2004): 205–228.

Wiktorowicz, Quintan. 2001. *The Management of Islamic Activism: Salafis, the Muslim Brotherhood, and State Power in Jordan*. SUNY Press.

Zainah Anwar. 2008. "Advocacy for Reform in Islamic Family Law" In *The Islamic Marriage Contract: Case Studies in Islamic Family Law*, ed. Asifa Quraishi and Frank Vogel. Cambridge, MA: Harvard University Press.

Zainah Anwar. 2008b. *Wanted: Equality and Justice in the Muslim Family*. Selangor, Malaysia: Musawah.

Zainah Anwar and Jana S. Rumminger. 2007. "Justice and Equality in Muslim Family Laws: Challenges, Possibilities, and Strategies for Reform." *Washington and Lee Law Review* 64:1529–49.

Zeghal, Malika. 2013. "Competing Ways of Life: Islamism, Secularism, and Public Order in the Tunisian Transition." *Constellations* 20.2: 254–274.

Zin, Najibah M. 2012. "The Training, Appointment, and Supervision of Islamic Judges in Malaysia." *Pacific Rim Law and Policy Journal*, 21: 115.

Zulficar, Mona. 2008. "The Islamic Marriage Contract in Egypt" In *The Islamic Marriage Contract: Case Studies in Islamic Family Law*, ed. Asifa Quraishi and Frank Vogel.

CASES CITED

Abdul Kahar bin Ahmad v. Kerajaan Negeri Selangor (Kerajaan Malaysia, intervener) & Anor [2008] 3 MLJ 617.

Adrianus Petrus Hertogh and Anor v. Amina Binte Mohamed and Ors [1951] 1 MLJ 12.

Amina Binte Mohamed v. HE Consul-General for the Netherlands [1950] 1 MLJ 214.

Azmi Mohamad Azam v. Director of Jabatan Agama Islam Sarawak & Ors [2016] 6 CJL 562.

Balbir bin Abdullah lwn. Mahadzir bin Mohd Nor, Jurnal Hukum 27 (1) at 53.

Berjaya Books Sdn Bhd & Ors v. Jabatan Agama Islam Wilayah Persekutuan & Ors [2013] MLJU 758.

Boto' Binti Taha v. Jaafar Bin Muhamed [1985] 2 MLJ 98.

Chang Ah Mee v. Jabatan Hal Ehwal Agama Islam & Ors [2003] 1 CLJ 458.

Che Omar bin Che Soh v. Public Prosecutor [1988] 2 MLJ 55.

Dalam Perkara Permohonan Perisytiharan Status Agama Si Mati Mohammad Abdullah@Moorthy a/l Maniam [2006] Jurnal Hukum 21 (2) at 210.

Dalip Kaur v. Pegawai Polis Daerah, Balai Polis Daerah, Bukit Mertajam & Anor [1992] 1 MLJ 1.

Dewan Pemuda Masjid Malaysia v. SIS Forum [2011] MLJU 518.

Hj Raimi bin Abdullah v. Siti Hasnah Vangarama bt Abdullah and another appeal [2014] 3 MLJ 757.

Indira Gandhi v. Pathamanathan A/L Krishnan (also known as Muhammad Ridzuan Abdullah) Judicial review No. 25-10-2009.

Jabatan Agama Islam Wilayah Persekutuan & Ors v. Berjaya Books Sdn Bhd & Ors [2015] 3 MLJ 65.

Kaliammal Sinnasamy v. Islamic Religious Affairs Council of the Federal Territory [2006] 1 MLJ 685.

Latifah bte Mat Zin v. Rosmawati bte Sharibun & Anor [2007] 5 MLJ 101.

Lina Joy v. Majlis Agama Islam Wilayah & Anor [2004] 2 MLJ 126.

Lina Joy v. Majlis Agama Islam Wilayah Persekutuan & Ors [2005] 6 MLJ 193.

Lina Joy v. Majlis Agama Islam Wilayah Persukutuan dan lain-lain [2007] 4 MLJ 585.

Md Hakim Lee v. Majlis Agama Islam Wilayah Persekutuan, Kuala Lumpur [1998] 1 MLJ 681.

Menteri Dalam Negeri & Ors v. Titular Roman Catholic Archbishop of Kuala Lumpur [2013] 6 MLJ 468.

Meor Atiqulrahman bin Ishak and Others v. Fatimah binti and Others [2006] MLJU 267

Mohd Syafiq Abdullah @ Tiong Choo Ting v. Director of Jabatan Agama Islam Sarawak & Ors [2015] MLJU 1150.

Muhamad Juzaili Mohd Khamis & Ors v. State Government of Negeri Sembilan & Ors [2015] 1 CLJ 954.

Myriam v. Mohamed Ariff [1971] 1 MLJ 265.

Nafsiah v. Abdul Majid [1969] 2 MLJ 174.

Nedunchelian V Uthiradam v. Nurshafiqah Mah Singai Annals & Ors [2005] 2 CLJ 306.

Ng Wan Chan v. Majlis Ugama Islam Wilayah Persekutuan & Anor [1991] 3 MLJ 487.

Ng Wan Chan v. Majlis Ugama Islam Wilayah Persekutuan & Anor [1991] 3 MLJ 174.

Persatuan Aliran Kesedaran Negara v. Minister of Home Affairs

Priyathaseny & Ors v. Pegawai Penguatkuasa Agama Jabatan Hal Ehwal Agama Islam Perak & Ors [2003] 2 MLJ 302.

Roberts v. Ummi Kalthom [1966] 1 MLJ 163.

Shamala Sathiyaseelan v. Jeyaganesh Mogarajah & Anor [2004] 2 MLJ 648.

Shamala Sathiyaseelan v. Jeyaganesh Mogarajah & Anor [2011] 2 MLJ 281.

SIS Forum v. Dato' Seri Syed Hamid Bin Syed Jaafar Albar (Menteri Dalam Negeri).

Soon Singh v. Pertubuhan Kebajikan Islam Malaysia (PERKIM) Kedah & Anor [1994] 1MLJ 690.

Soon Singh v. Pertubuhan Kebajikan Islam Malaysia (PERKIM) Kedah & Anor [1999] 1 MLJ 489.

State Government of Negeri Sembilan & Ors v. Muhammad Juzaili Bin Mohd Khamis & Ors [2015] MLJU 597.

Subashini a/p Rajasingam v. Saravanan a/l Thangathoray [2007] 2 MLJ 798.

Subashini a/p Rajasingam v. Saravanan a/l Thangathoray and other appeals [2008] 2 MLJ 147.

Sukma Darmawan Sasmitaat Madja v. Ketua Pengarah Penjara Malaysia & Anor [1999] 1 MLJ 226.

Tan Cheow Hong v. Fatimah Fong Abdullah@Fong Mee Hui

Tan Sung Mooi v. Too Miew Kim [1994] 3CLJ.

Teoh Eng Huat v. The Kadhi, Pasir Mas, Kelantan & Anor [1990] 2 MLJ 300.

Titular Roman Catholic Archbishop of Kuala Lumpur v. Menteri Dalam Negeri & Anor [2010] 2 CLJ 208.

Viran a/l Nagapan v. Deepa a/p Subramaniam [2014] MLJU 1391.

Viran a/l Nagapan v. Deepa a/p Subramaniam [2015] 3 MLJ 209.
Viran a/l Nagapan v. Deepa a/p Subramaniam [2016] MLJU 05.
Viran a/l Nagapan v. Deepa a/p Subramaniam [2016] 1 MLJ 585.
Zaina Abidin bin Hamid @ S. Maniam and Ors v. Kerajaan Malaysia and Ors [2009] 6 MLJ 863.
ZI Publications Sdn Bhd & Anor v. Kerajaan Negeri Selangor [2016] 1 MLJ 153.

STATUTES CITED

Administration of Islamic Law (Federal Territories) Act 1993
Administration of Muslim Law Enactment of Kedah 1962
Administration of Muslim Law Enactment of Malacca 1959
Administration of Muslim Law Enactment of Negeri Sembilan 1960
Administration of Muslim Law Enactment of Pahang 1956
Administration of Muslim Law Enactment of Penang 1959
Administration of Muslim Law Enactment of Perak 1965
Administration of Muslim Law Enactment of Perlis 1964
Administration of Muslim Law Enactment of Selangor 1952
Administration of Muslim Law Enactment of Terengganu 1955
Constitution (Amendment) Act 1976
Fire Arms (Increased Penalties) Act 1971
Guardianship of Infants Act 1961 (Revised 1988)
Islamic Family Law (Federal Territories) Act 1984
Law Reform (Marriage and Divorce) Act 1976
Malay Reservations Act of 1913
Malay Reservations Enactment Kelantan 1930
Malay Reservations Enactment Kedah 1931
Malay Reservations Enactment Perlis 1935
Malay Reservations Enactment Johore 1936
Malay Reservations Enactment Terengganu 1941
Muhammadan Offenses Enactment of Selangor 1938
Printing Presses and Publications Act 1984
Sabah Administration of Islamic Law Enactment 1992
Selangor Land Code 1891
Straits Settlements Enactment 5 of 1880
Syariah Civil Procedure (Federal Territories) Act 1998
Syariah Criminal Offences (Federal Territories) Act 1997
Syariah Criminal Procedure (Federal Territories) Act 1997
Syariah Criminal Offences (Selangor) Enactment 1995

Index

CPSIA information can be obtained
at www.ICGtesting.com
Printed in the USA
LVHW081157110319
610205LV00005B/398/P